Literary Lives

This classic and longstanding series has established itself making a major contribution to literary biography. The books in the series are thoroughly researched and comprehensive, covering the writer's complete oeuvre. The latest volumes trace the literary, professional, publishing, and social contexts that shaped influential authors—exploring the "why" behind writers' greatest works. In its thirtieth year, the series aims to publish on a diverse set of writers—both canonical and rediscovered—in an accessible and engaging way.

More information about this series at
http://www.palgrave.com/gp/series/14010

Linda Wagner-Martin

Walt Whitman

A Literary Life

Linda Wagner-Martin
University of North Carolina
Chapel Hill, NC, USA

Literary Lives
ISBN 978-3-030-77664-0   ISBN 978-3-030-77665-7   (eBook)
https://doi.org/10.1007/978-3-030-77665-7

This Palgrave Macmillan imprint is published by the registered company Springer Nature Switzerland AG
The registered company address is: Gewerbestrasse 11, 6330 Cham, Switzerland

Great is today, and beautiful,
It is good to live in this age ... there never was any better.
"Great Are the Myths,"

Walt Whitman

For My Children

Acknowledgments

Most of the quotations here from Whitman's writing are taken from the Library of America edition, *Whitman, Complete Poetry and Collected Prose*, edited by Justin Kaplan (noted as "Library" in references). I have chosen to use this 1982 (1995) text for its accessibility, in part because the Literary Lives series, founded so many years ago by Richard Dutton, was intended for undergraduate students as well as for the general reader. While I've drawn from more scholarly editions in cases where this edition does not reproduce the Whitman text (there is a supplemental primary bibliography for those sources), most of the Whitman material comes from this collection, which includes the first publication of Whitman's Leaves of Grass as well as the sixth publication (sometimes called the "deathbed edition"), published in 1891–92, and passages from the prose of his later years.

I am once again grateful to Ben Doyle, who was my editor for other of my Literary Lives books, and to Allie Troyanos, who saw this book through to its publication. I am also grateful to Justin Kaplan and Scott Donaldson, for their work in literary biography and their conversations about it, and to Jerome Loving, for his exhaustive biography of Whitman.

Chapel Hill   Linda Wagner-Martin
2021

Praise for *Walt Whitman*

"Using her intimate knowledge of both Whitman scholarship and nineteenth-century social and cultural history in a magisterial but also tactful way, Linda Wagner-Martin offers a reading of the life and work of Walt Whitman that is original and utterly persuasive. This book rewrites the story of a seminal figure in American literature and reconfigures our understanding of American culture in the nineteenth century."

—Richard Gray, Fellow of the British Academy, and author of *After the Fall: American Literature Since 9/11 (2011)*

Contents

1

Introduction

Few nineteenth-century writers are so often referred to in twenty-first-century publications. Former President Barack Obama recently gave testimony to the power of Whitman's identity as a prominent exploratory American artist. What Obama wrote in the introduction to *A Promised Land*, his 2020 memoir, was that as a college student, he envied "the America Tocqueville wrote about, the countryside of Whitman and Thoreau, with no person my inferior or my better: the America of pioneers heading west in search of a better life or immigrants landing on Ellis Island, propelled by a yearning for freedom."[1]

In 2019, international critic Paul Giles spent a large part of one chapter of his book *American World Literature* explaining why Whitman was the foremost American poet (even though Longfellow had lived on his income from poetry most of his life). As this British observer proposed, even though Longfellow's *Song of Hiawatha* sold 30,000 copies in the first six months of its publication in 1855 and Whitman's *Leaves of Grass* sold only a few copies that same year, it is Whitman who has come to represent the America of steadfast patriotic and humanistic beliefs. Much of *Leaves of Grass* gives the reader "Walt Whitman," a poet embodying the spirit and the self of America, just as his eloquent "When Lilacs Last in the Dooryard Bloom'd" crown President Abraham Lincoln the most beloved of the country's martyred leaders. Throughout his various editions of *Leaves of Grass*, Whitman insists on the

---

[1] Barack Obama, *A Promised Land*. New York: Crown, 2020: 14.

© The Author(s), under exclusive license to Springer Nature Switzerland AG 2021
L. Wagner-Martin, *Walt Whitman*, Literary Lives,
https://doi.org/10.1007/978-3-030-77665-7_1

1

embodiment of country through the physical body; he brought the physical into a poetry that had previously only sentimentalized that equation.[2]

Random attention by poets themselves has created and maintained the prominence of Whitman and his poems—as well as his prose, particularly "Democratic Vistas" and "Specimen Days"—so that few explanations are necessary when anyone refers to Whitman: Adrienne Rich borrows his sense of the country's landscape of "vistas of possibility"[3] whereas William Carlos Williams exudes his sense of brotherhood with "Chaucer, Villon and Whitman," a group he called "contemporaries of mind." More specifically, Williams called Whitman "a key man to whom I keep returning," claiming that he was "tremendously important in the history of modern poetry.....For God's sake! He broke through the deadness of copied forms which keep shouting above everything that wants to get said today drowning out one man with the accumulated weight of a thousand voices in the past."[4] The list is long of modern poets who helped Whitman maintain his currency as the prominent American poet of the nineteenth century. Poet C. K. Williams, in fact, recently wrote an entire book on Whitman.[5]

Besides the commentary of hundreds of poets, Whitman has been the subject of essays and books by nearly all of America's best literary critics and historians: Daniel Aaron, Floyd Stovall, Joel Porte, Betsy Erkkila, Gay Wilson Allen, F. O. Matthiessen, Phillip Callow, Ed Folsom, Kenneth M. Price, Edward Haviland Miller, Angus Fletcher, Ezra Greenspan, Vivian Pollack, C. Carroll Hollis, Justin Kaplan, Geoffrey Sill, Michael Moon, Joel Myerson, James E. Miller, Jr., Eve Kosofsky Sedgwick, Lawrence Buell, Robert K. Martin, David S. Reynolds, John Carlos Rowe, Susan Belasco, Edmund Wilson, Zachary T. Turpin, Jay Grossman, Richard Seery, Gary Schmidgall, Jerome Loving, M. Wynn Thomas, Newton Arvin, Emory Holloway, Douglas A. Noverr, Martin Klammer, Roy Harvey Pearce, Constance Rourke, Richard Chase, Leslie Fiedler, Roger Asselineau, William White, Michael Robertson, Shelley Fisher Fishkin, Daniel Hoffman, Henry Seidel Canby, Judith N. Shklar, Christine Stansell, M. Jimmie Killingsworth, Andrew Lawson, William Dow, Quentin Anderson, Mark Bauerlain, Paul Zweig, and others. One of the critics missing from this list is the postmodern author and critic William H. Gass, who posed one of the most significant questions

---

[2] Paul Giles, *American World Literature, an Introduction.* Chichester: Wiley, 2019: 76–79, 89–90.

[3] Adrienne Rich, "Six Meditations in Place of a Lecture," *What Is Found There: Notebooks on Poetry and Politics*, second edition. New York: Norton, 2003: 263.

[4] William Carlos Williams, "Preface," *Selected Essays of William Carlos Williams.* New York: Random House, 1954: n.p. and "Against the Weather," *Selected Essays:* 196–218.

[5] C. K. Williams, *On Whitman.* Princeton, NJ: Princeton University Press, 2016.

about the unique rhythms of Whitman's poems. In his seminal discussion of Emerson as poet, expressed through Emerson's essay "The Poet" (which Whitman heard in its oral version), and his intuitive reasoning that what Emerson really wanted in representing America in poetry was something he—Emerson—could not create. He was too rule-bound, too lean. But for Emerson, the American voice would be just that—*voiced*.

In Gass's words, "What Emerson wanted from poetry—masses of detail to drive a moral home; strong, swift strokes as if the writer were propelling a scull, yet a slow engorgement of the line which would lead to a kind of spasm of passion in the finally completed thought, with then a gentle ebb at the end to mark the close...."[6]

Gass believed that Emerson saw the country as gripped by the need to create self-definition, a definition which could be achieved only through freedom. The newness of the nation underscored "the implicit promise of democracy to exalt mankind, to praise as well as work the earth; and above all, the gift to that emerging individual of limitless opportunity—breathing space—space for rebeginning—space to the edge of every coast—space to infinity: each required the resettlement of language on the page, an equalitarian diction, a pioneering line, the big book, the great theme; each asked for energy and optimism." In Gass's interpretation, "This New World prose is prose which resembles talk of one kind or another: the tall tale, the loud spiel, or the sermon's moral prod; often it has the gentle swing of slow and somber reflection, the laudatory march of patriotic speech, or the unspoken assumptions of private conversation; and it is deeply marked—in theme, in pattern, rhythm, and diction—by the thumper's Bible; but there is always a point of origin, a human voice."

Gass then interpolates his own wide readings of nineteenth-century American literature as he points out that "nearly all the best American poets do write prose: Melville and Faulkner and James, Robinson, Thoreau, Eliot, and Frost. I mean that they remained *in the service of the sentence*. Even Whitman, to create his extraordinary and quintessentially American poetry, had to invent a prose which would explode into verse in contact with the page. Notice what happens when we hold one such poem in the good firm grasp of the paragraph:

> When I heard the learn'd astronomer, when the proofs, the figures,
> were ranged in columns before me, when I was shown the charts and
> diagrams, to add, divide, and measure then, when I sitting heard the

---

[6] William H. Gass, "Emerson and the Essay," *Habitations of the World: Essays*. New York: Simon & Schuster, 1985: 32.

astronomer where he lectured with much applause in the lecture-room, how soon unaccountable I became tired and sick, till rising and gliding out I wander'd off by myself, in the mystical moist night-air, and from time to time, look'd up in perfect silence at the stars."[7]

Gass sees different ways of approaching "the great theme" which America demands but he embroiders his description of Whitman's successful experiments with the hyperbolic "a prose which would explode into verse in contact with the page." Of the thousands of words written about Whitman's innovative (and evidently unsettling) poetic lines, the catalogues of subjects, the emphasis on the mundane, seldom has a critique described such an explosion. Whitman himself, retrospectively, talked about the way the 1855 *Leaves of Grass* was intended to represent "the new life of the new forms," i.e., to *be* America. "The Americans of all nations at any time upon the earth have probably the fullest poetical nature. The United States themselves are essentially the greatest poem. In the history of the earth hitherto the largest and most stirring appear tame and orderly to their ampler largeness and stir. Here at last is something in the doings of man that corresponds with the broadcast doings of the day and night. Here is not merely a nation but a teaming nation of nations. Here is action... and details magnificently moving in vast masses.... Here are the roughs and beards and space and ruggedness and nonchalance that the soul loves."[8]

Whitman stood nearly wordless before *his* America. The hyperbole here as he reflects on his creation—"a teaming nation of nations"—shows a love unbound by words, shaped not only by language but also by "roughs and beards and space." Diction succumbs to emotion. Great literature does not age; it rather provokes new and ever more relevant readings. In his 1985 essay about Emerson's and Whitman's writing, Gass brings a contemporary reading to texts that we have long thought, erroneously, were already complete.

Later, Whitman claimed that the poem of his life, his soul, could never have been written without his immersion in the Civil War and its aftermath,[9] but the crucial point remains: Whitman's *Leaves of Grass* was intentionally anchored in not only 'Song of Myself' but in his own human voice. Outrageous as most readers found his poetry, his cries, his exclamations, his yawp, the words and the lineage of the great poems of the 1855 *Leaves of Grass* were

---

[7] Gass, "Emerson and the Essay," *Habitations of the Word*, 33.

[8] Whitman, "Preface, 1855" to *Leaves of Grass, Leaves of Grass and Selected Prose*. New York: Modern Library, 1950: 441; hereafter cited as Modern Library.

[9] Jerome Loving clarifies that even though Whitman made that comment, he had published the first three editions of *Leaves of Grass* before the Civil War began. *Walt Whitman, The Song of Himself*. Berkeley: University of California Press, 1999: 22.

the true expression of what "Walt Whitman" not only was *as himself* but as what he saw to be the voice of the American *commoner*, a spirit as new to the world of literature as it was to the world of the truly human.

The best-known anecdote about Whitman's publishing, and publicizing, the first edition of *Leaves of Grass* ties him back to the *un*common—and conventional—literary establishment. Intent on making a name for his work, Whitman and his publishers had sent a paper-bound copy of the 1855 *Leaves of Grass* to Ralph Waldo Emerson, the leader of the country's literati at that time. Emerson responded positively but Whitman did not receive the letter for some months. When he did, he was so pleased that he included it (without Emerson's permission) in a segment of the book's second printing, and he also published the letter in the *Tribune*, again without Emerson's permission. The way some critics tell the story suggests chicanery, or outright duplicity; the exuberance of hearing from the great Emerson so positively might, however, be explained more naturally. Loving quotes the letter entire, and notes that late in 1855, Whitman and Emerson dined in New York together. That fact leads Loving to understand that Emerson did not hold the poet's use of his letter against him.[10]

The most recent re-telling of this story is Angus Fletcher's when he begins an assessment of Whitman's careful revisions of *Leaves of Grass* with his own mordant wit. Fletcher writes, "as if to demonstrate that he was just another rough and tough New Yorker, an inspired natural-talent Bowery Boy, Whitman expeditiously published Emerson's private letter along with a lengthy blurb commenting on Emerson's praise and on his own splendid ambitions. Never before or since have poetry and advertising come so close together...."[11]

---

[10] Loving, *Walt Whitman*, 188–190. Emerson's letter in full:

Dear Sir, I am not blind to the worth of the wonderful gift of "Leaves of Grass." I find it the most extraordinary piece of wit & wisdom that America has yet contributed. I am very happy in reading it, as great power makes us happy. It meets the demand I am always making of what seemed the sterile & stingy nature, as if too much handiwork or too much lymph in the temperament were making our western wits fat & mean. I give you joy of your free & brave thought. I have great joy in it. I find incomparable things said incomparably well, as they must be. I find the courage of *treatment*, which so delights us, & which large perception only can inspire. I greet you at the beginning of a great career, which yet must have had a long foreground somewhere for such a start. I rubbed my eyes a little to see if this sunbeam were no illusion; but the solid sense of the book is a sober certainty. It has the best merits, namely, of fortifying & encouraging ....

[11] Angus Fletcher, "The Book of a Lifetime," *A New Literary History of America*, ed. Greil Marcus and Werner Sollors. Cambridge, MA: Harvard University Press, 2009: 306.

2

The Pride of Family

Emerson's letter, according to his brother George, set Whitman up. It also felt as if the Brooklyn poet had earned a high school diploma. When Walt Whitman quit school at eleven, feeling that some teachers were less than happy with his work, he knew that whatever career lay before him was to be won through apprenticeships. He was already conscious of the deep debt that marked his family's life as they moved from rental house to rental house: he did not pretend to want or need more education.

He later wrote about the strengths of the Whitman family, as well as his mother's family, the Van Velsors, emphasizing their initial ownership of lands. Being a landowner was the calling card for status in the New Republic. The Van Velsors' farm was in Cold Spring, Long Island, New York State; the Whitmans' "500 acres, all good soil, gently sloping east and south ... at West Hills, Suffolk county."[1] Whitman traces his fathers' family arriving from England beginning with 1640. He avoids telling his readers, however, that by the time of his and his seven siblings' births, his family had lost the land and, in the blunt words of Michael Moon and Eve Sedgwick, the family was *poor*—"poor health, lack of money and adequate housing." These critics describe the "sad" letters Louisa Van Velsor Whitman wrote telling the story of a "nineteenth-century working-class Brooklyn woman's extremely difficult life, as she strives hopelessly to take care of herself and her children in the face of overwhelming experiences of disease and early death, intense emotional

---

[1] Walt Whitman, "Specimen Days," *Complete Poetry and Collected Prose*, ed. Justin Kaplan. New York: Library of America, 1982: 691–92. Hereafter referenced as Library.

© The Author(s), under exclusive license to Springer Nature Switzerland AG 2021
L. Wagner-Martin, *Walt Whitman*, Literary Lives,
https://doi.org/10.1007/978-3-030-77665-7_2

disturbance, unremitting physical labor, and want of material essentials for living—decent and ample food and living space."[2]

Of English and Dutch bloodlines, the Whitman children struggled to think they were lower middle class, but they lived well below that line. Walter Whitman, probably an alcoholic, lived a less-than-purposeful, chaotic life: Jerome Loving calls the family "dysfunctional."[3] Jesse was the first born in 1818, followed by "Walt" in 1819. Two daughters, Mary and Hannah Louisa, and an unnamed son who died in infancy followed. Then came the three brothers who were named after national heroes—Andrew Jackson, George Washington, and Thomas Jefferson. The fourth son, Edward, probably a Down's syndrome baby, was born last, when Louisa was forty. It was Edward who shared a room with Walt whenever his older brother lived in his parents' house. Several earlier commentators on the health of the Whitman children were dismissive: John Kouwenhoven said bluntly, "One brother was an epileptic, another died in a lunatic asylum, and one sister was thoroughly unstable."[4] As Justin Kaplan described the patriarch of the family, Walter "trained [his children] as radical Democrats, on the side of the farmer, the laborer, the small tradesman, and the 'people.'"[5] There is some suggestion that the father ruled with an iron hand, particularly when he was drinking. When Walt Whitman wrote about his family and his childhood, however, he suggested none of this controversy.

It was not rare that children left school in third or fourth grade. Wealthy families, often descended from the British, built children's lives around education—but for women, particularly, education meant reading and studying languages—not going to a school. When Walt Whitman secured a place as an errand boy in a father and sons law firm, he felt fortunate: he had his own desk, and when the younger partner presented him with a membership to a

---

[2] Michael Moon and Eve Kosofsky Sedgwick, "Confusion of Tongues," *Breaking Bounds: Whitman and American Cultural Studies*, ed. Betsy Erkkila and Jay Grossman. New York: Oxford University Press, 1996: 25–26.

[3] Loving, *Walt Whitman*, 29–30.

[4] John A. Kouwenhoven, "Introduction," Modern Library, ix. Drawing from Louisa Whitman's papers held at Duke University, Clarence Gohdes and Rollo G. Silver add this comment: "Edward, her youngest son, was feeble-minded and crippled .... Jesse, her oldest son, had fallen from the mast of a ship and after being hospitalized for six months seems to have recovered, but in 1860 overt signs of insanity developed, and at last his attacks became so violent that in December, 1864, he was committed to an asylum. Andrew, another son, a joiner by trade, who lived not far away with his wife Nancy and two little boys, was taken into the army but was soon discharged." *Faint Clews and Indirections*. Durham, North Carolina: Duke University Press, 1949: 183. Similar descriptions appear to this day, as in John Tytell's *Reading New York*. New York: Knopf, 2003: 118.

[5] Justin Kaplan, *Walt Whitman: A Life*. New York: Simon & Schuster, 1980: 56–57.

big circulating library, Whitman called it "the signal event of my life up to that time."[6]

Until recently, studies of American writing paid little attention to the class of its authors. But with the 2016 publication of historian Nancy Isenberg's *White Trash, The 400-Year Untold History of Class in America*, previously neglected elements such as family finances, the years and kinds of children's education, nutrition, and even cleanliness became significant. Isenberg shows that most of the founding documents of America are paternalistic, striving to prove that the United States differed from any British social models. The facts, however, proved that class strata and levels of poverty existed in the States just as they did in England: indentured servants, slaves, and the poor were generally seen as "human waste."

> Every era in the continent's vaunted developmental story had its own taxonomy of waste people---unwanted and unsalvageable. Each era had its own means of distancing its version of white trash from the mainstream ideal.[7]

American language itself helped to reveal class fissures. The poor in the States might be called "lubbers" and "clay-eaters," "crackers" and "rubbish," but they still were allowed to believe in "the American dream." As Isenberg notes, "Even now, the notion of a broad and supple middle class functions as a mighty balm, a smoke screen. We cling to the comfort of a middle class, forgetting that there can't be a middle class without a lower. It is only occasionally shaken up, as when the Occupy Wall Street movement of recent years shone an embarrassing light on the financial sector and the grotesque separation between the 1 percent and the 99 percent."

She continues that the propaganda of a classless, welcoming America continues to draw immigrants to it, but when they arrive, they find "not a land of equal opportunity, but a much less appealing terrain where death and harsh labor conditions awaited most migrants."[8]

The earliest immigrants to the United States may have been able to keep their landholdings but as the Whitman narrative showed, hanging on to prosperity was hard. Walt Whitman remembered both the acreage his paternal family owned, as well as the stable of horses his mother's family maintained for so long. But by the early nineteenth century, even though more recent immigrants could be looked down upon—partly because of their lack of language skill, as well as their differing cultural practices—immigrants

---

[6] Whitman, "Specimen Days," Library, 699.

[7] Nancy Isenberg, *White Trash*. New York: Viking, 2016: 2.

[8] Isenberg, *White Trash*, 3, 14.

from England and Holland who arrived in America early in the seventeenth century were no better off than very recent migrants. What was contributing to Whitman's sense of superiority was the color of his skin, and the memory of the family's financial history.

In 2020 came Isabel Wilkerson's revealing history of class on an international basis. She titled her book with the somewhat shocking rubric *Caste, The Origins of Our Discontents. Caste* was a word seldom applied to economic levels within the United States: Wilkerson's study changed that. Clearly and reasonably, she announced,

> Caste is more than rank, it is a state of mind that holds everyone captive, the dominant imprisoned in an illusion of their own entitlement, the subordinate trapped in the purgatory of someone else's definition of who they are and who they should be.[9]

Wilkerson studies India, Germany, the United States and other national cultures, pointing out that skin color is never a single characteristic. She writes bluntly about the twelve generations of slavery that existed in America "from 1619 to 1865 …. Legal and sanctioned by the state and a web of enforcers." It was the victims who were punished—for living. They could not escape. "Against this ordained caste, all Americans who were *not* African slaves were "better."[10] Skin color was a powerful inscription.

Yet as we saw from Whitman's reconstruction of his ancestry, he knew how privileged he was to be Caucasian—he could "pass" wherever and whenever he liked. Living in the various parts of New York City was also a protective situation: there were, as he often said, a myriad of races and nationalities of people in that comparatively small geographic area. Eventually, however, as Wilkerson says, a person's recognition of class (or caste) changes behavior:

> When you are caught in a caste system, you will likely do whatever it takes to survive in it. If you are insecurely situated somewhere in the middle—below the very top but above the very bottom--you may distance yourself from the bottom and hold up barriers against those you see as below you to protect your own position. You will emphasize the inherited characteristics that rank higher on the caste scale.[11]

In Whitman's case, as we have seen, creating his family legend through their land ownership helped to establish a birthrite of property—and therefore

---

[9] Isabel Wilkerson, *Caste, The Origins of Our Discontents*. New York: Random House, 2020: 290.
[10] Wilkerson, *Caste*, 44–45.
[11] Wilkerson, *Caste*, 327.

propriety. As he read and studied, observed, and listened, he was finding ways to propel himself out of a class he would rather disguise. Written language was his route to higher placement in New York's world of the literate. As he confessed in his narrative of his life, although when he was young, he sometimes debated, by the time he was working in printing and publishing, he preferred to listen. He was Whitman the *observer*, not the *converser*.

Whitman felt lucky to get work learning the printing trade. Although his father was a carpenter, so that his sons could work in that trade, Whitman had an instinct for language. He saw, almost intuitively, how important newspapers were in the changing lives of Americans—even to people who were barely literate. He itched to be a part of the world of what was happening—or at least of the *news* about those happenings. As he told the story of his first apprenticeship,

> Went to work in a weekly newspaper and printing office, to learn the trade. The paper was the 'Long Island Patriot,' owned by S. E. Clements, who was also postmaster. An old printer in the office, William Hartshorne … was a special friend of mine …. The apprentices, including myself, boarded with his grand-daughter. I used occasionally to go out riding with the boss, who was very kind to us boys; Sundays he took us all to a great old rough, fortress-looking stone church, on Jocalemon street …. Afterward I work'd on the 'Long Island Star,' Alden Spooner's paper.[12]

Because of his mother's poor health, the Whitmans moved "back to the country," but Walt kept one foot in Long Island, especially during summers.

As Whitman approached his eighteenth birthday, he was working as a "compositor" in printing offices in New York, and down in Queens and Suffolk counties, Long Island, where he sometimes "boarded round. (This latter I consider one of my best experiences and deepest lessons in human nature … and in the masses.)".[13]

With the country undergoing severe financial unrest—banks failing, people losing homes—Whitman decided to take up teaching in the one-room district schools, with their irregular calendars. Little detail exists about Whitman's teaching years though his contracts were for several months at a time: Jerome Loving says that for a five months contract, Whitman earned $72.20. Loving also counts eight separate district schools contracts between summer, 1836, and spring, 1841, ranging from East Norwich to Woodbury.

---

[12] Whitman, "Specimen Days," Library, 699.
[13] Whitman, "Specimen Days," Library, 700.

As a teacher, Whitman believed corporal punishment was unnecessary, and he did not in those years smoke or drink.[14]

Other sources suggest that Whitman returned to the newspaper world in late 1840. According to critic William Dow, for the next decade Whitman wrote for or edited the *Aurora*, the *Evening Tattler*, the *Statesman*, the *New York Sun*, the *New York Mirror*, the *Brooklyn Evening Star*, the *New Orleans Daily*, the *Brooklyn Freeman*, and the *Brooklyn Daily Times*.[15] In Dow's assessment, Whitman was in the Jacksonian lower middle-class as he earned a living from his printing. Dow charts the expansion of those skills: not only was Whitman an accomplished printer, he was soon to become the publisher of essays, short stories, and an occasional poem (usually conventional in form).

In 2006 Andrew Lawson wrote a book important for any consideration of Whitman and class. His *Walt Whitman and the Class Struggle* emphasized that much of Whitman's writing showed his "lower-middle-class reading formation." The polyglot and sometimes surprising language in even his first *Leaves of Grass* is, according to Lawson, revelatory of Whitman's lack of learning, and he notes that the poet's use of language parallels the educations gathered by "largely self-educated clerks of the antebellum metropolis." These men knew too well the value (socially and morally) of the classical education they would never be able to get (or only in scraps); their education would, instead, be "haphazard." Their identities would remain "fragmented." Lawson states, "*Leaves of Grass* manifests the creative haphazardness, the eclectic taste, and the capacity for syncretic combinations of information from diverse fields of knowledge."[16]

Seeming less assured than this discussion suggests, Lawson contends that there remains a mystery about Whitman's "class identity." For all his use of mixed diction, of borrowed phrasing, of inappropriate phrases from other languages, the power of *Leaves of Grass* manages to shake off these questions about class. After discussions about the poet's choices of language, and given that Lawson repeats that *Leaves of Grass* is a text of "profound oddity and obliqueness," he finally concludes that the book shows Whitman's own "conflicted social space." He continues:

> Whitman is not actually a member of the 'working class' but an artisan possessed of a skilled trade and a measure of independence. Leaving school

---

[14] Loving, *Walt Whitman*, 38–39.

[15] William Dow, *Narrating Class in American Fiction*. New York: Palgrave Macmillan, 2009: 229. He usefully lists a number of Whitman's editorials through the decade that show his political and aesthetic positions.

[16] Andrew Lawson, *Walt Whitman and the Class Struggle*. Iowa City: University of Iowa Press, 2006: xxiii–iv.

at the age of 12 (sic), he began as an apprentice printer …. he did not labor in the factories and sweatshops of Manhattan, and in his career as a journalist he gained increasingly in 'respectability' and reputation. It is more accurate, I think, to see Whitman as belonging to the antebellum lower middle class: a class location that is more complex and indeterminate than that of the 'proletarian' class.[17]

For all the assumption of a more polished façade that Whitman tries to project, says Lawson, his work, like his pose, shows him "a provincial outsider who steps across the metropolitan threshold—uncertain of his ground but determined to make his mark." He is never easy in his accumulation of, and use of, cultural capital; he is, in fact, "in estranged relation to it."[18]

William Dow sees Whitman as one of the most genuine of America's lower-class writers. Dow analyzes Whitman (as well as Jack London, Stephen Crane, Rebecca Harding Davis, and others) from the perspective of the classically proletarian, making this distinction: that Whitman effectively bridged the gap between the country's change from "the old master and apprentice paradigm" to what Dow describes as "a seemingly unbridgeable gap between capital and labor."

For Dow, Whitman became a part of "a new middle class (Whig) ideology of competitive individuation. As a response to these changes, the 1855 *Leaves of Grass*, while championing the cause of individual potential and freedom, holds that labor as opposed to property should be the dominant feature of the social order in which all work, both manual or mental, should be recognized and rewarded equally, while fraternal association and apprenticeship should still serve as the structuring principles of society."[19] For Dow, Whitman accepts his authenticity as a "worker" whereas for Lawson, the poet tries—somewhat consistently—to hide that identity.

Accepting his class position, Whitman makes his poetry from his knowledge as someone far removed from easy or ready money.

Accepting Whitman as a somewhat naïve writer, Dow establishes what he sees as the ruling principles of his groping toward art. He states that it is Whitman's understanding that work governs lives and that movement within class structures—through good work—is possible. He also reads Whitman's writing as a key to his economic beliefs, considering that his journalism is built on his "class vocabulary, [an entity] that is ceaselessly displayed,

---

[17] Lawson, *Walt Whitman*, xv.
[18] Lawson, *Walt Whitman*, xiv.
[19] Dow, *Narrating Class*, 17.

recontextualized and deferred." Within Whitman's journalism, such a vocabulary holds. Once he turns to poetry, however, his attempts to become more conventionally literary mar his choices.

His veneration for Emerson is particularly troublesome, Dow claims:

> As a 'worker' among many other workers, Whitman's incarnational poet, a mixture of buoyant self-expression and anxious assertion, follows his obsession with social, sexual, and racial exchanges, and asserts a commitment to lower-middle-class respectability and independence.[20]

Dow makes clear that Whitman's obvious belief in the supremacy of nature was never meant to oppose Emerson's Transcendentalism, but rather to move in a current that aligned with that more elitist belief.

Referencing Whitman's love of the ferry operators and the Broadway omnibus drivers, Dow points out that no one before had ever written about such classes, that until Whitman was in his forties, he "was a typical worker—carpenter, printer, and sometimes newspaper editor—who avidly participated in the party politics of his time. He was a firm advocate and voice of artisan republicanism."[21] Even as Emerson is calling for a new intellectual elite, Whitman contentedly draws from what he already sees in his own well-populated world. Emerson gives his readers nature as landscape, often unpopulated; Whitman presents to his readers a landscape filled with all kinds and classes of people. And while Emerson's point of view is admonitory, representing a speaker far advanced from his listeners, Whitman speaks in mixed (and sometimes euphoric) levels of language. Dow says,

> Whitman grounds the transparent, transcendent, Emersonian soul, suspicious of human context and craving 'infinite relations,' in the solidity and fragility of the human body, and into a classed body and world.[22]

Beginning with Whitman's insistence that he is, himself, one of the "roughs" of his world, this critic turns to his employment of language, noting that Whitman's choices of vocabulary portray him "as one of the people and that [simultaneously] of the people's leader, an itinerate bard 'Stuffed with the stuff that is coarse, and stuffed with the stuff that is fine.'"[23] In using both

---

[20] Dow, *Narrating Class*, 3, 17.
[21] Dow, *Narrating Class*, 23, 33.
[22] Dow, *Narrating Class*, 21.
[23] Dow, *Narrating Class*, 29.

low and high levels of language, Whitman shows a kind of searching within existing language for expressions of an often-maligned working-class fervor.

Above all, Whitman drew from his years of journalism to insist that factual information was essential. He never maligned "the news," and realized how important that information was to the middle and lower classes, separated from much of the intellectual world available through lectures and libraries. As he set in print the long preface for his 1855 publication of *Leaves of Grass*, he used the two-column printing style common to newspapers. It was as if through his form he was telling readers that what he had to say about poetry was, in fact, "news."

When Joel Porte, a superior Emerson critic, describes the differences between Whitman and Emerson, he emphasizes Emerson's unchallenged intellectual position. He surmises that in the summer of 1855, Whitman's sending a copy of *Leaves of Grass* to Emerson benefited from his timing: Emerson was at a low point in his own writing career: "in general, his capacity for new enthusiasms had diminished considerably .... therefore, Whitman reanimated, electrically, this old longing which might become dormant but could never quite die out in Emerson." What *Leaves of Grass* suggested was that Whitman, a man completely unheard of, might have the capability of stringing "worlds like beads" together in his writing.[24]

It was clear to Emerson, in reading through the twelve poems that comprised the first edition of Whitman's *Leaves of Grass*, that whoever this poet was, he had absorbed much of Emerson's own favorite essays: "Nature," "Self-Reliance," "The Poet," as well as Emerson's over-arching idea of "the representative man." As Whitman explained in the "Preface" to "*Leaves of Grass*," he—read, this poet—was a kind of archetypal American pioneer, a poet whose language spoke for all American men. And in this assumption of the "student of Emerson" role, Whitman resembled Henry David Thoreau. As Porte points out, eventually Emerson would withdraw from both Thoreau and Whitman. But in 1855, he greeted the latter with surprising warmth. And when Thoreau visited Whitman in 1856, he was somewhat taken aback when the poet described himself as "a man representing America."[25]

Whitman's first edition of *Leaves of Grass* opens with the two strongest poems. Both untitled then, they became "Song of Myself" and "A Song of Occupations," and the pair drove home unquestionably the direction Walt Whitman would take throughout his coming work. "Song of Myself" crystallizes his love of the natural person, nature itself, the universe in accord

---

[24] Joel Porte, *Representative Man: Ralph Waldo Emerson in His Time*. New York: Columbia University Press, 1988: 323.

[25] Porte, *Representative Man*, 325.

with humanity. Most of the critical readings of Whitman's work—to this day—focus on this lengthy, memorable poem. But coming a close second is "A Song of Occupations," a work that will be less frequently noticed later because it appears to be only lists of workmen and workwomen, people at their tasks, dominated by the routines of those jobs, sparked with the variety of task-building. If "Song of Myself" captured the most salient of human questions about the universe, "A Song of Occupations" might be called the grist to enumerate a bevy of well-oiled machines. (It became "A Song for Occupations" in later versions of the collection.)

In Whitman's first *Leaves of Grass*, "Song of Myself" is the first poem in the collection, and "A Song of Occupations" is the second. The remaining ten poems are shorter, somewhat repetitious in format, and unsurprising in language. By the time of Whitman's eighth publication of *Leaves of Grass*, the 1881–1882 "deathbed edition," "Song of Myself" still appears in the first book, though it is not *first* in that grouping but *last*. One searches for "A Song for Occupations," however: it comes more than sixty poems later than "Song of Myself," and it is placed in a group all titled with the prefatory words, "A Song for" so that the *group* seems to be linked. The prominence through isolation that this poem *of* or *for* "occupations" had held in 1855 is now blurred. Among the new poems added within the first books of this "deathbed" edition are several that replicate Whitman's interest in enumeration of the common properties of countries, classes, affects—"I Hear America Singing," "Starting from Paumanok," "I Sing the Body Electric," "Salut au Monde!" "Song of the Open Road," "Crossing Brooklyn Ferry" and "A Song of Joys." For readers of *Leaves of Grass* in 1855, however, the narrative of that slim poem collection was encapsulated in its opening duet of extraordinarily long poems.

Angus Fletcher concentrates on the impact of "Song of Myself," calling the poem "an impossible act to follow. On the other hand, if we take Whitman at his word, which is the word of history as he understood his own life in history, we discover another picture: a *Leaves of Grass* not falling off from its first edition but instead fulfilling the 'Song's' self-expressive rhapsody according to a very different poetic vision, one that would require nothing less than a whole lifetime to achieve its purpose. That formal aim seems to be what Whitman wanted to achieve—the book of a lifetime, which meant a book in several editions....His different editions were imagined from the beginning as falling into a continuous, endlessly worked-over process."[26]

---

[26] Fletcher, "The Book of a Lifetime," 306–7.

Agreeing with the shocked critics who commented on Whitman's "completely novel free verse," Fletcher notes the poem's *energy*, its "wildly associative use of suddenly discontinuous images." He discusses the changing titles of separable poems, but he sees the lifetime process as one that *can* be categorized. These are the four principal directions of the later versions of Whitman's *Leaves of Grass*:

> ...the free-form personal elegy; the variegated hymns or chants categorizing democratic themes (for example, the second, untitled chant of 1855 becomes 'Poem of the Daily Work of the Workmen and Workwomen of These States' to be finally named 'A Song for Occupations'; the myriad lyrics, usually much shorter ('Calamus' and 'Children of Adam'); and finally "the vital but virtually fragmentary miniatures [titled] 'Thought' or 'Thoughts.'[27]

Fifty years before Fletcher, Richard Chase set out a prolegomenon about not only Whitman but about "Song of Myself." Calling it America's "first modern poem," he contrasted it with one of the best-known British poems, Wordsworth's "Prelude," which he considers much more autobiographical. Chase's point, however, is that in 1855, "Song of Myself" was meant to be a corrective to such genteel and conventional poems. Rather, "Song of Myself" shows the contradictions within the American spirit—as well as within America as country. "Song of Myself" made the reader think of prose rather than poetry. It brought the *city* into an important poetic experience. And it is also comic, having what Chase describes as "a purely lawless gaiety and upwelling wit." The comedy is surprising because Whitman's pervasive theme was "the plight and destiny of the self."[28]

While readers have been studying Whitman's poems for over 165 years, and critics such as Chase and many others have made irrefutably accurate comments about his *oeuvre*, there is something about our need as *readers* to find words ourselves as part of a good reading process. Whitman shared this need, I think, writing toward the end of his life, that he still admired *Leaves of Grass* because in it he "had my say entirely my own way ... [he places his own work within other texts, saying] American poetry must extend further to express American individuality ... the great pride of man in himself.... a pride indispensible to an American. I think it not inconsistent with obedience, humility, deference, and self-questioning."[29]

[27] Fletcher, "The Book of a Lifetime," 310.
[28] Richard Chase. *Walt Whitman*. Minneapolis: University of Minnesota Press, 1961: 13, 17–18, 45.
[29] Walt Whitman, "A Backward Glance O'er Travel'd Roads," Library, 657, 666.

3

Whitman's Romance with Work

For David Herreshoff, Whitman's energetic pursuit of learning to be a skilled worker seemed very ordinary within his nineteenth-century culture. Many other critics, however, had seen the lives of such authors as Bronson Alcott, Henry David Thoreau, and Ralph Waldo Emerson as the norm, and treated their writings as logical outgrowths of their educational milieu. These men were steeped in the wealth that colleges had to offer. Their writing was eloquent, provocative, certainly representative of real literacy. Those same critics had understood that Whitman's leaving school at eleven meant, for him, a very different learning process. Yet they still treated his more than twenty years as a printer, a country school teacher, and a carpenter as something of an anomaly. When they read his poems about the American worker in the first edition of *Leaves of Grass*, they seemed puzzled at his emphases. As Herreshoff points out, however,

> "Like many who worked in the rapidly expanding American economy of the years of his adolescence and young manhood, Whitman became a jack of several trades. At ten [sic] he was an office boy for a lawyer and a doctor .
>
> . .[Then] he was learning the printing trade. In 1835, at age 15 and 16, he worked as a printer. [The next 14 years he taught and edited and wrote.]

L. Wagner-Martin, *Walt Whitman*, Literary Lives, https://doi.org/10.1007/978-3-030-77665-7_3

"After becoming a Free Soil Democrat, he edited the *Brooklyn Freeman* in 1849. He ran a printing office and stationery store, free-lanced, and built houses on speculation."[1]

Herreshoff is a literary critic, not an economist, so he builds his conclusions from his reading of Whitman's second poem, "A Song of Occupations." But he also includes the appeal of "Song of Myself" to show the contrast and what seemed to be readers' bewilderment over the poet's emphasis here on workers and their lives. It was a commonplace that most readers had responded to the opening of "Song of Myself."

> I celebrate myself, and sing myself,
> And what I assume you shall assume,
> For every atom belonging to me as good belongs to you.[2]

The interrogation of the universe by a sentient human mind is a common poetic theme—it is also a common religious theme. The human impulse to claim control and, more importantly, to celebrate *understanding* draws the reader in both rhythmically and syntactically.

Whitman names no author until later in this first poem, when "Walt Whitman, an American, one of the roughs, a kosmos" makes his entrance. But we warm to the unnamed poet as we read, "Born here of parents born here from parents the same, and their parents the same,/ I, now thirty-seven years old in perfect health begin …." The reader feels assured that the poem expresses how a writer—male, mid-life, descended from native stock—may be someone *becoming* a poet, a person of the literary world. Quickly the poem explains that, regardless of the poet's place, this poet is involved in physical work: "Apart from the pulling and hauling stands what I am."

In "Song of Myself," readers remember the early meditation on the grass, and the later elaboration of the power of the natural world, as the poet explains,

> I am enamoured of growing outdoors,
> Of men that live among cattle or taste of the ocean or woods,
> Of the builders and steerers of ships, of the wielders of axes and mauls, of the
> drivers of horses,
> I can eat and sleep with them week in and week out.

---

[1] David Sprague Herreshoff. *Labor into Art: The Theme of Work in Nineteenth-Century American Literature.* Detroit, MI: Wayne State University Press, 1991: 118.

[2] Whitman, "Song of Myself" (untitled in his first edition, *Leaves of Grass, First and "Death-Bed" Editions*, ed. Karen Karbiener. New York: Barnes and Noble, 2004:29–91. All quotations in this chapter from this edition.).

Given as Walt Whitman is to declaiming about the natural world, he later says,

> To behold the daybreak!
> The little light fades the immense and diaphanous shadows,
> The air tastes good to my palate.

Modest in his claims, and apparently in his aims, the poet reminds his readers "I think I will do nothing for a long time but listen .... I witness and wait." He explains further,

> "Behold I do not give lectures or a little charity,
>   What I give I give out of myself .... "He earlier had contextualized these couplets, "Logic and sermons never convince,/The damp of the night drives deeper into my soul.//Only what proves itself to every man and woman is so,/ Only what nobody denies is so.

The fact that "Song of Myself" is read as a more religious treatise than most of Whitman's early poems appears to be the result of the way critics have emphasized certain segments: even when Whitman features the role of God, as here, there is little overt "religious" statement:

> Why should I wish to see God better than this day?
> I see something of God each hour of the twenty-four, and each moment then,
> In the faces of men and women I see God, and in my own face in the glass;
> I find letters from God dropped in the street, and every one is signed by God's name;
> And I leave them where they are, for I know that others will punctually come forever and ever.

Sections of "Song of Myself" have prepared the reader for Whitman's second poem, "A Song of Occupations." Early on in that work, Whitman explains, "Neither a servant nor a master I,/ Offspring of ignorant and poor, boys apprenticed to trades,/ Young fellows working on farms and old fellows working on farms,/ ... but nigher and farther the same I see,/None shall escape me and none shall wish to escape me."[3] Repositories of knowledge as they are, workers impart their skills to the reader, who speaks to "You work-women and workmen of these States having your own diverse and strong life,/ And all else giving place to men and women like you."

---

[3] Whitman, "A Song for Occupations" (untitled in his first edition, *Leaves of Grass, First and "Death-Bed" Editions*, ed. Karen Karbiener. New York: Barnes and Noble, 2004: 91–101. All quotations in this chapter from this edition.).

Whitman makes clear in "A Song for Occupations" that he values all sources of education: "What is seen or learned in the street, or intuitively learned,/ What is learned in the public school—spelling, reading, writing and ciphering …. The usual routine …. the workshop, factory, yard, office, store, or desk." Moving away from the more visible spiritual explorations of "Song of Myself," Whitman here charts the normal, the common. He does this with no derogation.

Herreshoff's reading of Whitman's second poem moves in two directions: he isolates the segments of its content that relate visibly to the world of work and, by doing so, suggests links between Whitman and Karl Marx. He sees similarities in philosophy, with both men relating closely to the eighteenth-century Enlightenment. Rather than emphasizing their differences, Herreshoff sees Marx and Whitman as proponents of a Jeffersonian democratic ideal, as in Whitman's emphasis above on "obedience, humility, deference." He calls "A Song for Occupations" a "manifesto," in fact, echoing one of Whitman's earlier titles for the work, which was "A Manifesto for the Workers of the United States." Other of his earlier titles for the poem were "Poem of the Daily Work of the Workmen and Workwomen of These States," "To Workingmen," "Song of Trades and Implements," and "Chant of Mechanics."[4]

Moving in a second direction, Herreshoff sees affinities between Whitman's two great opening poems, "Song of Myself" and "A Song for Occupations." He quotes such lines from the former as "I am the teacher of athletes" to set up Whitman's lack of such specifics in the second poem. Similarly Herreshoff comments on the fact that three lines taken from "Song of Myself" are later expanded into sixteen lines in "A Song of Joys," a poem that seems closely related to "A Song for Occupations."

> The boatmen and clamdiggers arose early and stopped for me,
> I tucked my trouser-ends in my boots and went and had a good time,
> You should have been with us that day round the chowder-kettle.

Whitman expands the initial fishing scene into three segments. The first begins "The work of fishermen, the work of the eel-fisher and clam-fisher." Then the second long passage begins "Another time in warm weather out in a boat, to lift the lobster-pots where they are sunk with heavy stones." The third expansion surrounds the poet figure with "the quick veering and darting of fifty skiffs, my companions." Here, as in all Whitman's passages using the trope of the fisherman, that figure is seldom solitary: he is a man among

---

[4] Herreshoff, *Labor into Art*, 126.

friends, other men, also fishermen, men and boys "who love to be with me,/ By day to work with me, and by night to sleep with me." In the expansion that Herreshoff notes, Whitman creates a community of searchers, all looking for a means of finding income as well as friendship.[5]

Another of Herreshoff's tactics for reading these two poems is his discussion of the lithograph which Whitman chose as frontispiece. The simple workman, dressed as if for daily duties, appears to intentionally *mis*represent a writer. He looks straight at his reader, not assuming any kind of intellectualized pose. He is, by any definition of the word, *common*. Herreshoff segues from this observation into a discussion of several of Whitman's poems about children, "There Was a Child Went Forth," "Out of the Cradle Endlessly Rocking," "A Song of Joys" as he continues to place the education theme within his subject matter categories.

> There was a child went forth every day,
> And the first object he look'd upon, that object he became.
> Not the sea coast, but a barnyard pond. ...

In Herreshoff's reading, even the word "loafe" when Whitman used it carried no implication of "rest"—it was rather the human means of learning, learning from whatever surrounded the human consciousness, and in this critic's assessment, it suggested "contemplating work, taking in work's sights, sounds, smells." He uses Whitman's poem "I Hear America Singing" as an illustration of this belief, calling the "songs expressive of the free development of each worker"—and pointing out that there are "no bosses singing" in this poem.[6]

It is in "A Song for Occupations" that Whitman perfects the true catalogue that marks so much of his poetry. The last third of this poem becomes a song of naming, as this segment of listing shows:

> Manufactures.. commerce . . engineering . . the building of cities, and every
>   trade carried on there . . and the implements of every trade,
> The anvil and tongs and hammer . . the axe and wedge . . the square and
>   mitre and joiner and smoothingplane,
> The plumbob and trowel and level . . the wall-scaffold, and the work of
>   walls and ceilings . . or any mason-work:
> The ship's compass . . the sailor's tarpaulin . . the stays and lanyards,
>   and the ground-tackle for anchoring or mooring,

---

[5] One might borrow a few lines from Emory Holloway's second volume of Whitman's "uncollected poetry and prose," to cite his lines, "I will not descend among professors and capitalists–/I will turn the ends of my trousers around my boots, /and my cuffs back from my wrists, and go with drivers and boatmen/ and men that catch fish or work in the field. I know they are sublime" (p. 68).

[6] Herreshoff, *Labor into Art*, 118–19.

The sloop's tiller . . the pilot's wheel land bell . . the yacht or fish-smack . .
   the great gay-pennanted three-hundred foot steamboat under full headway,
   with her proud fat breasts and her delicate swift-flashing paddles;
The trail and line and hooks and sinkers . . the seine, and hauling the seine . . .
.

Herreshoff's important emphasis on what Whitman saw as the power of work and the learning that comes with it is one corrective to the malaise of incomprehension that some critics have created: even though Whitman thought himself the world's best observer of people in their daily surroundings, he was not infallible. And despite biographers' commenting on his long absences from whatever physical work he did, having to be brought back to the print shop after too long a lunch break, for example, Whitman felt that his time was put to good use: his "loafing" was giving him contemplative time, with or without accurate information.

The years between 1840 and 1855, when Whitman published the first slim *Leaves of Grass* and made his surprising mark on the American literary world, were somewhat schizophrenic. His brothers wondered why he didn't just build houses and take advantage of the city's housing boom. His need to write was, however, taking him in a myriad of publishing directions: involved in the temperance movement, he wrote short fiction and temperance essays, leading up to his 1842 novel, *Franklin Evans*. He wrote a variety of William Cullen Bryant-type poems, sometimes reprinting work he had earlier published elsewhere. Seemingly frustrated with the blandness of his teaching experiences, Whitman had been writing stories and columns, such as his ten-part series, "Sun-Down Papers, From the Desk of a Schoolmaster," published in three different newspapers over half a year. According to Loving, he may have been looking for an identity for his voice, though the essays were not about teaching. In this biographer's view, they reflected Whitman's somewhat late coming to maturity—meditating on the use of time, on a friend's suicide, on fashion, and on the nobility of the working-class. In the third essay "He chides the worker about seeking 'to hide what he is' by aping the manners 'of those whom he foolishly supposes to be his superiors, merely because they are of no use in the world, have small and soft hands, and never bend themselves down to the practice of vulgar industry or labor."[7] Here in the late months of 1840, a few years before he published "Intelligence of the Working People," Whitman was acknowledging the significance of class in human behavior.

More and more of Whitman's efforts were going into short fiction and poems, neither marked by noteworthy innovation. His short fiction was

---

[7] Loving, *Walt Whitman*, 46–47.

usually moralistic (and much of that, as well as his journalism, was unsigned). It often revolved around an unloving father and a preferred elder son, one or the other troubled by alcohol.

Sorting through the decade of the 1840s is difficult: Whitman was also selling work as a penny-a-line journalist though he could sometimes sell fiction for two dollars a page (the rate for the *Democratic Review*). He also sold fiction and poetry to *Evening Tattler, Brother Jonathan,* and *New World*. The decade was a mélange of Whitman's searching for remunerative, and public, success. His efforts brought him to feel that he was building some identity in the world of journalism, though he had no way to maintain stable finances. He often returned to live in his parents' house—although when he could afford to board, he boarded well.

New York was flourishing as the center of yellow journalism. If Whitman was not at work as a printer, he was publishing his own writing. His name was becoming known. For a brief time in 1842, he became editor of the new *Aurora*.[8]

Jerome Loving sees the development of Whitman's intellectual and aesthetic talents in a focused way. He states,

> The year 1842 was pivotal in Whitman's development as a poet. Not only did he first hear (and probably read) Emerson then, but he had the opportunity to expand his fiction and poetry skills into the essay form, which in the *Aurora* was allowed to run to two columns, each 21 inches long. His subject expands almost exponentially from a moralism focused on death and family relationships to a world stage upon which all nationalities and types interact. It is from the essay, more than anywhere else perhaps, that Whitman's use of free verse came into being. He democratized the Emersonian essay by giving the 'emblem of nature' a viable (and virile) body.[9]

Whether or not this assessment is completely accurate, it suggests Whitman's development as more of an intellectual than as a newsman. Writing essays meant providing more rationale than simple fact; it also meant allowing Whitman to return to his earlier interest in debate, in the use of subjective reasoning.

It was in 1842 as well that Whitman wrote *Franklin Evans*, a serial feature for. *New World*. Interest in temperance was high, as evidenced by the "Great Mass Temperance Meeting" at Tompkins Square in November, 1841. Published as a slim special issue, *Franklin Evans; or The Inebriate, A Tale of*

---

[8] Loving, *Walt Whitman*, 50–56. Loving believes that Whitman left his editorial post voluntarily but he summarizes the controversy.

[9] Loving, *Walt Whitman*, 60.

the Times sold close to 20,000 copies at ten copies for a dollar. Whitman took his $75 gratefully and was pleased, later, at receiving another $50. The novel was advertised as the work of "a Popular American Author," and the title page named the author as "Walter Whitman."

Franklin Evans is a Whitman-like figure, leaving Long Island to come to New York. Tempted by all the urban pleasures, including drink, he finally leaves his life with prostitutes and marries a "good woman." Unfortunately, his alcoholism sickens her and she dies quickly. Then Evans moves South and marries a Creole ex-slave. But then he falls in love with a white woman and the Creole has her rival murdered.

Loveless, Evans returns to New York, where an old employer has left him a partial inheritance—Whitman suggests that the remainder of Evans' life is stable because he has taken both the "Old Pledge" and the "New Pledge." Freed from his alcoholism, he becomes a sane, sober New Yorker. Not only a temperance story, *Franklin Evans* gives the reader a fantasy romance, complete with rare outspokenness about skin color.

Common life is exposed in *Franklin Evans*. Although Evans has become a drunk, he lives a secret life: the novel has him surrounded by good male companions, some of whom also drink. Most men are plagued by "occupational mobility" because they must move to follow work. The dialogue represents working-class camaraderie, expression which women cannot enter: the women are peripheral. New York itself, in this novel, has become not a progressive city but rather a haven for polyglot immigrants—Evans speaks of "a Catholic invasion" which is occurring.[10]

Continuing the temperance theme is Whitman's *The Madman*, the first (and only) installment of which appears in the *Washingtonian*, a temperance paper, January 18, 1843. The opening introduces two male characters, Arden and Barcourse, whose sexual orientation is blurred. Jerome Loving sees some of Whitman's traits in Barcourse, a figure reminiscent of Edgar Allan Poe's "William Wilson." Fragmentary, too, is Whitman's next tale of men's friendship, *The Fireman's Dream: With a Story of His Strange Companion*, published in the *Sunday Times & Noah's Weekly Messenger* of March 31, 1844. Dreamlike, this fantasy concerns a young fireman and a Native American man. The part-time fireman is an apprentice cabinet maker who leaves Brooklyn for a trip to Hoboken. After a fall which leads to an injury, he imagines that he has become the Native American he saw en route. Educated and apparently white, the latter man mourns his lost culture, his lost family. In both these

---

[10] Christopher Castiglio and Glenn Hendler, "Introduction," *Franklin Evans*, 2007.

unfinished fictions, Whitman probes the physical compatibility—almost the fusion—of two male characters.[11]

Another story from the same period is *The Child and the Profligate*, again a re-working of a common popular narrative, often appearing in British fiction—of the child mired in poverty and therefore subject to predators of obvious kinds.[12] In 1927 Thomas Ollive Mabbott edited *The Half-Breed and Other Stories by Walt Whitman*, a collection complete with frontiersmen, deformed hunchbacks, and Native American characters. More stoic than some of Whitman's earlier romances, this group of stories professes so-called "native" resilience, as when Arrow-Tip comments that "Death is but a puff of air and in the distance lie the Green Hunting Grounds of the honest Indian. They are fair."[13] Among the other stories in this collection are "Richard Parker's Widow" (a story Poe called "admirable") and "Shirval, A Tale of Jerusalem."

Whitman's practice of learning to write moralistic fiction was a preoccupation of his fourth decade. Although readers today benefit from the burgeoning practice of electronically archiving the quantity of not only his stories but his journalism, the fact that Whitman during his thirties saw that his destiny would lie in the field of language rather than in building and construction is clearly stated. About that emphasis he did not waver.

In his last published essay, in fact, Whitman describes the period of his thirties as his coming to a real sense of ambition—"to take part in the great melee, both for victory's prize itself and to do some good." He also spells out what he means by "victory's prize":

> a feeling or ambition to articulate and faithfully express in literary or poetic form, and uncompromisingly, my own physical emotional, moral, intellectual, and aesthetic Personality, in the midst of, and tallying, the momentous spirit and facts of its immediate days, and of current America—and to exploit that Personality, identified with place and date, in a far more candid and comprehensive sense than any hitherto poem or book.[14]

Discussion about Whitman's fiction has been re-energized with the discovery in 2016 of his 1852 novel, *Life and Adventures of Jack Engle; An Auto-Biography*. Perhaps the most common of his fictional characters, Engle, an

---

[11] Loving, *Walt Whitman*, 75–86. See Loving for descriptions of "Eris: A Spirit Record," "Dumb Kate," "My Boys and Girls," "Boys and Girls," Arrow-Tip," "The Half-Breed: A Tale of the Western Frontier," "Richard Parker's Widow," and others.

[12] Christopher Castiglia and Glenn Hendler, "Introduction," *Franklin Evans*, 2007.

[13] Whitman, "Arrow-Tip," *The Half-Breed and Other Stories*, 1927, 71.

[14] Whitman, "A Backward Glance o'er Travel'd Roads," Library, 657–58.

orphan, begins in poverty but comes through his education process a lawyer, set to find *right* in the legal world. Whether Charles Dickens or Horatio Alger was Whitman's model, Jack Engle survived all kinds of chicanery and criminality, not all of it within legal circles. The clearest impression of what Whitman tried to create was that good conquers evil, or at least most of it.

By 1852, Whitman had progressed no further toward his lifetime goals than he had a decade earlier. Indeed, in 1852 the $125 that he had made from *Franklin Evans* looked reasonably attractive, as did those 20,000 copies the earlier novel had sold. Despite the housing boom in New York, Whitman resisted the pressure to build houses; he was still intent on becoming a writer.[15]

Written in a combination of quasi-literary style (with heavy British echoes) and aimed at the marginally literate, *Jack Engle* was a combination of romance, revenge fantasy, and detective story. Fast-paced, it paired Jack with the truly innocent young woman, his beloved Martha, and forced readers to recognize that the most evil of the villains was himself a lawyer. Jack narrates his own story.

Published anonymously in six installments by the New York *Sunday Dispatch*, *Jack Engle* did not do as well as *Franklin Evans* had. Whitman had written it so that his knowledge of housing construction came into play; and he set it in Brooklyn and New York, on the Brooklyn ferry, and in Camden, New Jersey. One of the villains, ironically, was a Quaker—a dimension that most readers did not understand (Whitman loved the Quaker ancestry of his maternal grandmother, Amy). In many ways Whitman seemed to be trying to personalize the somewhat tired plot. Turpin describes the book as a "rags-to-riches (or rags-to-respectability) fiction, about an orphan whose 'luck and pluck' lift him out of poverty. But he gains his respectability out of his sincere empathy with the poor." Turpin sees it as a "social reform novel."[16]

According to Ted Genoways, who reviewed the publication in the *New York Times Book Review*, "Jack Engle" "is a piece of pure pulp, a city mystery that offers a twisty tour through the underbelly of 19th-century New York but makes no pretense toward lasting literary merit." As Genoways reminds us

---

[15] Zachary Turpin quotes in the introduction to this text a comment by George Whitman, who did not hide his impatience with his older brother's stubbornness: "Walt wanted more than a mere livelihood: he never would make concessions for money—always was so. He always had his own way, or took it. There was a great boom in Brooklyn in the early fifties, and he had his chance then, but you know he made nothing of that chance. Some of us reckoned that he had by this neglect wasted his best opportunity, for no other equally good chance ever after appeared."
"Introduction," *Life and Adventures of Jack Engle*, 2017: viii.

[16] Zachary Turpin, "Introduction," *Life and Adventures of Jack Engle*, xv.

that reader sentiment in 1852 may have differed radically from any twenty-first-century opinion, his calling the novel "pure pulp" may not work even for today's readers. He goes on to say that this work relates well to Whitman's aims at the time: "Whitman can be said to have invented not only American literature but also the American author—setting the mold for generations of visionaries willing to strip bare in search of essential truths.

The pitfall for readers, of course, is in confusing an author's *persona* with the author's *person*."[17]

Moving indiscriminately through more than 160 years of critical views of Whitman and his work, these contemporary assessments leave us acknowledging the distance readers today have come from the mid-nineteenth century, and how fiction then was sorted and judged. The literary landscape from 1840 to 1852, when *Jack Engle* appeared, and then in 1855, when Whitman first printed *Leaves of Grass*, charging a somewhat exorbitant $2 for each copy of the slim book, was one of the most fertile periods in American literary history. The congruence of new and more open attitudes about social behavior and more questioning of religious beliefs merged with experimental writing from France and England, and the notion of formalism in writing began to disappear: Emerson's essays set the mark for prose that conveyed philosophical ideas with eloquence. As Whitman would write in one of his last essays, *Leaves of Grass* was meant to be the same kind of deep experiment as

> our American republic itself ... with its theory. (I think I have at least enough philosophy *not* to be too absolutely certain of any thing, or any results.) In the second place, the volume [*Leaves of Grass*] is a *sortie*—whether to prove triumphant, and conquer its field of aim and escape and construction, nothing less than a hundred years from now can fully answer. I consider the point that I have positively *gained a hearing* ... .[18]

The explosion of new writing in essays, fiction, and poetry blurred Whitman's perception then, as it did that of most readers. Even as Nina Baym points out that during these years leading up to the Civil War, nearly half the publications in poetry were written by women,[19] the prominence in the annals of literary history still focuses on writing by men—the "Fireside poets" and the "Schoolroom poets" were geared to express common sentiments so that readers might quote, orate, and agree. William Cullen Bryant's important

---

[17] Ted Genoways, "A Common Language," *NYTBR*, September 3, 2017: 21.

[18] Whitman, "A Backward Glance O'er Travel'd Roads," Library, 657.

[19] Nina Baym, "The Rise of the Woman Author," *Columbia Literary History*, 305.

anthology, *Selections from the American Poets,* appeared in 1840 and even though Whitman had long admired Bryant—partly because he was also a lawyer and the editor of an important New York newspaper for fifty years,– he found the work there gathered from Longfellow, Poe, Whittier, Holmes, and Lowell, among others, very predictable. He thought that some of his own poems, appearing in the New York papers, were easily as effective.

But he also understood that he did not belong within the educated New England circles. Witness the publication from 1840 to 1844 of the highly-regarded periodical *The Dial,* a composite of essays and arguments written by the expected few. Not only was Whitman not from the right kind of family, he also had never traveled abroad. As Henry James later said, the problem is the "thinness of the New England atmosphere." In that place with its "simple social economy," a person may dwell largely on the self. In contrast, James viewed his well-traveled father as having an intellect that was "extraordinarily complex and worked out and original."[20]

All around Whitman, books were becoming best-sellers. Susan Warner's *The Wide, Wide World* in 1850 broke all American publication records; and Harriet Beecher Stowe's *Uncle Tom's Cabin,* 1852, became a *cause celeb* among Abolitionists. "Nineteenth-century America," notes Thomas Wortham, "was intensely conscious of itself as a literary culture."[21] The gates to literary fame were well-guarded, however, and not many writers without good educations and social connections gained entry.

Repeatedly, Whitman saw his writing ignored.

Elite literary readers here at mid-century were following the "moral histories" written by Nathaniel Hawthorne—"The Birth-mark" in 1843; *The Scarlet Letter* in 1850; *The House of Seven Gables* in 1851 and *The Blithedale Romance* in 1852. A good many readers were following the charismatic stories by Edgar Allan Poe. Quietly, Herman Melville found wide readership for his tales of exotic lands in *Typee,* 1846, and *Mardi,* 1849. Although his *Moby-Dick* was to change the dimensions of the American novel when it appeared in 1851, it sold less well than his more popular books. Though not a fiction writer, Henry David Thoreau expanded the reach of travel writing and the essay with *Walden* in 1854. Whitman, reading these works, realized how far from any popular success his work remained.

It was ironic in some ways. From the time he had been given his circulating library card, Whitman had been reading romances. He talks easily about

[20] Henry James, *Notes of a Son & Brother,* 1904, 4, 6.
[21] Thomas Wortham, "William Cullen Bryant and the Fireside Poets," *Columbia Literary History,* 288.

all the novels of Sir Walter Scott, as well as the *Arabian Nights*.[22] Jerome Loving includes many references to Whitman's reading habits, which are wide ranging but often focused on "romances"—British and French as well as American. George Sand, Madame Dudevant, with her *Consuelo* (1842–1844) and its sequel, *The Countess of Rudolstadt* (1843–1845), as well as her novels *The Journeyman Joiner* (1840) and *The Devil's Pool* (1848), were staples for Whitman, for example. *Consuelo* in translation, running to 800 pages, was a favorite with both Whitman and his semi-literate mother. Not accidentally, the title character of *Journeyman* dresses like a simple worker and speaks plainly, as if on intimate terms with those around him. Perhaps not so effulgent as "Walt Whitman" in *Leaves of Grass*, he at least shares the poet's love of the common and the real, however one describes the normality of the working-class.[23]

Whitman's biographer also comments on his somewhat esoteric choices of reading matter. While he preferred George Sand to Victor Hugo, he did read the latter. He seldom read Edgar Allan Poe, and thought Hawthorne's short stories less good than his novels. He developed an interest in Bernhard S. Ingemann, particularly *The Childhood of King Eric Medved,* 1828, and even proposed doing a translation of that work for a New York paper. The novel was based on not only dreams and knowledge acquired while sleeping but also on adherences to basic principles of Danish democracy.[24]

Andrew Lawson, considering sources for what he sees as Whitman's unpredictable thinking, blames his reading for some of his beliefs, saying that Whitman "was the product of a course of wide, undirected, necessarily haphazard reading." He looked for texts that satisfied what Lawson terms "a gnawing class consciousness." Part of his development stemmed from the fact that his family was downwardly mobile, and was falling lower than what they considered the lower middle class. Whitman looked for narratives that would explain such a pattern.[25]

In William Dow's assessment, Whitman's journalism during the 1840s parallels the kinds of choices he will make in the poems of the first *Leaves of Grass*. Form is never uniform or predictable. "Everything in *Leaves* reflects

[22] Whitman, "Specimen Days," Library, 699.

[23] Loving, *Walt Whitman,* 161, 180. Loving also points out that during 1852, Whitman had built the Myrtle Street house, where he ran both a printing business and a bookstore. It is during those months of running the small bookstore that Whitman came back to exploring fiction of the world. Loving then shows the sequence of Whitman's housing—he next built two houses on Cumberland Street, and one on Skillman Street. Just six weeks before the publication of *Leaves of Grass* in 1855, he bought a house in his mother's name for $1840 cash, and moved his family into it just before his father died on July 11, 1855.

[24] Loving, *Walt Whitman,* 163.

[25] Lawson, *Walt Whitman,* xx, xxii, xxiv.

Whitman's interest in obliterating boundaries between cultural and class levels and subverting narrative expectations (abrogating normal rules of punctuation, providing no titles for the twelve separate poems, etc.). Form, as the bearer of meaning, thus becomes the "content" of the text rather than the container of content. While form is the poet's contesting of class (the poet refuses to draw a perimeter around sexual, social, class ties), it is also an engagement in which the poetic self and the reader's interaction with class is acted out."[26]

Dow sees similarities between Whitman's best journalism of the 1840s and his achievement in the long poems that open *Leaves of Grass*: "modeled dramatic storytelling, relied on vivid and concrete descriptions, deployed narrative devices to engage the reader in the described scene, depended on vernacular constructions, advertised its own self-reflexivity, and expressed an engaged interest in the world of fact. The need for recognizing the literariness in general and the subjectivity in particular in Whitman's journalism corresponds to the necessity for seeing the 'flesh and blood reporter' and the implicit construction of this reporter in *Leaves*." Further, says Dow, "Whitman's journalism provides a blueprint for his class sympathies in *Leaves*. If by critical consensus, his journalism was quite undistinguished, didactically moralistic, and conventional .... there are consistent reformist and sympathetic stances on female labor, working-class rights, and the plight of the poor that assail both his journalism and *Leaves*."[27]

The way all this operated in Whitman's journalism in particular was that he insisted on *change*. He not only saw the injustices, he wanted to *right* them. By the time of writing poetry for *Leaves*, Whitman inveighs against "those who piddle and paddle here in collars and tailcoats," instead choosing to honor the man "with his rolled up sleeves":

> Many sweating and ploughing and thrashing, and then the chaff for payment receiving,
>   A few idly owning, and they the wheat continually claiming.[28]

Whitman himself wrote about his love for the common American in many places and in many ways. It was no enigma: he said it in the "Preface" to the 1855 *Leaves of Grass*, as he described his relationship with what he called "the common people":

---

[26] Dow, *Narrating Class*, 36–37.
[27] Dow, *Narrating Class*, 37.
[28] Dow, *Narrating Class*, 38.

Their manners speech dress friendships—the freshness and candor of their physiognomy—the picturesque looseness of their carriage ... their deathless attachment to freedom—their aversion to anything indecorous or soft or mean—the practical acknowledgment of the citizens of one state by the citizens of all other states—the fierceness of their roused resentment—their curiosity and welcome of novelty—their self-esteem and wonderful sympathy—their susceptibility to a slight—the air they have of persons who never knew how it felt to stand in the presence of superiors—the fluency of their speech—their delight in music, the sure symptom of manly tenderness and native elegance of soul ... their good temper and openhandedness—the terrible significance of their elections—the President's taking off his hat to them not they to him— these too are unrhymed poetry. It awaits the gigantic and generous treatment worthy of it.[29]

Much that Whitman says in this long preface is not repeated until his very last writings—he published it with the first *Leaves of Grass*, the 1855 edition of the twelve untitled poems. None of the subsequent printings of the collection ever included this remarkable opening, but it is currently available in all editions of the Whitman *oeuvre*.

Whitman echoes it—at least implicitly—in one of his last poems, "The Commonplace,"

> The commonplace I sing,
> How cheap is health! How cheap nobility!
> Abstinence, no falsehood, no gluttony, lust;
> The open air I sing, freedom, toleration,
> (Take here the mainest lesson—less from books—less from the schools,)
> The common day and night—the common earth and waters,
> Your farm—your work, trade, occupation,
> The democratic wisdom underneath, like solid ground for all.[30]

---

[29] Whitman, "Preface," Library, 6.
[30] Whitman, "The Commonplace," Library, 651.

4

To Travel

It did not bother Whitman, that he never made it to Europe or England. None of his family traveled so far although the older relatives repeated stories they had heard about Holland and Britain. Cosmopolitanism was not high on the Whitman list of priorities, but somewhat accidently, in 1848 when Whitman was offered an editorial post with *The New Orleans Daily Crescent*, he went to Louisiana with alacrity—and his younger brother Jeff accompanied him.

As an integral part of the print culture, Whitman knew that many of his associates had crossed the Atlantic and he was, at a minimum, curious about other cultures. He often spoke of travel somewhat figuratively and when his *Leaves of Grass* appeared in 1855, there is a sense that he had made various travels earlier in his life. A passage from the latter part of "Song of Myself" is illustrative:

> I tramp a perpetual journey,
> My signs are a rain-proof coat and good shoes and a staff
>   cut from the woods;
> No friend of mine takes his ease in my chair,
> I have no chair, nor church nor philosophy;
> I lead no man to a dinner-table or library or exchange …
> My right hand points to landscapes of continents, and
>   a plain public road.

© The Author(s), under exclusive license to Springer Nature
Switzerland AG 2021
L. Wagner-Martin, *Walt Whitman*, Literary Lives,
https://doi.org/10.1007/978-3-030-77665-7_4

> Not I, nor any one else can travel that road for you,
> You must travel it for yourself ... .[1]

Karen Karbiener points out legitimately that living in Brooklyn and Manhattan from the 1820s on was almost like traveling extensively. The growth was phenomenal; for someone as observant as Whitman, he noted all the dramatic changes as soon as they occurred. Brooklyn in 1823 was a city of only 7000 people. By 1855, it was the fourth-largest city in the nation. Manhattan grew from 123,706 in 1820 to 813,669 in 1860. Then the city was mostly below Fourteenth Street but building moved northward until, in 1851, plans were developed for a "central park," which would begin at 59th Street. In 1850 five new rail lines were incorporated as one. Paralleling that growth was the explosion of omnibus availability. In 1853 that system carried over 100,000 people daily.[2]

Impressed with all the knowledge Whitman displayed about his city and its parts, this critic accepts his clear satisfaction with his life. She quotes,

> This is the city .... and I am one of the citizens:
> Whatever interests the rest interests me .... politics, churches,
>   newspapers, schools,
> Benevolent societies, improvements, banks, tariffs, steamships,
>   factories, markets,
> Stocks and stores and real estate and personal estate.

She also makes partial lists of some of the news stories he wrote during the 1840s: The opening of the Croton Aqueduct, which brought running water to city residents; the Astor Place Opera House riots, in which more than twenty people were killed in 1849; everything that happened in the "Bloody Sixth" ward and the crime-infested, impoverished streets of Five Points. He often went to the city opera houses, to the Museum of Egyptian Antiquities and the Phrenological Cabinet of the Fowler Brothers and Samuel Wells. And of course his work was in "Newspaper Row," just east of City Hall Park.[3]

But even city-proud Walt Whitman knew that his life during his 20 s and 30 s would have been changed immensely had he found some way to travel to Europe. Therefore, even though Karbiener considers Whitman's taking a job in New Orleans "impetuous," he had just lost a position in New York and, an important consideration, the offer from the New Orleans paper included

---

[1] Whitman, "Song of Myself," Library, 82.

[2] Karen Karbiener, "Introduction," *Walt Whitman, Leaves of Grass* (New York: Barnes and Noble, 2004), xxxi.

[3] Ibid., xxxii.

a $200 advance for travel expenses. There was no way any New York offer would have included such a cash stipend.

As biographer Jerome Loving contextualizes the story, New Orleans already had six daily papers, but Sam McClure and A. A. Hayes were starting this new daily independent of their earlier work. Well-funded, the *Crescent* would have only a small staff and many of its stories would be coming from New York coverage (creating ties with New York papers would be part of Whitman's role). A port city that was also a military base, New Orleans was home to wealthy planters and tourists traveling the Mississippi.

Whitman would do double duty as a printer, as would the fourteen-year-old Jeff, who was already an apprentice printer.

After the Whitmans traveled down the Mississippi on the steamship *St. Cloud,* Whitman wrote a three-part account of their February journey titled "Excerpts from a Traveller's Note Book." They had gone by rail to Baltimore and Cumberland and then by stagecoach over the Allegheny Mountains, taking the steamboat from Wheeling, West Virginia, down the Ohio River to the Mississippi. The two-week trip was inordinately slow because the steamboat was also a cargo ship.[4]

They found a moderate hotel, The Tremont House, in the American section of New Orleans, next door to the stunning St. Charles Theatre with its seating capacity of over 1000, and across from the *Crescent* office. Nearby were the offices of Pierson & Bonneval, Auctioneers, which sold land, machinery, and slaves.[5] As Whitman would write in "I Sing the Body Electric,"

A man's body at auction,
(For before the war I often go to the slave-mart and watch the sale,)
I help the auctioneer, the sloven does not half know his business.[6]

There is little of Whitman's writing in the *Crescent* to assess, a situation that suggests that he worked as an exchange editor and printer, alongside his brother Jeff, rather than as a news writer. One essay, unsigned, has been

---

[4] Loving, *Walt Whitman*, 114–18. Loving points out that while the Whitmans were not in steerage with immigrant travelers, they had probably booked second-class passage. But they could observe the celebrity—and the clothes—of the first-class passengers.

[5] Ibid., 119.

[6] Whitman, "I Sing the Body Electric," Library, 123 and the full page that follows. On page 124 a passage begins, "A woman at auction ... ." The image recurs in "Song of Myself" as well, "The quadroon girl is sold at the stand" and there are several lengthy passages there about African American men. The most moving is "I am the hounded slave .... I wince at the bite of the dogs,/ Hell and despair are upon me .... crack and again crack the marksmen./ I clutch the rails of the fence .... my gore dribs thinned with the ooze of my skin" (Library, 63).

identified as his because of its many references to New York. "The Inhabitants of Hotels" states early on that "There is no actual need of a man's
traveling around the globe in order to find out a few of the principles of
human nature." It also seemed, according to the writer, unnecessary to attend
any college. The bar scene in New Orleans covered blocks and blocks, with
men in evening dress drinking and smoking Havana cigars. The easiest haven
for newspapermen was the St. Charles Hotel, in the Quarter, not far from the
French Market.

There were many performances that Whitman attended at the St. Charles
Theatre,—Julie Dean, the Collyer actors who performed a semi-nude "Model
Artists" show—but Jeff was young and increasingly homesick. He and Walt
did not hear from their mother for the first six weeks of their stay in New
Orleans, and since they were accustomed to living and talking with her—and
eating her cooking—they felt very much adrift. Jeff was sometimes bothered
with dysentery since the Southern city was never noted for its cleanliness.

After three months in New Orleans, the Whitmans made an elaborate plan
for their return trip home. At odds with the Louisiana sentiment about slaves
as well as political events in Mexico, Europe, and the States, Walt Whitman
proposed to the *Crescent* owners that he leave their employment—after a
dispute over salary he felt he was owed.[7]

Both the Whitmans started their return back on *The Pride of the West* May
27, 1848; they spent some time in St. Louis before boarding the steamer
Prairie Bird to La Salle and then went by canal to Chicago, where they spent
several days. Most enthusiastic about the miles and miles of prairie, the poet
later wrote numerous poems and a series of prose poem paragraphs about
the natural scene that seemed to stem from this exuberant experience. Sailing
across Lake Michigan on the *Griffith*, enjoying the Wisconsin shore with its
many small towns, they then visited Milwaukee and the Michigan Upper
Peninsula—Mackinaw—before entering Lake Huron. After Lake Michigan
came Lake Erie, where the water was rougher than it had been on the other
Great Lakes, and Whitman admitted to sea sickness. Spending the night of
June 11 in Cleveland, Whitman walked the streets after dark and found that
even this Midwestern city had tolerable advantages. Later the two explored
Buffalo, New York and spent time at Niagara Falls. Then they traveled by
train to Albany and after a day's journey down the Hudson River, they finally
reached their parents' house on Adams Street near Myrtle Avenue late in the
evening."[8]

---

[7] Loving, *Walt Whitman*, 134–35.

[8] Loving, *Walt Whitman*, 139–40. The biographer draws as well on Whitman's answers to questions
posed to him by the *New Orleans Picayune*, compiling information on its fiftieth anniversary in 1887.

When Whitman himself wrote specifically about this time spent traveling the States, rather than talking about the stay as of three-months duration, he claimed he was gone *two years* and called the experience "a leisurely journey and working expedition." In quick sentences he described traveling "through nearly every one of the Middle, Southern, and Western states, and to Louisiana and Texas." With the exception of Texas, his geographical listing is close to accurate. He adds more detail in describing their return trip: "plodded back northward, up the Mississippi, and around to, and by way of the great lakes, Michigan, Huron, and Erie, to Niagara falls and lower Canada, finally returning through central New York and down the Hudson; traveling altogether probably 8000 miles this trip, to and fro."[9] Again, Whitman's mileage is less of an exaggeration than one might suppose, since the routes followed natural terrain and riverways, without benefit of any highways.

Whitman's responses to the *Picayune* questionnaire is characteristically detailed. He notes the price of an acre of land in Illinois, for instance, before telling his readers about "La Salle," Illinois:

> ... "we went on board a canal-boat, had a detention by sticking on a mud bar, and then jogg'd along at a slow trot, some seventy of us, on a moderate-sized boat. (If the weather hadn't been rather cool, particularly at night, it would have been insufferable.) Illinois is the most splendid agricultural country I ever saw; the land is of surpassing richness; the place par excellence for farmers. We stopt at various points along the canal, some of them pretty villages. ... . "

He continues, after spending the night in Chicago, "At 9 the next forenoon we started on the "Griffith" up the blue waters of Lake Michigan. I was delighted with the appearance of the towns along Wisconsin. At Milwaukee I went on shore, and walk'd around the place. They say the country back is beautiful and rich. (It seems to me that if we should ever remove from Long Island, Wisconsin would be the proper place to come to.) The towns have a remarkable appearance of good living, without any penury or want. The country is so good naturally, and labor is in such demand .... Sunday Morning, June 11—We pass'd down Lake Huron yesterday and last night, and between 4 and 5 o'clock this morning we ran on the "flats," and have been vainly trying, with the aid of a steam tug and a lumbering lighter, to get clear again. The day is beautiful and the water clear and calm. Night before last we stopt at Mackinaw, (the island and town,) and I went up on the old fort, one of the oldest stations in the Northwest. We expect to get to Buffalo

---

[9] Whitman, Through Eight Years, "Specimen Days," Library, 705.

by tomorrow. The tug has fasten'd lines to us, but some have been snapt and the others have no effect. We seem to be firmly imbedded in the sand .... We are now on Lake Erie, jogging along at a good round pace. A couple of hours since we were on the river above. Detroit seem'd to me a pretty place and thrifty. I especially liked the looks of the Canadian shore opposite and of the little village of Windsor, and, indeed, all along the banks of the river. From the shrubbery and the neat appearance of some of the cottages, I think it must have been settled by the French. While I now write we can see a little distance ahead the scene of the battle between Perry's fleet and the British during the last war with England. The lake looks to me a fine sheet of water. We are having a beautiful day. ...".[10]

One of the benefits of Whitman's travel was, obviously, sheer knowledge. He wrote quickly about the natural sights of the South, as well as the varieties of people who seemed to him to be classically "Southern." His new knowledge appears in "Song of Myself" and other poems from *Leaves of Grass,* particularly such paeans to nature as "I Saw in Louisiana a Live-Oak Growing," as well as "The Prairie-Grass Dividing," "To a Stranger," and "To the East as to the West," among others. In the "live-oak" poem, for instance, he finds a sonorous and long line that sets a leisurely pace for reflection, and the poem balances its second half with the first as if the poet would create a type of sonnet. "I Saw in Louisiana" projects the satisfied voice of an observant poet-traveler:

> I saw in Louisiana a live-oak growing,
> All alone stood it and the moss hung down from the branches,
> Without any companion it grew there uttering joyous leaves
>   of dark green,
> And its look, rude, unbending, lusty, made me
>   think of myself,
> But I wonder'd how it could utter joyous leaves
>   standing alone there without its friend near, for
>   I knew I could not,
> And I broke off a twig with a certain number of leaves
>   upon it, and twined around it a little moss,
> And brought it away, and I have placed it in sight in my room ... .[11]

The combination of the personal expression with the reflection of a beauty of nature creates a kind of essay in lines. Just as Whitman was to draw from his knowledge of effective language when he composed the long-lined poems

---

[10] Whitman, "New Orleans in 1848," Library, 1202–4.
[11] Whitman, "I Saw in Louisiana," Library, 279–80.

of the 1855 *Leaves of Grass*, so here he modifies that line to resemble more conventional "fireside" poems, drawing in the reader so that the voice in the poem seems natural. He starts this segue to the human by having the tree "utter" those "joyous" dark green leaves. The speaker's tactile joining with the fertile tree, as he breaks off a twig to preserve, is a kind of reciprocity.

Long after Whitman was writing the hundreds of poems that he continuously added to his *Leaves of Grass*, he wrote a substantial number of short passages about a natural scene—birds, trees, a river. He does not name this form—does he consider it a poem in paragraph form? A type of mini-essay? For instance, Whitman titles this description "A Meadow Lark:"

> March 16.—Fine, clear dazzling morning, the sun an hour high, the air just tart enough. What a stamp in advance my whole day receives from the song of that meadow lark perch'd on a fence-stake twenty rods distant! Two or three liquid-simple notes, repeated at intervals, full of careless happiness and hope. With its peculiar shimmering-slow progress and rapid-noiseless action of the wings, it flies on a ways, lights on another stake, and so on to another , shimmering and singing many minutes.

In "Clover and Hay Perfume," Whitman seemingly draws from the 1848 trip into the Middle West, when he was so amazed at the quantity of grain that Illinois fields produced. He does not disguise that point of origin, emphasizing that even the birds differ from those further east.

> July 3rd, 4th, 5th.—Clear, hot, favorable weather—has been a good summer— the growth of clover and grass now generally mow'd. The familiar delicious perfume fills the barns and lanes. As you go along you see the fields of grayish white slightly tinged with yellow, the loosely stack'd grain, the slow-moving wagons passing, and farmers in the fields with stout boys pitching and loading the sheaves. The corn is about beginning to tassel. All over the middle and southern states the spear-shaped battalia, multitudinous, curving, flaunting— long, glossy, dark-green plumes for the great horseman, earth. I hear the cheery notes of my old acquaintance Tommy quail; but too late for the whip-poor-will, (though I heard one solitary lingerer night before last.) I watch the broad majestic flight of a turkey-buzzard, sometimes high up, sometimes low enough to see the lines of his form, even his spread quills, in relief against the sky. Once or twice lately I have seen an eagle here at early candle-light flying low.

Precision is not lost in Whitman's word choice. In a passage titled "Sundown Lights," he begins with the description that "This is the hour for strange effects in light and shade—enough to make a colorist go delirious—long spokes of molten silver sent horizontally through the trees." The humor that sometimes enters Whitman's long lists of describers—even if at times such a tone seems out of place—surfaces frequently here as he addresses himself to a natural scene.

Occasionally the poet writes a description that merges into a kind of diary, as in "Thoughts Under an Oak—A Dream." Dated June 2, this description includes the writer as a participant in a more involved way than in some of his drawings of nature:

"This is the fourth day of a dark northeast storm, wind and rain. Day before yesterday was my birthday. I have now enter'd on my 60ᵗʰ year. Every day of the storm, protected by overshoes and a waterproof blanket, I regularly come down to the pond, and ensconce myself under the lee of the great oak; I am here now writing these lines. The dark smoke-color'd clouds roll in furious silence athwart the sky; the soft green leaves dangle all round me; the wind steadily keeps up its hoarse, soothing music over my head—Nature's mighty whisper. Seated here in solitude I have been musing over my life—connecting events, dates, as links of a chain, neither sadly nor cheerily, but somehow, to-day here under the oak, in the rain, in an unusually matter-of-fact spirit.

But my great oak—sturdy, vital, green—five feet thick at the butt, I sit a great deal near or under him. Then the tulip tree near by—the Apollo of the woods—tall and graceful, yet robust and sinewy, inimitable in hang of foliage and throwing-out of limb; as if the beauteous, vital, leafy creature could walk, if it only would. (I had a sort of dream-trance the other day, in which I saw my favorite trees step out and promenade up, down and around, very curiously—with a whisper from one, leaning down as he pass'd me, *We do all this on the present occasion, exceptionally, just for you.*).[12]

The strain of dream-knowledge or sheer fantasy that was inherent in some of the discussions of Transcendentalism seldom reached critics who read Whitman. Had Emerson still lived when Whitman was writing these meditations on nature, or more aptly, the natural world as it became an integral part of Whitman's world, he would have been among the first to applaud Whitman's reach. Instead, what became the dominant discussion about Whitman's months in New Orleans during 1848, much later than the various outrages about his creation of poetic form, was the investigation of the poet's sexuality—as well as his sexual preferences. The blatant mentioning of the sexual act—and, obviously, the sexual organs—was part of what made Whitman so objectionable. Some readers took the easiest course and simply tossed the 1855 *Leaves of Grass* into a trashcan. Others read any language of sexuality as if it were metaphoric. But just as nobody could miss the poet's

---

[12] Whitman, "Specimen Days," Library, 815–16.

interest in the body, accompanied by what some readers would consider that body's legitimate sexual functions, reading "Song of Myself," the first poem to appear in the first printing of *Leaves of Grass,* meant thinking about sex—sex throughout modern living, sex in America, sex as Whitman wrote about it, and sex that still remained objectionable for reading. To read "Song of Myself" meant being faced with sex: ten lines into the poem, Whitman colors the atmosphere with a rich perfume, of which he says "I am in love with it," followed by this rhapsodic set of lines that are much more than suggestive:

> I will go to the bank by the wood and become undisguised
>   and naked,
> I am mad for it to be in contact with me.
>
> The smoke of my own breath,
> Echos, ripples, and buzzed whispers .... loveroot,
>   silkthread, crotch and vine ... .[13]

Throughout this long and generally arresting opening work, Whitman brings us to thoughts of sex, often with no warning. He plans that the reader accepts the ubiquity of sexual thoughts: he never apologizes for their appearance. Whitman's point is that the genitals are a part of his body, just as the "thrust" of trying to reach physical closeness is germane to not only friendship but to life. As the stanza above closes,

> A few light kisses ... . a few embraces ... .a reaching
>   around of arms,
> The play of shine and shade on the trees as the supple
>   boughs wag,
> The delight alone or in the rush of the streets, or along the
>   fields and hillsides,
> The feeling of health ... . the full-noon trill ... . the
>   song of me rising from bed and meeting the sun.

Seven years before the publication of *Leaves of Grass,* then, what Whitman's biography tells readers is that he traveled thousands of miles to New Orleans where he had been offered work. Even in one of his greatest nature poems, "I Saw in Louisiana a Live-Oak Growing," the solitary character who envies the tree mentions "my own dear friends," "manly love," and the fact that the tree produces its abundant life "without a friend a lover near." The swift denouement makes the reader re-think the poem, and one who knows about

---

[13] Whitman, "Song of Myself," Library, 27.

the time spent in New Orleans ties Whitman's trip to this "Louisiana" mode, not so different from the effusive sex in "Song of Myself" but seemingly tied more specifically to his trip south. As Scott Donaldson recently asked in his study of literary biography, "What happened to Whitman on his trip to New Orleans?".[14]

Literary criticism moves through various stages: in the mid-nineteenth century, sexuality, and particularly homosexuality, was a topic few genteel critics would discuss. More recently, rather than using the term *homosexuality*, critics such as Caleb Crain or Kristin Boudreau or Cindy Weinstein have written studies of "sympathy" or "empathy," about writers focused on American men. Harold Aspiz studied *Walt Whitman and the Body* while Vivian Pollack wrote about *The Erotic Whitman*. M. Jimmie Killingsworth wrote early about *Whitman's Poetry of the Body: Sexuality, Politics, and the Text*. Before that Joseph Cady published his essay "Not Happy in the Capitol: Homosexuality and the *Calamus* Poems." Betsy Erkkila, Gary Schmidgall, Glenn Hendler, and Michael Moon were other sensible pioneers. Jerome Loving suggests that the word "homosexual" was not being used until the 1890s,[15] although he notes that Whitman's biographers have worried these questions for generations.

Some of this controversy parallels the difference of opinion to do with Whitman's interest in—and participation in—the politics of the mid-nineteenth century, especially as it influenced the American Civil War. In Whitman's case, because he became so personally involved with the soldiers and survivors of the actual war battles, beginning in 1862, there is a tendency to ascribe more knowledge of and interest in politics than his news articles may support. What this level of critical controversy means is that the close perusal of the quantity of electronic resources now available come into scholarly play, and eventually some definitive statements will be helpful to the general reader.

Whitman himself described the paths his poetry and human interests took as he worked toward writing what would become his book of life: decades after the first printing of *Leaves of Grass*, the poet wrote,

> Long I thought that knowledge alone would suffice me—
>   O if I could not but obtain knowledge!

---

[14] Scott Donaldson, *The Impossible Craft*. University Park: Pennsylvania State University Press, 2015: 100.

[15] Loving, *Walt Whitman*, 270. He also notes that "slept with" might have a reference to "a contingency sleeping arrangement in a working-class neighborhood," and be literal. He also sees some of the poet's objectionable sexual references to stem from class. "I Sing the Body Electric" comes directly from "the poet's Brooklyn and Long Island experiences." See 202–3.

Then my lands engrossed me—Lands of the prairies, Ohio's
land, the southern savannas, engrossed me—
For them I would live—I would be their orator ... .[16]

The list continues, but in retrospect, even the poet sees how central those months traveling to and from Louisiana had been as he developed the new kind of poetry that would appear only seven years after the New Orleans trip.

[16] Whitman, "Calamus.8," "Poems Excluded from the 'Death-Bed' Edition," *Leaves of Grass,* Barnes and Noble Classics, 755.

5

Leaves of Grass, 1855

It was a book few people were ever going to see. In the midst of the years after Whitman returned from New Orleans, he still played with the idea of writing a book, *his* book: his strong opinions and somewhat narrow political views had just led to the loss of several newspaper jobs and, as Jerome Loving said, Whitman had to be recognizing that he was being undermined by "his relative poverty and uncertainty about finding a satisfying profession."[1] As his siblings had long known, for Walt, it was never just about the money.

Ironically, when he returned to New York in June of 1848, he brought with him some savings. He bought land and built a few houses—but he was also looking for work as a newspaperman. His absence over the spring had seemingly wiped out any name recognition he had accumulated. When he wrote late in life about the years between 1848 and 1855, the year he published *Leaves of Grass*, he said only,

> "Commenced putting *Leaves of Grass* to press, for good—after many MSS. doings and undoings—I had great trouble in leaving out the stock 'poetical' touches—but succeeded at last."[2]

There was more going on than this note suggests. Whitman seemed to be exploring new areas—he went to opera and theatre and concerts. Loving says, "the notebooks leading up to *Leaves of Grass* imply that Whitman was awash

---

[1] Loving, *Walt Whitman*, 41.
[2] Whitman, "1852–54," Library, 1297.

L. Wagner-Martin, *Walt Whitman*, Literary Lives, https://doi.org/10.1007/978-3-030-77665-7_5

in romantic ideas about arts and the artist,"[3] but he also was searching for employment. He republished some stories and sketches. He worked as a free-lancer, profiting from his trip to Louisiana in his ten-part series, "Letters from a Travelling Bachelor" for the *New York Sunday Dispatch*. He sometimes lived in Greenport, an old whaling village. He tried to establish a new penny-paper, but the politics and a damaging fire at nearby buildings interfered. While he was editing the last of his papers, the *Freeman*, he finished building the home on Myrtle Street that housed his bookstore. Eventually he lost the *Freeman*. He then started an advertising sheet, *Salesmen and Traveller's Directory for Long Island*, which quickly failed.[4]

According to his notebooks, by 1852 Whitman was working toward the poems—or the rhythmic prose, however he conceived of this writing—that would comprise *Leaves of Grass*. Along with experimenting with new writing styles, he was reconstructing some family history that was proving useful. His mother's Quakerism, and her reverence for the mystical preachings of Elias Hicks, was one source of Whitman's new ways of tapping into language. It is probably true that Whitman's family was not quite so unread or so untutored as their low economic class suggested. Louisa was a strong and caring woman who had grown up a Quaker, living among the natural beauties of her family's farm. She loved animals and for years was a successful horseback rider. If Whitman now, using his financial cushion and his profits from building, spent time feeling less pressured to "work" in a newspaper office, perhaps he was learning a more leisurely approach to the worlds of both nature and spirit.

Several biographers have mentioned what Whitman called mysterious "perturbations" which helped him create *Leaves of Grass*. He spoke of this somewhat mystical state of mind as "great pressure, pressure from within" that caused him to feel an urgency—"that he must do it."[5]

It was not as if Whitman surrounded himself with people who cared about aesthetic principles; observers commented that they didn't *know* about his poetry writing, or even about the publication of *Leaves of Grass*. Aimed at readers who might have fewer sophisticated skills than those who normally read verse, Whitman's poems were still *poems*—and for most of his friends and his family members that language seemed obscure, indirect, and bewildering. Given that situation, he worked pretty much in secret. Finally, he felt that he was ready to put his lines of poetry—all still untitled—and their extremely long "Preface" into print.

---

[3] Loving, *Walt Whitman*, 162.

[4] Loving, *Walt Whitman*, 143–47.

[5] Justin Kaplan, *Walt Whitman, A Life*. New York: Simon & Schuster, 1980:185.

The publication date for *Leaves of Grass* was July 4, 1855. The *American* poem, the "new" American poem, was—as Whitman expressed it through the long "Preface"—this work, a rhapsodic flood of words that were not titled, not subdivided, an almost impenetrable whirl of language that should be read aloud. Whitman knew what *oratory* meant, and he saw the oratorical qualities in the pages he had written. He later admitted to friends that *he* read his work out loud as a matter of course: the American language was language written to be *heard*.

As Karen Karbiener stated, Whitman understood that this process demanded privacy, a sorting through of drafts and pages, a collection and a recollection. "Purposefully dropping out of workaday life and common sight suggests that Whitman may have intended to obscure the details of his pre-*Leaves* years, and there is further evidence to support the idea that Whitman consciously created a 'myth of origins.'" Drawing from Whitman's early critics, she describes the poet's "clean-up" processes, when he destroyed significant amounts of manuscripts and letters, reminding himself to "not name any names." He also advised, "Make no quotations, and no reference to any other writers.—Lumber the writing with nothing."[6]

Once Whitman had his poems together, each in a format he approved, he had difficulty finding a printer to do the work. He arranged with friends at Andrew and James Rome's print shop at Cranberry and Fulton streets and, as part of that arrangement, set some of the type himself. (He knew he would be paying the entire cost.) The small booklet was eventually distributed by Fowler and Wells in Manhattan, the group that had performed Whitman's phrenological reading. There are no sales records; there were barely any sales. In Loving's emphasis on place, he describes the site of the printers, "the Ryerson Streets and the Mrytle Avenues of Brooklyn... a fairly reliable microcosm of the United States." He adds that *Leaves of Grass* foreshadows Whitman's crossings on the ferry: "The motion is back and forth rather than forward. The journey of the soul is therefore relative—with time and distance availing for nothing. The imagery also reflects a real, physical journey, for Whitman often took the ferry for the fresh air."[7]

Karbiener too points out how aligned Whitman's poetry was to his democratic beliefs, quoting from the "Preface": "This is what you shall do: Love the earth and sun and the animals; despise riches, give alms to everyone that asks, stand up for the stupid and crazy, devote your income and labor to others; hate tyrants; argue *not* concerning God, have patience and indulgence toward the people; take off your hat to nothing known or unknown or to any man

---

[6] Karen Karbiener, "Introduction," *Leaves of Grass*. New York: Barnes & Noble, 2004: xxvii.
[7] Loving, *Walt Whitman*, 178–79, 207.

or number of men, go freely with powerful uneducated persons and with the young and with the mothers of families, read these leaves in the open air every season of every year of your life, re-examine all you have been told at school or church or in any book, dismiss whatever insults your own soul, and your very flesh shall be a great poem and have the richest fluency not only in its words but in the silent lines of its lips and face and between the lashes of your eyes and in every motion and joint of your body."[8]

For Karbiener, Whitman's aim was to "shake awake a slumbering, passive nation and inspire a loving, proud, generous, accepting union of active thinkers and thoughtful doers." For William Dow, Whitman's poetry truly stemmed from his political beliefs. In his lexicon "'democracy' stands less for a realizable mode of government than it does for a conception of the classed body, personal relations, and erotic intimacies that could be shared by anyone able to interpret him." His choices of words reflect this motivation: "in the poem Whitman uses a language that itself functions as an *act,* not a *report* of one.... *Leaves of Grass* is therefore resistant to any kind of social marginality."[9]

It became more than a cottage industry—trying to describe how Whitman's seemingly innovative approach to poetics both stemmed from existing poetry and influenced the next decades of typically "American" art. Richard Chase emphasized that all the elements of a poem were there—parallelism, repetitions of word, image, or idea, and "counterbalance of phrases and lines... cycles of statement and restatement, the restatement providing the poem with momentum because it not only restates but at the same time amplifies, modulates, or qualifies what has been said and prepares us, it may be, for the next rhythmic cycle."[10] In the past thirty years, now that Whitman's poetry is being taken more and more seriously, the critical consensus has come to be that his "poetics" was not nearly so original as had been thought. Angus Fletcher sees Whitman as developing his language out of then-emerging forms in both the United States and England; Kenneth Price considers Whitman's prosody as less a break from tradition than a modification of traditional forms. Stephen Cushman took on the argument that form was less the issue than the fact that Whitman still used "alliteration, anaphora, assonance, apostrophe, parallelism, and personification." For Theo Davis, writing as recently as 2016, he sees what Whitman creates as "a string of emblematic gestures, cut and set together in a way that constrains our ability to understand them as representative." Davis uses the term "ornamentation" and finds in it the practice that gives Whitman's lists their distinctive

---

[8] Karen Karbiener, "Introduction" including Whitman's "Preface," *Leaves of Grass,* xxxvii.

[9] Karbiener, "Introduction, xxxviii; Dow, *Narrating Class,* 18.

[10] Chase, *Walt Whitman,* 16.

character—"they are so laden with clauses as to overflow with an abundance that piles over the content of the words."[11]

It became the task of M. L. Rosenthal and Sally M. Gall, writing in 1983, to create a new category for Whitman, that of the creator of the American "long poem." By placing "Song of Myself" (and what they saw as Whitman's other major poems, "Drum-Taps" and "Calamus") in the company of works by Hart Crane, William Carlos Williams, Anne Sexton, Sylvia Plath, W. D. Snodgrass, Robert Lowell and others, these critics set new parameters for a successful work. Their analysis made the earlier pronouncements of Chase and others—that Whitman wrote the first "modern" American poem—more defensible. If fragmentation and collage had become the modern structural principle for both prose and poetry—a reflection of the effusion of thoughts, stories, polyglot languages, and unwritten emotions that ran rampant through the city streets, then Whitman had become a prognosticator of modernism in the United States.

These critics rehearse the way *Leaves of Grass* developed—without poem titles, with no break indications. The 52 divisions of "Song of Myself" came later, as did spacing, as did the numbering of its 372 sections. It was as if Whitman changed what he thought would be reader perceptions as the poems in *Leaves of Grass* grew and developed. He was learning to think of frames for his words.

Rosenthal and Gall emphasize "tonalities" in "Song of Myself." Out of the "sheer variety" of tone, they chart that this poem "starts exuberantly and yet ceremonially, its speaking sensibility that of a man bursting with health and self-regard who is yet a bard chanting formulaically." Its language is of "delighted choice." They find seven major tonal groupings within "Song of Myself," seeing sections 21-29 as a climactic group. Early on, Whitman uses "a language of almost unbearable sensation."

Then the poet speaks of death and decay, emphasizing the "barbarity and pathos of war." This is the downward movement into despair and then to "a form of darkened reaffirmation."[12] Such an incisive reading brings the task Whitman undertook in the years leading to the publication of *Leaves of Grass*

---

[11] Angus Fletcher, *A New Theory of American Poetry: Democracy, the Environment, and the Future of Imagination*. Cambridge, MA: Harvard University Press, 2004; Kenneth M. Price, *Whitman and Tradition: The Poet in His Century*. New Haven, CT: Yale University Press, 1990, 21; Stephen Cushman, *Fictions of Form in American Poetry*. Princeton: Princeton University Press, 1993, 125; Theo Davis, *Ornamental Aesthetics: The Poetry of Attending to Thoreau, Dickinson, and Whitman*. New York: Oxford University Press, 2016, 142, 153.

[12] M. L. Rosenthal and Sally M. Gall, *The Modern Poetic Sequence*. New York: Oxford University Press, 1983: 25–44.

into relief: the structure, reflective of the poet's strategy, was always carefully polished.

It was also overwhelming. Effusive, blatant, cheering on the nondescript readers who saw the heart of its language as exuberance:

> "This is the city. . . . and I am one of the citizens;
> Whatever interests the rest interest me. . . . politics, churches, newspapers, schools,
> Benevolent societies, improvements, banks, tariffs, steamships, factories, markets,
> Stocks and stores and real estate and personal estate. . ."

A few segments later, the poet announces, "Sermons and creeds and theology. . . . but the human brain, and what is called reason, and what is called love, and what is called life."

Part of the ebb and flow of meaning in the poem accrues from repetition. Whitman had earlier stated,

> "Behold I do not give lectures or a little charity,
> What I give I give out of myself."

As an aside, the poet announces, "I think I will do nothing for a long time but listen."

He continues in an admonitory vein,

> "Logic and sermons never convince,
> The damp of the night drives deeper into my soul.
>
>
> Only what proves itself to every man and woman is so,
> Only what nobody denies is so."

Always positive in his plans, the poet explains to his reader:

> "I am enamoured of growing outdoors,
> Of men that live among cattle or taste of the ocean or woods,
> Of the builders and steerers of ships, of the wielders of axes and mauls, of the drivers of horses,
> I can eat and sleep with them week in and week out."[13]

---

[13] Whitman, "Song of Myself," Library, 79, 75, 59, 56, 40.

Whitman does not just draw up lists, however, he tells the stories of many of his characters. William Dow pointed out that much of Whitman's storytelling came from the newspaper accounts of those he was reading about: "Whitman did not have to go out 'into the field' because he was permanently living in the field."[14]

Dow comments that Whitman uses a "working class" language, one with elements of the "disorderly, fleshy, sensual, democratic presence embodied.

He speaks in idioms but he also commands a position of leadership: above all, he does not want to sound like a European."[15] With less specificity, Theo Davis sees Whitman's language choices as part of his "ornamentation," his means of writing as if both poet and poem "were adorning the world." For Whitman, Davis says, literary form "is part of lived experience."[16]

As to the stories Whitman includes in "Song of Myself" and all his other early poems, their presence has forced critics to play biographer more often than not. We have seen his mention of selling slaves at auction in New Orleans. Yet there are several more impressive passages that deal with Whitman's relationship to African Americans—and to force those passages into a discussion of slave or non-slave does a disservice to the poem. Early on, Whitman writes

> "The negro holds firmly the reins of his horses....
>   the block swags underneath on its tied-over chain,
> The negro that drives the huge dray of the stoneyard. . . .
>   steady and tall he stands poised on one leg on the stringpiece,
> His blue shirt exposes his ample neck and breast and loosens
>   over his hipband,
> His glance is calm and commanding. . . . he tosses the slouch
>   of his hat away from his forehead,
> The sun falls on his crispy hair and moustache. . . . falls on the black
>   of his polish'd and perfect limbs,
> I behold the picturesque giant and love him. . . . and I do not
>   stop there,
> I go with the team also. . . ."[17]

Thinking specifically of what Whitman had written in his "Preface" to the 1855 collection, one can see the fragility of his capturing a sense of reality through memory: the details of the scene bring this figure to life. In the "Preface," he had written that these would be his subjects in poetry:

---

14 Dow, *Narrating Class*, 10.
15 Dow, *Narrating Class*, 24, 29.
16 Theo Davis, *Ornamental Aesthetics*, 155–56.
17 Whitman, "Song of Myself," Library, 37.

"men and women and the earth and all upon it are simply to be taken as they are, and the investigation of their past and present and future shall be uninterrupted and shall be done with perfect candor.... For the eternal tendencies of all toward happiness make the only point of sane philosophy."[18]

Critics have often commented about the lengthy story of the Fall of the Alamo, a marvel of set description that foreshadows some of Whitman's later writing in *Drum-taps*. But it may be the smaller stories that have caused the most questioning, since readers are eager to find links between subject matter and writer. In the case of Whitman's assumed story about the runaway slave, for example, a reader wants to place that account in the New Orleans time frame—though it could have happened anywhere in the northeast as well (or it could, more likely, be imaginary).

"The runaway slave came to my house and stopped outside,
I heard his motions crackling the twigs of the woodpile,
Through the swung half-door of the kitchen, I saw him
    limpsey and weak,
And went where he sat on a log, and led him in and assured him,
And brought water and filled a tub for his sweated body and bruised feet,
And gave him a room that entered from my own, and gave him
    some coarse clean clothes,
And remember perfectly well his revolving eyes and his
    awkwardness,
And remember putting plasters on the galls of his neck and ankles;
He staid with me a week before he was recuperated and
    passed north,
I had him sit next to me at table. . . . my firelock leaned in
    the corner."[19]

Messianic in tone, the poet places himself in the role of a savior—yet because the comfort he provides is so simple, so negligible, it does not call attention to his generosity. For the reader of "Song of Myself," a passage from a later section might be brought into this scene. Whitman writes a commonplace testimonial:

"Why should I wish to see God better than this day?
I see something of God each hour of the twenty-four, and each moment then,
In the faces of men and women I see God, and in my own face in the glass;
I find letters from God dropped in the street, and every one is signed by

---

18 Whitman, "Preface," Library, 16.
19 Whitman, "Song of Myself," Library, 35–36.

God's name;
And I leave them where they are, for I know that others will punctually
  come forever and ever."[20]

Whitman's ability to weave disparate segments into intricate patterns appears
everywhere in "Song of Myself." After the perfectly paced description of the
runaway slave, above, he segues to one of the more famous of his descriptions
of men ("Twenty-eight young men bathe by the shore") and then appears the
description of "The negro holds firmly the reins of his four horses," quoted
earlier.

But, as if in a summary metaphor, comes

"The wild gander leads his flock through the cool night,
Ya-honk! he says, and sounds it down to me like an invitation;
The pert may suppose it meaningless, but I listen closer,
I find its purpose and place up there toward the November sky."[21]

When Whitman had instructed future readers to return to his book every
year, he was surely underscoring the various kinds of richnesses woven
through the many pages of even that slim *Leaves of Grass*.

To be even-handed, one might chart Whitman's separate poem segments
about women, particularly mothers, in a similar manner, but these are mostly
one or two lines of description. Moving from "Song of Myself" through "A
Song of Occupations" and the rest of the 1855 volume, it is only in the poem
"Faces" where Whitman writes a comparable portrait of a woman:

"Behold a woman!
She looks out from her quaker cap. . . . her face is clearer and
  more beautiful than the sky.

She sits in an armchair under the shaded porch of the farmhouse,
The sun just shines on her old white head.
Her ample gown is of creamhued linen,
Her grandsons raised the flax, and her granddaughters spun it
  with the distaff and the wheel.

The melodious character of the earth!

---

[20] Ibid., 88.
[21] Whitman, "Song of Myself," Library, 38.

The finish beyond which philosophy cannot go and does not
    wish to go!
The justified mother of men!"[22]

There are many more passages that relate to women—though these, too, are usually mothers or a parent paired with the father; single women characters (separate from families) are rare in Whitman's poetics, even as he develops hundreds of new poems for the successive collections of *Leaves of Grass*. The paucity of women, in fact, might need to be considered when the supposed "romances" of his New Orleans months come into question.

---

[22] Whitman, "Faces," Library, 128.

6

Whitman's Life as "Poet"

Getting *Leaves of Grass* published in 1855 was the first visible step in Whitman's moving into the literary arena as a *poet*. For all the attention the slim book received, it was something of a wonder that Whitman felt properly launched, though as we have discussed, his receiving Emerson's letter of praise—that, alone—would have kept him writing. Edward Everett Hale reviewed *Leaves of Grass* in *Putnam's Monthly*, saying that somehow "Yankee transcendentalism and New York rowdyism" had managed to "fuse and combine."[1]

Whitman would have liked the phrase "New York rowdyism" because, more and more often, he claimed the great city's influence on his aesthetics. Those American voices his poems were trying to replicate were all speaking with Northern urban accents. They were breaking into each others' statements, mirroring the confused sounds of people speaking—sometimes without waiting for replies—"Jostling me through streets and public halls. . . ./Crying by day Ahoy from the rocks of the river. . . ./Swinging and chirping over my head,/Calling my name from flowerbeds or vines or tangled underbrush,/Or while I swim in the bath. . . . or drink from the pump at the corner. . . . or the curtain is down at the opera. . . . or I glimpse at a woman's face in the railroad car. . . ."[2]

---

[1] Michael J. Colacurcio, "Idealism and Independence," *Columbia Literary History of the United States*, ed. Emory Elliott. New York: Columbia University Press, 1988: 219.

[2] Whitman, "Song of Myself," Library, 80–81.

© The Author(s), under exclusive license to Springer Nature Switzerland AG 2021
L. Wagner-Martin, *Walt Whitman*, Literary Lives,
https://doi.org/10.1007/978-3-030-77665-7_6

The poet as city dweller lists his leisurely walking, "Through the gymnasium. . . . through the curtained saloon. . . . through the office or public hall. . . . Looking in at the shop-windows on Broadway the whole forenoon. . . . pressing the flesh of my nose to the thick plate-glass,/Wandering the same afternoon with my face turned up to the clouds. . . .

> "Hurrying with the modern crowd, as eager and fickle as any,
> Hot toward one I hate, ready in my madness to knife him. . .
> Storming enjoying planning loving, cautioning,
> Backing and falling, appearing and disappearing,
> I tread day and night such roads. . ."
> Ever the narrator, Whitman describes "a call in the midst of the crowd. . .
> Ever the eaters and drinkers. . . . ever the upward and downward sun. . . . ever
>   the air and the ceaseless tides,
>   Ever myself and my neighbors, refreshing and wicked and real. . . .
> And as he nears a pause in his listing, the voice of Whitman notes:
>   My words are words of a questioning, and to indicate reality;
> This printed and bound book. . ."[3]

Whitman creates an unusual *stop* here as all this physical movement crystallizes into the oasis of his *book*. Usually thought of as more of a conglomerate poem, including natural scenes, seascapes, and bucolic landscapes, the source of "Song of Myself" again and again comes from the city. A different kind of energy, as William Sharpe writes about the aesthetics of city writers:

> "in the city no self can be held apart from the urban whirl. . .that
> observer and the objects he sees engender each other."[4]

One effect of this reciprocity is that the writer's imagination transcends the limits of the visibly physical.

This critic sees the years immediately after 1855 as Whitman's best writing about "Mannahata," and along with "Song of Myself," he chooses to discuss "Crossing Brooklyn Ferry" and other of the "Calamus" poems. His point seems to be that Whitman's days *as a New York poet* brought him some of his most accomplished writing. Whitman's attempts to reinscribe himself as the Manhattan poet brought a new capaciousness to his expression. He had previously emphasized the poet's communication skills but in these works

---

[3] Whitman, "Song of Myself," Library, 62–63, 75–76.
[4] William Chapman Sharpe, *Unreal Cities*. Baltimore, MD: Johns Hopkins University Press, 1990: 69–70.

he immersed his readers/listeners in the process of coming to language. A different critic sees Whitman's catalogues and listings as homage to the new art of photography. Reading through long sequences of description in these first poems has the same effect as looking through a photograph album, or to watching a video montage. When Whitman titles one of the first poems "Faces," he is surely thinking of visual effects.[5]

Excited that his book would appear, Whitman immediately began adding new poems to his collection. Just as quickly, however, disappointed at the lack of sales, he decided he erred in pricing his slim book at $2. So he changed its cover and removed the elegant touches, packaging the next 200 copies to sell for $1. The 800 copies of the first print run were nearly all, eventually, destroyed. So, to the literary world's confusion, Whitman published two printings of *Leaves of Grass* in 1855. The second printing did not change any of the poems in their original arrangement, but Whitman added a *before*-section that included three of *his* very positive, anonymous "self-reviews."

Just a year later, in 1856, came the official "Second Edition" of *Leaves of Grass*.

Excited by the results of his current writing, Whitman here included the letter from Emerson in a promotional section entitled "'Leaves Droppings.'" In 1860 appeared the Third Edition, and two impressions of the same work were printed. In this collection, which was much expanded from the original 1855 book, Whitman used special titles for groupings that helped readers follow thematic patterns.

To summarize the subsequent editions running through the 1860s, 1870s, and 1880s, I quote here from Karbiener's listing.[6]

Whitman saw his "poem" as continually developing, as indeed it did. By the time of the full collection in the early 1880s, the twelve original

---

[5] Karen Karbiener, "Introduction," *Leaves of Grass*, xl.

[6] "1865 (*Drum-Taps*): A separate book of poems on the Civil War, not initially part of *Leaves of Grass* but an important later addition.

1865–1866 (Sequel to *Drum-Taps*): Bound in with *Drum-Taps* after Lincoln's death.

1867 (Fourth Edition): *Leaves of Grass* poems, plus the annexes "Drum-Taps," "Sequel to Drum-Taps," and "Songs before Parting."

1871, 1872, 1876 (Fifth Edition): Published in Washington, DC, in 1871 with ten new poems, and republished again later that year with the separately paginated section *Passage to India*, also published as a separate volume that year. The 1872 impression contains the annexes "Passage to India" and "After All, Not to Create Only." The 1876 impression came out in two variants: *Leaves of Grass, Author's Edition, with Portraits and Intercalations*, and *Leaves of Grass, Author's Edition, with Portraits from Life*; a companion volume entitled *Two Rivulets* accompanied both.

1881, 1882, 1883, 1884, 1888, 1889, 1891–1892 (Sixth Edition): The 1881 plates were used in all subsequent impressions of *Leaves of Grass* during Whitman's life-time." Karen Karbiener, "Introduction," *Leaves of Grass*, 161–62.

poems—the core of *Leaves of Grass*—had grown to a book of more than four hundred poems. The original twelve poems, though sometimes changed, were placed carefully as if *scattered* throughout the long volume. Subsequently added poems were included though some had been separated by stanzas: they had, through Whitman's revisions, become very different works, their titles changed on occasion. The poem that later became "Song of Myself"—untitled in the 1855 edition, as were all the poems—was in the 1856 edition called "Poem of Walt Whitman, an American." By the time of the "Death-Bed" edition, which was finally printed in 1891–1892, tracking a single title through this panoply of poems was difficult.

The evidence of Whitman's need to select and revise, sorting through this assemblage of poems, adding in some passages, taking out others, lies in the monumental last collection, which is now considered the definitive *Leaves of Grass*.

In studying these changes, the critic can see without question that Whitman had a clear idea of what his poetry was meant to be saying: there was nothing imitative, nothing hesitant, nothing indefinite, in *Leaves of Grass*.

In the late 1850s, however, when so few readers even knew what *Leaves of Grass* indicated, Whitman was feeling his way toward competency. For all the somewhat sentimental readings of the word "grass," with its native link to the American scene, and its mystical link to spiritual energy, as well as a poetic link to the interrogation that Whitman plays with in "Song of Myself," it may be that Jerome Loving's definition of the way a professional printer would think about "grass" wins the day. Loving notes that when printers were killing time, they sometimes printed up materials just for practice—"grass" in that jargon meant "compositions of dubious value." The word 'leaves" shared the same printer's doubleness—*pages* as well as *bundles* of paper. It would come as little surprise if Whitman's ironic titling of his book was meant to suggest a kind of double meaning.[7]

Without realizing that his July 4 publication of *Leaves of Grass* might *not* change his life, Whitman had planned carefully for both the book and his subsequent time as an author. He had purchased his family's home for cash, putting the property in his mother's name. There would be no mortgage payments to owe, and he could plan ahead for the low property taxes. He could not plan ahead for his father's death, which occurred just a week after *Leaves of Grass* appeared, but the ailing head of the family had not been able to earn much income for months. Whitman knew supporting his mother

[7] Loving, *Walt Whitman*, 179.

and his youngest brother, Eddy, would fall at least partly to him, and he was satisfied with his sharing Eddy's room whenever he lived at home.

Loving speculates that there was a great deal of comfort in living with Louisa and Eddy. Whitman enjoyed the stability of a normal home: meals were plentiful, nights were long and restful, and yet his days were his own, and he traveled around the city as he liked, frequenting the public baths, seeing friends. (He later recalled his visits to the beach at Coney Island, "at that time a long, bare unfrequented shore, which I had all to myself, and where I loved, after bathing, to race up and down the hard sand, and declaim Homer or Shakespeare to the surf and sea-gulls by the hour."[8]) His biographer points out that Whitman often praised the regularity of the trains, the expectations of New Yorkers as they lived their comparatively steady lives in the milieu, a place where things *did* work—his attitudes from his journalism seldom varied.

Some of the time, however, when life for the Whitmans was placid, the poet would move his own house—and his stacks of paper—out to Greenport, where he lived even more modestly than did his family. As he had written in one of his "Travelling Bachelor" essays, he enjoyed the privacy of living alone, and he had always felt comfortable enclosed in the natural world. But even then, he kept his finger on the pulse of New York: "he preferred the city for the construction of the complete person."[9]

For Whitman to continue writing new poems at a pace equal to the work he had done before 1855 meant that he was prioritizing his thinking and writing. What he now considered his life's work did not take any kind of a back seat to his role as the family's wage earner. His mind was filled with lines of poetry. Loving gives as one example that when he returned home from New Orleans, Whitman began working on the poem that eventually would become "Crossing Brooklyn Ferry." His notebooks from the early 1850s show that some of his notes then migrated into patterns that finally became parts of "Song of Myself." Yet he did also create the very meaningful city poem ("Crossing Brooklyn Ferry"). An observer might think of a process of gestation: months of considering language, images, scenes, in order to crystallize meaning.[10]

He had learned that he could always make money writing as a freelancer, though some papers were less compatible than others. And if worse came to worse, there was construction, and he sometimes helped with projects that made use of one or another of his brothers—none of them consistently

---

[8] Whitman, "Specimen Days," Library, 566.
[9] Loving, *Walt Whitman*, 147.
[10] Ibid., 149.

employed, as a rule. Just getting by was no hardship to a man recently turned forty, a man who knew his aims and his responsibilities and who was content with a life that moved to his own plan. But there were also new social paths that Whitman found appealing. More distinguished than writing for newspapers, being a poet had brought him back into some of the relatively interesting social paths that for a time had been closed to him.[11]

The intellectual circles that might have begun to include him were slow to respond, however. He attended some of Emerson's talks and readings, and shared an occasional meal with him when he stayed at a New York hotel. Through Emerson, he had met both Henry David Thoreau and Bronson Alcott—but of that group he wrote, with some disappointment, "all had the same manner. . . . they meant me to see they were willing to come only so far: that coming an inch beyond that would mean disaster to us all."[12]

When Alcott decided to visit Whitman at his mother's house on October 4, 1856, the men had a good conversation and Alcott enjoyed Louisa's dinner (though she served beef and discovered to her confusion that Alcott was a vegetarian). A month later, Alcott brought Thoreau and a lady friend—but they then missed Whitman. They returned the following day and Louisa sent the group upstairs to Whitman's room, which he shared with Eddy. Somewhat surprised at the unkemptness of the house, Alcott wrote later about the unmade bed, with "the vessel scarcely hidden underneath. A few books were piled disorderly over the mantel-piece. . . the walls were very rude." Whitman spoke then of his pleasure in "visiting the public baths daily even in midwinter, and riding atop omnibuses up and down Broadway, beside the driver."[13]

With no apparent connection to Whitman's *Leaves of Grass*, the often out-of-work poet found himself a part of the inner circle at the German bar and eatery in Greenwich Village. Pfaff's, housed at 647 Broadway, welcomed children as well as parents, laborers as well as doctors and lawyers, anyone who entered—women as well as men. One social observer listed some of the women who were regulars—actress Ellen Gray, dancer Lola Montez, and journalist Juliette Beach, as well as Ada Isaacs Menken, herself a progressive poet, and Ada Clare, "the Queen of Bohemia" and a regular contributor to Henry Clapp, Jr.'s *Saturday Press*, the print organ that represented Pfaff's tight-knit society.

---

[11] Lawson, *Walt Whitman*, 82. According to Lawson he was no longer invited to Anne Lynch's Waverly Place salon.

[12] Whitman, WWCIII, 403, in Loving, *Walt Whitman*, 403.

[13] Loving, *Walt Whitman*, 224–25; and see *Journals of Bronson Alcott*, 278–94.

Informal and blessedly inexpensive, Pfaff's served the best German wines in the city, but it was more famous for German lager in steins and strong coffee, accompanied by beef, German pancakes, sausages, and cheeses, the food served on "fine china and genuine silver flatware." What it created was "a gas-lit, smoke-filled basement, its floor covered with sawdust," a cordial circle where people told stories and ate and drank in good fellowship—without any pressure to buy more and more drinks. The bar was known for its affability, the kindly caring of Pfaff himself, and a kind of studied privacy—ambience that never threatened anyone.

When Walt Whitman took the ferry from Brooklyn and spent long hours of the night at Pfaff's, he was enjoying the comfort of his usual friends—Charles Chaunsey, an importer, Benjamin Knover, a "clerk," Charles Kingsley, in training for sailing, Nat Bloom, a cartman, Henry Clapp, Jr, founder-editor of the *Saturday Press*, and the younger Fred Grey, eventually a doctor like his father but for this time, the founder of the "Fred Gray Association," perhaps New York's first society for gay men.[14]

Throughout his life, Whitman was often attracted to groups of younger men—those about to choose a profession or join a service, make decisions that would shape the rest of their lives. It is in that pattern that he became an enthusiast for the members of the "Fred Grey Association."

It is Karbiener who calls Whitman "an active participant in street culture," as she discusses his friendships with what she terms "semi-literate" working men. She sees his interest in becoming a participant in Pfaff's Cellar and its table-in-the-round as an illustration of his belief that a new concept of "nationhood" needed to be held together by love, empowered by the institution of "the dear love of comrades," to borrow a line from one of his *Calamus* poems. She summarizes, "Pfaff's was the first public space in which Whitman claimed to feel "at home." From 1858 to 1862, he was there almost every night."[15]

As a critic of his poetry, she is particularly interested in the fact that the years she cites above parallel the period when he is writing new poems, almost furiously, to add to later editions of *Leaves of Grass*. By the time Whitman brings out the 1860 edition, he has added 120 new poems, chiefly grouped under the titles that caused the most legal issues whenever *Leaves of Grass* was being reprinted—"Children of Adam" and "Calamus." Clearly, the

---

[14] See Delia Cabe, *Storied Bars of New York: Where Literary Luminaries Go to Drink*. New York: Countryman, 2017: 21–30; Karen Karbiener, "Whitman at Pfaff's: Personal Space, A Public Place, and the Boundary-Breaking Poems of *Leaves of Grass* (1860)," *Liberators of New York*, ed. Sabrina Fuchs-Abrams. Newcastle on Tyne: Cambridge Scholars Press, 2009: 1–38; and *Whitman Among the Bohemians*, ed. Joanna Levin and Edward Whitley. Iowa City: University of Iowa Press, 2014.
[15] Karbiener, "Whitman at Pfaff's," 2–3.

years following the first publication of Whitman's book were upsetting and disappointing, even as they were also energizing.

Once Whitman's "barbaric yawp" had begun making its way through the several echelons of New York (and Boston) readers, he began to have more confidence that his decision to publish *Leaves of Grass* was the right move in 1855 and again in 1856. He revealed in "Crossing Brooklyn Ferry" that immediately after the book appeared, he felt grave reservations, speaking in that poem about "dark patches" and, further, a kind of remorse: "The best I had done seem'd to me blank and suspicious."

"Children of Adam" with its sixteen poems (including the much longer and more explicit "I Sing the Body Electric" from the original book) seemed newly offensive to the few readers who had already read *Leaves of Grass*. The human body, so lovingly portrayed from the start of Whitman's poetry, now was given a more overt sexuality. Thoughts of sex began in the opening poem, "To the Garden the World," a short poem that, despite its somewhat Biblical context, seems heretical.

If, as the poet suggests, this tactile earth is "the garden," then Whitman's addressing the opening poem to his "*potent* mates, daughters, sons" is more than a sly signal. Procreation is the health of the world. The poet memorializes "the life of their bodies" as he wakens from a slumber and finds himself "Amorous, mature. . . my limbs and the quivering fire that ever plays through them, for reasons, most wondrous,/Existing I peer and penetrate still."

If the poet needed to describe intercourse any more vividly than his use of this description, the closing two lines cement the act:

> "By my side or back of me Eve following,
> Or in front, and I following her just the same."

Whitman follows this description with an even more flamboyant poem, its title drawn from its first line, "From Pent-up Aching Rivers." Quickly into the poem the reader is told about "the hungry gnaw that eats me night and day":

> "From my own voice resonant, singing the phallus,
> Singing the song of procreation,
> Singing the need of superb children and therein superb grown people,
> Singing the muscular urge and the blending, the bedfellow's song . . .".[16]

---

[16] Whitman "From Pent-up Aching Rivers," Library, 248–49.

As much a narrative as many of Whitman's poems, here the poet shows the nature of sexual coupling as he describes "the mystic deliria, the madness amorous, the utter abandonment." A later synopsis of his story:

"I love you, O you entirely possess me,
O that you and I escape from the rest and go utterly off, free and lawless,
Two hawks in the air, two fishes swimming in the sea not more lawless than we;)
The furious storm through me careering, I passionately trembling. . . . ."

After these two new poems, Whitman places the much revised and extended "I Sing the Body Electric," one of the original 1855 poems. Notice how changed some of these sections are, as here in the opening.

The 1855 Version:

"The bodies of men and women engirth me, and I engirth them,
They will not let me off nor I them till I go with them and respond to them and love them.

Was it dreamed whether those who corrupted their own live bodies
        could conceal themselves?
And whether those who defiled the living were as bad as they who
        defiled the dead?

The expression of the body of man or woman balks account,
The male is perfect and that of the female is perfect."

The 1860 Version:

"I sing the body electric,
The armies of those I love engirth me and I engirth them,
They will not let me off till I go with them, respond to them,
And discorrupt them, and charge them full with the charge of the soul.
Was it doubted that those who corrupt their own bodies conceal themselves?
And if those who defile the living are as bad as they who defile the dead?
And if the body does not do fully as much as the soul?
And if the body were not the soul, what is the soul?"

Whitman does more than just repeat the title as his opening line here: he divides the poem into sections so that the above lines constitute all of part I. Then part II opens,

"The love of the body of man or woman balks account, the body itself balks
    account,
That of the male is perfect, and that of the female is perfect.

The expression of the face balks account,
But the expression of a well-made man appears not only in his face,
It is in his limbs and joints also, it is curiously in the joints of his hips and
    wrists,
It is in his walk, the carriage of his neck, the flex of his waist and knees,
    dress does not hide him,
The strong sweet quality he has strikes through the cotton and broadcloth
To see him pass conveys as much as the best poem, perhaps more,
You linger to see his back, and the back of his neck and shoulder-side."

Beginning with the word "discorrupt" in the fourth line, Whitman presumes
the reticence that readers have about the physical, but he quickly pairs that
physical manifestation with the *soul*. Some of these quoted lines are very
close to those in the 1855 version—which, at the end—brings the soul into
the meditation, but the subtle changes in rhythm and emphases creates a
movement that seems new. Throughout his 1860 poem, Whitman re-uses
the stories from the first poem, the old farmer, for example, but the salience
of the over-all pace changes the poem's effect. The earlier version of the poem
has 118 lines, while the later version runs to 165 lines. Among the additions,
the most striking is the long paean to the female body which, in 1860, closes
the poem (and leads to the new fourth poem, "A Woman Waits for Me.")
The 1860 poem closes in this way, some lines omitted:

"Womanhood, and all that is a woman, and the man that comes from woman,
The womb, the teats, nipples, breast-milk, tears, laughter, weeping, love-looks,
    love-perturbations and risings,
The voice, articulation, language, whispering, shouting aloud,
Food, drink, pulse, digestion, sweat, sleep, walking, swimming, ...
The curious sympathy one feels when feeling with the hand the naked meat
    of the body,
The circling rivers the breath, and breathing it in and out,
The beauty of the waist, and thence of the hips, and thence downward
    toward the knees,
The thin red jellies within you or within me, the bones and the marrow
    In the bones,
The exquisite realization of health;
O I say these are not the parts of poems of the body only, but of the soul,
O I say now these are the soul!"[17]

---

[17] Whitman, "I Sing the Body Electric," Library, 258.

Readers could not avoid seeing the clear connections between poems as Whitman linked one outspoken verse with the next, and having the titles as guides made them even more self-conscious.

Among the many new poems grouped under "Children of Adam," even today's reader might blanch a bit at the sexualized language. Word choice is most provocative in the earlier poems among the sixteen, which are the longest. The last poems of the group seem to be summaries of a kind, as is the three-line "I Am He That Aches with Love." The closing poem, "As Adam Early in the Morning," is another, serving as a closing so that the poet can repeat,

> "Touch me, touch the palm of your hand to my body as I pass,
> Be not afraid of my body."

Whitman opens the "Calamus" segment with a poem that emphasizes friendship among men. "In Paths Untrodden" he speaks of "comrades," of "athletic love," and of a man "escaped from the life that exhibits itself." Rather than the *sixteen* poems of "Adam," "Calamus" includes *fifty-one* poems. From the original dozen poems of 1855, he here draws "A Song for Occupations," which had been the second poem in the original *Leaves of Grass*. There are several other poems from that 1855 version here as well. "Salut au Monde!,"added in the 1856 printing, is his promise to international respect and love. Also from the 1856 printing are "Crossing Brooklyn Ferry," "Song of the Open Road," "Song of the Broad-Axe" and "A Song of the Rolling Earth."

The sexuality so concentrated in "Children of Adam" is missing here, partly diluted through the inclusion of so many earlier poems. The voice of Whitman praising country, people, workers, philosophers, and the religious reassures the reader, even though in the new poems within "Calamus," there is less physical and sexual energy. What the reader sees in the opening half of the "Calamus" section is a shorter, more prosaic poem, still voice-oriented but with few surprises. For example, one sequence of these shorter poems leads the reader to question if these are poems at all.

"Sometimes with One I Love" brings the title into the poem as first line:

> "Sometimes with one I love I fill myself with rage for fear I effuse
>   unreturn'd love,
> But now I think there is no unreturn'd love, the pay is certain one
>   way or another,
> {I loved a certain person ardently and my love was not return'd.
> Yet out of that I have written these songs.}"

Similarly, "O You Whom I Often and Silently Come" also shares the title as first line:

> "O you whom I often and silently come where you are that I may be
>   with you,
> As I walk by your side or sit near, or remain in the same room with you,
> Little you know the subtle electric fire that for your sake is
>   playing within me."

A third new poem, "That Shadow My Likeness," echoes the same direct speech but includes more varied topics, and speaks for one of the rare times about Whitman's financial fears:

> "That shadow my likeness that goes to and fro seeking a livelihood,
>   chattering, chaffering,
> How often I find myself standing and looking at it where it flits,
> How often I question and doubt whether that is really me;
> But among my lovers and caroling these songs,
> O I never doubt whether that is really me."[18]

There is more ambivalent sexuality in the poems Whitman wrote to open this section, poems such as "Whoever You Are Holding Me Now in Hand," placed as the third poem in this grouping. From the fifth stanza, the poet segues into the sexual,

> "Here to put your lips upon mine I permit you,
> With the comrade's long-dwelling kiss or the new husband's kiss,
> For I am the new husband and I am the comrade."

Another of the early poems, "For You O Democracy," opens,

> "Come, I will make the continent indissoluble,
> I will make the most splendid race the sun ever shone upon,
> I will make divine magnetic lands,
>   With the love of comrades,
>   With the life-long love of comrades. . . ."

Quickly following that poem comes "These I Singing in Spring," in which the opening title line is completed

---

[18] Whitman, 3 poems from "Calamus," Library, 285–86.

"collect for lovers,
{For who but I should understand lovers and all their sorrow and joy?
And who but I should be the poet of comrades?). . . ."

Walking with those he loves, some living and some dead, Whitman announces,

"(O here I last saw him that tenderly loves me, and returns
    again never to separate from me,
And this, O this shall henceforth be the token of comrades,
    This calamus-root shall,
Interchange it youths with each other! Let none render it back!)"[19]

One of the poems that relates directly to a possible homosexuality is the calm and pristine "Behold This Swarthy Face":

"Behold this swarthy face, these gray eyes,
This beard, the white wool unclipt upon my neck,
My brown hands and the silent manner of me without charm;
Yet comes one a Manhattanese and ever at parting kisses me lightly
    on the lips with robust love,
And I on the crossing of the street or on the ship's deck give a kiss
    in return,
We observe that salute of American comrades land and sea,
We are those two natural and nonchalant persons."[20]

Placement here indicates a link to his mention of a partnership in the sedate "I Saw in Louisiana a Live-Oak Growing," which follows this poem directly. Then Whitman places "To a Stranger," which opens "Passing stranger! You do not know how longingly I look upon you. . . ." If not as immediately sexual as the poems in "Children of Adam," this grouping may be seen as an expression of longing rather than fruition.

Whitman recalls that when he traveled to Boston in March of 1860 so that he might oversee the printing of the third edition of his book at the publishing house of Thayer and Eldridge, he walked on the Boston Common with Emerson. Emerson, who had seen some of the new poems, argued that he should "expurgate" the "Children of Adam" poems—and to his plea Whitman "said no, no."[21]

---

[19] Whitman, "These I Singing in Spring," Library, 272–73.
[20] Whitman, "Behold This Swarthy Face," Library, 286.
[21] Whitman in "Chronology," Library, 1348.

Judging from the long letter which Whitman had sent to Emerson as a belated reply to his praise of the initial *Leaves of Grass*, their commerce was less than candid. Whitman assumes a confident pose as he explains to his benefactor that of the first print run, "a thousand copies," "they readily sold." He goes on in that paragraph to explain that he thinks several thousand of the 1856 *Leaves of Grass* should be adequate, and he can see that such a large regular printing would continue to be called for. The truth of a continual small sale does not enter the picture—though one would suppose that Emerson doubted such an account.[22]

For cultural critic John Tytell, Whitman's heavily sexual poems in "Children of Adam" make him a true pioneer: "No voice in our literature before Whitman had been nearly as personal, as excessive and irreverent, as baldly extravagant."[23]

Karen Karbiener sees Whitman as, in these poems, letting readers into his most private existence, a move which few poets have ever accomplished. She notes that he "assumes our presence." In many of the "Calamus" poems, he is "at home": "private life is exposed to common light." In so doing, Whitman "reconceptualized his literary project." The new poems "challenged common understanding of the boundaries between public and private" and opened a broad new path of meaning between writer and reader.[24] But for Whitman in the mid-1850s, he was less worried about any reader's reaction than he was about finding even a few readers who could be talked into buying a copy of *Leaves of Grass*.

---

[22] Whitman, "Letter to Emerson, August 1856," Library, 1327.
[23] John Tytell, *Reading New York*. New York: Knopf, 2003: 105.
[24] Karbiener, "Whitman at Pfaff's," *Literature of New York*, 11–12.

7

Family and the American Civil War

It may be comfortable for the twenty-first-century reader of Whitman's poems to believe that Whitman's writing so overtly about human sexuality, in the service of his evident adoration of the physical body, was one reason for the disdain and the outright disapproval of readers in the 1850s and 1860s. Such a rationale allows us to talk about prudery, squeamishness, and insult; it reinforces the legacy of superior taste through good educations and, effectively, of classed behavior.

For a number of expert critics of American poetry, Whitman's sexualized poetry in the 1860s was to be predicted: this was a poet of omnivorous appetites, a writer who was not about to censure himself or his language. As Edwin Fussell wrote with clear acceptance and praise in his 1973 *Lucifer in Harness*, Whitman "simply draws upon whatever vocabularies he likes, mainly the American vernacular, but also archaisms, poeticisms, neologisms, foreign borrowings, new coinages, slang ...." Fussell creates the term "American Eclectic" to describe the poet's linguistic style. He later notes, correctly, that no matter the sources of his "psychedelic" borrowings—or their effects—Whitman as poet "maintains an attitude of imperturbable tranquility."[1]

For Josephine Miles, one of this country's earliest critics of poetry *as poetry*, the most interesting thing about Whitman is his repetitious use of common words. She lists the fifty most used of these: "arm, beautiful, body, city,

---

[1] Edwin Fussell, *Lucifer in Harness*. Princeton, NJ: Princeton University Press, 1973: 123. He does not emphasize Whitman's use of the sexual.

L. Wagner-Martin, *Walt Whitman*, Literary Lives, https://doi.org/10.1007/978-3-030-77665-7_7

come, day, death, earth, eye, face, full, go, good, great, hand, hear, joy, know, land, life, light, long, look, love, male, man, night, old, pass, poem, read, rest, rise, sail, sea, ship, sing, soul, stand, strong, sun, take, thing, think, time, voice, war, woman, word, work, world, year, young."[2] Using this early computerized count—so helpful to the then-fashionable "concordances" of published works, Miles suggests that Whitman's poetry fell into her category of the "sublime." She explains, "The sublime poet tries not to do its theme justice but to *suffuse* it, to overwhelm it with the poet's passion. Such poetry has its specific complex of traits: an epithetical, phrased, participial, and compounding sentence structure, an unrhymed or irregular ode line, a vocabulary of passion and magnitude." She finds that such a poet draws on a "vocabulary of cosmic passion and sense impression," an "internal rather than external patterning of sound," and that the effect is "an exceptionally panoramic and panegyric verse, emotional, pictorial, noble, universal and tonal, rising to the height of heaven and feeling in the style traditionally known as grand or sublime." Whitman's reliance on one-syllable words, evocative of passionate belief and simple (even if) noble ideas, leads to his consistent word choices.

As sophisticated as her use of the computer, Miles' drawing together a number of earlier British poets with Whitman's practices served as one corrective for his apparent "strangeness" as a nineteenth-century American poet. It did little to dispel what seemed to be the Whitman poems' unfamiliarity to American readers who were more interested in prose, especially in the rolling sentences of the essay.

For British critic Denis Donoghue, list-making served a number of purposes. He chose as his favorite Whitman poems "Song of Myself," "Crossing Brooklyn Ferry," "Whoever You Are Now Holding Me in Hand," "Out of the Cradle," "As I Ebb'd with the Ocean of Life," "Tears," "On the Beach at Night," "Vigil Strange," "Reconciliation," "Lo, Victress on the Peaks," "When Lilacs Last," "The Sleepers," "There Was a Child Went Forth," "The Dalliance of the Eagles," and "Give Me the Splendid Silent Sun." While a few of these poems are from "Drum-Taps," and the memorable eulogy for Abraham Lincoln deserves to be known by all readers of the English language, most of this critic's choices are from the earlier printings of *Leaves of Grass*—1855, 1856, and 1860. Only a few are taken from the more controversial "Children of Adam" or "Calamus" groupings. Even for critics of poetry, the existence of the 400 poems that comprised Whitman's *oeuvre* was a problem in comprehension.

---

[2] Josephine Miles, *Eras and Modes in English Poetry*. Berkeley: University of California Press, 1957: 56–57, 202.

Donoghue's phrase to describe Whitman was based on themes, calling him "America's mythic poet"—admitting that no other poet then could take on that role. "The problem is how to cope with a *myth*. A mythic figure in literature is someone who in common opinion is thought to exceed his works and may be deemed, as a personality, to replace them."[3]

For Andrew Lawson, there is no need to gloss over the sometimes erratic choices Whitman made. He confronts what he calls the poet's "aggressively mixed diction, its pointed, perhaps even charged confrontations between high and low registers." He concludes that Whitman could not help using these "low registers" because that was his customary level of speaking. He was—naturally, financially, and educationally—at the bottom end of normal speech, and he drew heavily on "jargon, cant, and slang." According to Lawson, Whitman knew himself to be an outsider among those who listened to—or read—Emerson's lectures. His trying to gain that essayist's approval was always a part of his pretense, whether linguistic or social.

Lawson describes Whitman's politics during the 1840s, following the Panic of 1837, when he joined "the breakaway Equal Rights faction of the Democratic party, known as the locofocos, named after a brand of friction matches its members used when the power was turned off after a Tammany Hall meeting." The nickname for this party was "loafers," and that layer of the Democratic party was far from elite. Lawson underscores Whitman's frequent use of the verb "loafe," pointing to its obvious irony.[4]

Now that Whitman's 1856 letter to Emerson appears readily in print, the reader can see his choices in prose that could be classified as "low," and in some cases, "ironic." He begins with a flat statement that a more polished writer might have couched more subtly, saying,

> The genius of all foreign literature is clipped and cut small, compared to our genius …. Old forms, old poems, majestic and proper in their own lands here in this land are exiles.

But he then moves to a description of what *American* letters must include, drawing from a calculated jumble of seemingly chaotic nouns, many of them "low":

---

[3] Denis Donoghue, *The American Classics: A Personal Essay*. New Haven, CT: Yale University Press, 2005: 180–81. He also adds a somewhat ironic assessment, saying that one needs to read the poems as *poems* "rather than national anthems, hymns, manifestos, or campaign speeches."

[4] Lawson, *Walt Whitman*, xiv, xvii–xviii.

[The American poet must recognize] "the sturdy living form, the men and women of These States, the divinity of sex, the perfect eligibility of the female with the male, all the States, liberty and equality, real articles, the different trades, mechanics, the young fellows of Manhattan Islands, customs, instincts, slang, Wisconsin, Georgia, the noble Southern heart, the hot blood, the spirit that will be nothing less than master, the filibuster spirit, the Western man … the eye for forms, the perfect models of made things, the wild smack of freedom, California, money, electric-telegraphs, free-trade, iron and the iron mines—recognize without demur those splendid resistless black poems, the steam-ships of the sea-bound states, and those other resistless splendid poems, the locomotives, followed through the interior states by trains of rail-road cars."[5]

What we might term Whitman's "tactic of effusion" dominates each section of his letter, which opens tellingly with his metaphor that shows the distinguished essayist and poet that he, Walt Whitman, knows a great deal *about* publishing in its physical manifestation. Early in the letter, he writes, again, effusively.

Of the twenty-four modern mammoth two-double, three-double, and four-double cylinder presses now in the world, printing by steam, twenty-one of them are in These States. The twelve thousand large and small shops for dispensing books and newspapers—the same number of public libraries, any one of which has all the reading wanted to equip a man or woman for American reading—the three thousand different newspapers … the story papers, various, full of strong-flavored romances, widely circulated--the one-cent and two-cent journals---the political ones, no matter what side—the weeklies in the country—the sporting and pictorial papers—the monthly magazines, with plentiful imported feed—the sentimental novels … the low-priced flaring tales, adventures, biographies—all are prophetic … I am not troubled at the movement of them, but greatly pleased …. What a progress popular reading and writing has made in fifty years![6]

Who except a printer would understand his opening? By inclusion, Whitman gives Emerson insight into the way most people obtain books and papers, the crucial role of libraries for those who cannot afford to purchase books; after all, Whitman once owned a bookstore. He not only was a printer and publisher, but he also wrote for most of the kinds of outlets he here names.

---

[5] Whitman, "Letter to Ralph Waldo Emerson," Library, 1334.
[6] Whitman, "Letter to Ralph Waldo Emerson," Library, 1329. There is also an extensive discussion of the absence of *sexual* matter in American writing, in which Whitman notes the need of "an avowed, empowered, unabashed development of sex" (1334).

By implication, Walt Whitman *is* an American man of letters. Even as he calls Emerson "Master" in this letter, one sees that *Whitman*, his supposed disciple, is a differently equipped *master* of American publishing.

In his closing section, Whitman presents another argument. Still conscious that he has never toured Europe or England, he here draws on his lengthy trip to and through Louisiana. As he emphasizes to Emerson how great America is (the 1850s was becoming a period of lamenting the country's diversity and undisciplined behavior), he segues into a list of the country's parts:

> Always America will be agitated and turbulent. This day it is taking shape, not to be less so, but to be more so, stormily, capriciously, on native principles, with such vast proportions of parts! As for me, I love screaming, wrestling, boiling-hot days. Of course, we shall have a national character, an identity .... With Ohio, Illinois, Missouri, Oregon—with the states around the Mexican Sea—with cheerfully welcomed immigrants from Europe, Asia, Africa—with Connecticut, Vermont, New Hampshire, Rhode Island—with all varied interests, facts, beliefs, parties, genesis—there is being fused a determined character ... each indeed free, each idiomatic, as becomes live states and men .... *Such character is the brain and spine to all, including literature, including poems.* Such character, strong, limber, just, open-mouthed, American-blooded, full of pride, full of ease, of passionate friendliness, is to stand compact upon that vast basis of the supremacy of Individuality—the new moral American continent ....

Although much of Whitman's prose is lost to time, it is clear that he omitted his first literary statement about his country, and his love for it and its people, which was the "Preface" to the 1855 *Leaves of Grass*, not because he no longer believed in it but because he had found places to publish—or at least to express—those beliefs in other ways. In this letter to Emerson he rehearses a shorter version and makes more specific arguments than he earlier had in the "Preface."

Whitman's expression here, though characteristically exuberant, was not so different from what was being written by a more elite set of authors: the promise of America, the ability of all classes of its citizens, the almost overwhelming output of its writers. Many people were making statements and promises about the direction of America and its literature. As Jack Saltzman sees the period, however, "Melville and Hawthorne were more concerned with understanding the Self than the *American* Self. Others— Emerson, Thoreau, Whitman—wanted to define the nature of the American, but could best do so by making clear what was wrong with America .... From Emerson's rhetoric of self-reliance to Thoreau's search for an honest man to Whitman's ever-increasingly solitary singer, the voice of the writer makes clear America's unsettled state. The problem is political, sexual, and, above all, moral."[7]

The set of arguments that Whitman chose to make in his letter to Emerson answers a number of his insistences in his essays. Emerson was writing for a white and highly classed readership, one recognizable as stemming from the cultures of the Northeast; Whitman strikingly includes the immigrant populations as "Americans." He focuses on the "workmen" and "workwomen," not the highly educated. He gives many lines to charting the lives of black characters, prostitutes, Western men, mothers, the visibly poor.

While Emerson discusses "decorum," Whitman talks about "screaming." Whitman thinks he can win any argument with the restrained Emerson through effusive prose. In contrast, Emerson talks about his admiration for the poetry of Oliver Wendell Holmes, stressing his "wit, force, and perfect good taste."[8] It was a compliment Whitman knew he would never hear, just as he could imagine Emerson shuddering at his praise of "passionate friendliness." Although he called Emerson "Master" in this letter—and elsewhere—he saw the very separate ways that, even as friends, they would choose to walk.

Caution was not in Whitman's vocabulary. *Prudence* was not a trait he wanted to develop. Economically, he could never attain any sense of fashion—and after the hard depression of 1851, he was having more and more difficulty paying what bills he had. As Andrew Lawson described Whitman's economic circumstances, because a family's reputation stays reasonably stable, the Whitmans continued to be thought of as landholders— somehow, Walter Whitman's being a builder seemed an extension of the landowning class. For Walt Whitman, however, becoming a newspaperman (and first, a printer) showed no such continuity. He was seen as living marginally, particularly when he moved from one job to another, and from one boarding house to others.

Society saw Walt Whitman as "a newspaperman who had failed to progress … through a lack of 'polished' acquaintance." He had failed in the important game of politics. And his choosing to become a poet did nothing to improve his social, or his financial, position.[9]

It became clearer and clearer that Emerson shared that cultural frame. One of his sorrows about American life was its ingrained anti-intellectualism. He wrote, "our America has a bad name for superficialness. Great men, great

---

[7] Jack Salzman, "Literature for the Populace," *Columbia Literary History of the United States*, ed. Emory Elliott. New York: Columbia University Press, 1988: 549.

[8] Thomas Wortham, "William Cullen Bryant," *Columbia Literary History*, 283.

[9] Lawson, *Walt Whitman*, 9, 82.

nations have not been boasters and buffoons ...."[10] Jarred as he often was by Whitman's use of slang, cant, and too-familiar phrasing, Emerson eventually lost interest in what his younger Brooklyn friend was writing. For Whitman, his consciousness that Emerson had misgivings about him and his work, and his sense of his failure at maintaining the kind of decorum Emerson admired, was a constant.

The same season that he wrote his letter to Emerson, Whitman wrote and set in proof sheets his personal political tract. The work was titled "The Eighteenth Presidency!" and subtitled "Voice of Walt Whitman to each Young Man in the Nation, North, South, East, and West." Although not dedicated to Emerson, the treatise fills in some of the gaps in Whitman's letter. It declares the common people of These States (his usual phrase for "America") the heart and soul of the country. Accordingly, Whitman declares, "I expect to see the day when ... qualified mechanics and other young men will reach Congress and other official stations, sent in their working costumes, fresh from their benches and tools, and returning to them again with dignity."[11]

In Whitman's idealized world, "nothing gives place and never ought to give place except to its clean superiors." He sees in this large underclass "rude and undeveloped bravery, friendship, conscientiousness, clear-sightedness, and practical genius." He does not, sadly, see such traits in the current officeholders—nor "among all the literary persons."

He laments the current thinking that a person should be evaluated in terms of "respectability." He then puts forth ways of changing nominations and voting laws, and real change in thinking about leadership. He also calls for an end to political parties because, in his words, "America has outgrown parties." Those who control them think too small. Even the best of groups at the start will succumb to corruption, and then the party "ripens and rots with the rest."[12]

Whitman closes his oration with his angry comments about slavery. There is no argument: "Man cannot hold property in man." Whitman refers to the 350,000 slave holders in the country, set against the thirty million American citizens. "Shall no one among you dare open his mouth to say he is opposed to slavery, as a man should be? .... Do the 350,000 expect to bar forever all preachers, poets, philosophers—all that makes the brain of These States, free literature, free thought, the good old cause of liberty? Are they blind? Do they

---

[10] Jack Salzman, "Literature for the Populace," *Columbia*, 549–50.

[11] Whitman, "The Eighteenth Presidency!" Library, 1307.

[12] Whitman, "The Eighteenth Presidency!" Library, 1308, 1317. Whitman's poem "To the States," from the 1860 *Leaves of Grass*, repeats these ideas (Library, 415).

not see those unrelaxed circles of death narrowing and narrowing every hour around them?"

As he comes to a close, Whitman asks directly, "You young men of the Southern States! Is the word *abolitionist* so hateful to you, then? Do you not know that Washington, Jefferson, Madison, and all the great Presidents and primal warriors and sages were declared abolitionists?"

He then moves to "You young men! American mechanics, farmers, boatmen, manufacturers, and all work-people of the South, the same as the North! *You are either to abolish slavery, or it will abolish you.*"

This argument needs to be circulated not among the educated, because they already understand that slavery is wrong. But "the great masses of the mechanics, and a large portion of the farmers, are unsettled, hardly know whom to vote for, or whom to believe."

Almost after the fact, Whitman puts the American choice into an international context, saying "Freedom against slavery is not issuing here alone, but is issuing *everywhere.*"[13]

Part of Whitman's attention to slavery here in 1856 is that he has talked about the economic argument of land ownership through this essay (as well as often in his political writings for the news). Here he does the same, stating historical cycles that his own family experienced.

"A few generations ago, the general run of farmers and work-people like us were slaves, serfs, deprived of their liberty by law; they are still so deprived on some parts of the continent of Europe. Those who are free here … are free through deeds that were done, and men that lived …. The men and deeds of these years also decide for generations ahead, as past men and deeds decided for us." Whitman frequently used the word "slaves" to describe the white poor, and as he struggled monthly to earn a living, and as he watched his own family engage in the same struggle, his language became more pointed. He also cleared the air about "craft" in this essay, stating that "American craft" is "subtler than Italian craft," and is possibly "the subtlest craft on earth."[14] Taking to task the upper-class opinion about European skills and values when compared with American, Whitman interjects this definitional statement seemingly out of nowhere.

We have seen how frequently Whitman mentioned the Western states—especially California—as a definite source of hope. He seemed to see a new kind of intelligence and independence in the men he called "Western." "As the broad fat States of the West, the largest and best parts of the inheritance of the American farmers and mechanics, were ordained to common people

---

[13] Whitman, "The Eighteenth Presidency!" Library, 1319, 1321–24.
[14] Whitman, "The Eighteenth Presidency!" Library, 1315.

and workmen long in advance by Jefferson, Washington, and the earlier Congresses, now a far ampler west is to be ordained. Is it to be ordained to *workmen*, or to the *masters* of workmen? Shall the future mechanics of America be serfs? Shall labor be degraded, and women whipt in the fields for not doing their work? …. Workmen! Workwomen! These immense national American tracts belong to you; they are in trust with you."

Prescient as Whitman's discussion is here in 1856, Nancy Isenberg verifies the ongoing economic controversy over slavery in the states, with the passage of the Fugitive Slave Law in 1850—and the fact that land ownership in the West was not held at such a premium as it was in the more settled East. She notes that in the new West, "at least 35% of the population owned *no* real estate, and there was no clear path to land and riches among the lower ranks of workers.[15] These landless citizens were called "squatters" and were pictured as living in crude huts, distrusting any city's more civilized people, and practicing degenerate habits of breeding. Unfortunately, *class* was already a permanent fixture throughout the United States and even poor farmers heading west faced what seemed to be "a new breed of aristocrats: shrewd land speculators and large cotton and sugar planters."

Back in the eastern states, "To be lower class in rural America was to be one of the landless—"in effect, because of the Whitman family's continuous moving, they could have been considered "squatters" and "crackers."[16] No amount of Whitman's rhetoric changed those facts. As he engages in his dialogue with Emerson, both in his lengthy letter and in this political treatise (by implication), he writes what may well be the most insulting section of his "Eighteenth Presidency" essay. As he laments the kind of political leadership the United States has been facing, with presidents both old and utterly conventional, he thinks ahead to the next election and exclaims,

"I would be much pleased to see some heroic, shrewd, fully-informed, healthy-bodied, middle-aged, beard-faced American blacksmith or boatman come down from the West across the Alleghenies, and walk into the Presidency, dressed in a clean suit of working attire, and with the tan all over his face, breast, and arms."[17] It was just a year earlier that Whitman had chosen the likeness that showed himself as a new kind of poet, dressed as a working man, bearded, unprepossessing, large and brawny. Perhaps his identification of himself with the workingman was not just a pose. And by 1860, with Abraham Lincoln having been elected President—so that he was, indeed,

---

[15] Nancy Isenberg, *White Trash*, 112.
[16] Nancy Isenberg, *White Trash*, 103–7.
[17] Whitman, "The Eighteenth Presidency!" Library, 1308.

Whitman's "eighteenth president," even his electors saw Lincoln as a "Western" man, the product of a self-administered law degree, running his two-man law firm in Illinois, (later growing a beard but throughout poorly dressed and poorly mannered) and filling all too well the image of a bumpkin.

In this essay as well, Whitman begins to be more explicit about the qualities he sees in young men. The promise of a relatively untaught person, but one who could learn the virtues of friendship and trustworthiness, seemed more desirable than many traditionally approved personal traits. Whitman writes about the young man he envisions, "his daring step approaches the arctic and antarctic poles, he colonizes the shores of the Pacific, the Asiatic Indies, the birthplace of languages and of races, the archipelagoes, Australia; he explores Africa, he unearths Assyria and Egypt, he re-states history, he enlarges morality, he speculates anew upon the soul, upon original premises; nothing is left quiet ...."[18]

And it is clear that Whitman admires those who understand technology of whatever kind. His use of the term "mechanics" specifies a technological person, as he clearly thought of his own training in the complicated printing press, or the engineer who kept the trains running. Whitman speaks to this adaptability as a common underpinning within a mid-nineteenth-century America: "Landmarks of masters, slaves, kings, aristocrats are moth-eaten .... Frontiers and boundaries are less and less able to divide men. The modern inventions, the wholesale engines of war, the world-spreading instruments of peace, the steamship, the locomotive, the electric telegraph, the common newspaper, the cheap book, the ocean mail are interlinking the inhabitants of the earth together as groups of one family—America standing, and for ages to stand, as the host and champion of the same, the most welcome spectacle ever presented among nations .... Never was justice so mighty amid injustice; never did the idea of equality erect itself so haughty and uncompromising amid inequality, as to-day. Never were such sharp questions asked as to-day. Never was there more eagerness to know; never was the representative man more energetic ...."[19]

As he had written in a poem that later was removed from the final version of *Leaves of Grass*, Whitman's ideal young men's culture was aboard ship:

Ship Ahoy!
In dreams I was a ship, and sail'd the boundless seas,
Sailing and ever sailing—all seas and into every port, or out

[18] Whitman, "The Eighteenth Presidency!" Library, 1324. Reflecting this energy and wisdom of the young, America itself, says Whitman, "is a proud, young, friendly, fresh, heroic nation of thirty millions of live and electric men" (1325).

[19] Whitman, "The Eighteenth Presidency!" Library, 1324.

upon the offing,
Saluting, cheerily hailing each mate, met or pass'd, little or big,
"Ship ahoy!" thro' trumpet or by voice—if nothing more,
        some friendly merry word at least,
For companionship and good will for ever to all and each.[20]

While it is certainly possible to find in Whitman's near-obsession with the young men of New York, those he often lectures to in his prose and deifies in his poems, it is also possible to see him as a man out of step with his contemporaries—who either have no sense of the greatness of this country, or no physical energy to try to equip themselves to take advantage of that greatness—but, upon scrutiny, able to locate the traits he cherishes among younger men. It is also possible that there was much less sexual longing in Whitman's admiration than some twentieth-century critics have suggested.

We might think of Whitman's politics as being encapsulated in his characters—or at least in his country, often represented by that country's people. Except when he was phrasing a somewhat formal essay, he instead focused on the *stories* that fueled his knowledge about America. Jerome Loving says that Whitman was never an abolitionist. During the 1840s and 1850s, there were nuances to that position of hating the practice of slavery. The truth may have been that Whitman, being so entrenched in the people and work of New York City, may have known less about the existence of American slavery. He did not see it; what he saw was the plight of the many poor Americans, whose lot was governed by their own work and habits and practices—*poverty*, however, was not the same thing as slavery. For Whitman, says Loving, "everything went back to the good order and diversity of the urban unit as it confronted the challenges of democracy and capitalism— good ferries, reasonably priced fares, trains to the Greenwood cemetery or as far away as Greenport, the development of a park and Revolution Memorial at Fort Greene, fair pay for sewing women, instruction on the dangers of alcohol consumption (but no prohibition laws; here he parted company with a much more famous reformer, Horace Mann), the doings of the local churches, respect for firemen, and (even) the unfortunate, if not completely "evil," aspects of slavery.'[21]

More directly to political writing, Loving explains that "As late as 1846 Whitman thought the abolitionists were doing more harm than good." He thought all the attention was holding back changes that might have come naturally. In a December 29 piece, he wondered "why the 2,700,000 black

[20] Whitman, "Ship Ahoy!" Library, 1257.
[21] Loving, *Walt Whitman*, 105, 110.

slaves in America got all the abolitionists' sympathy while the fate of fifty millions of white men [in Russia and Austria], physically as good as their owners, don't seem to attract the slightest attention." By the fall of 1847, the Democratic party had broken into several parts and—for Whitman as well as at least two of his brothers—choosing between the Barnburners and the Hunkers led to a kind of neutrality, if not apathy, about the slavery issue. Whitman lost his job as editor of the *Eagle* over his failure to take a stand on abolition.[22]

Newspapers and newswriters stood against all slavery because "they did not want to see free labor degraded." Because Whitman was visible, in 1848 he was appointed one of fourteen delegates to represent the radical Democrats of King's County at the state Free-Soil presidential convention in Buffalo (he was a Barnburner). Then Whitman became editor of the *Freeman,* funded by some Brooklyn free-soilers, chief among them Judge Samuel B. Johnston, known for his aiding fugitive slaves in New York. Following the August convention, where Martin Van Buren was the nominee, the *Freeman* (like many of the people connected with it) was not truly anti-slavery. "Whitman's position was part-abolitionist, part free-soiler, and the paper's name probably referred to white workingmen, or "freemen," rather than blacks, who were known as "freedmen." Generally, his editorial position was that slaves were to be freed (or at least the institution of slavery kept out of the new territories) so that white labor not be demeaned by having the slaves do for nothing what the whites did for wages."[23]

Having lost his editorship of several papers, Whitman became a consistent freelancer. Following his political views is harder in the 1850s but he seemed to be training himself to write about music, painting, drama—all the burgeoning American arts. It was probably not the case that he found politics less interesting, but rather that covering aesthetic topics became more germane to his thinking about serious literature. Eventually, he developed a number of new ideas about writing what he was to call the *American* poem.

---

[22] Loving, *Walt Whitman,* 110–11.
[23] Loving, *Walt Whitman,* 143–44.

8

The Horrors of American War

Political skirmishes on paper were not important to the building angers that fed America's Civil War. Few observers expected that there would be a war at all—and those that accepted its inevitability predicted the fighting would take only a few days. The South had no resources; observers thought their military would run. The North had more men, more arms, and more money. Yet everyone who enlisted was a novice at what was about to occur: no one could predict, no one could train soldiers, no one could find arms or lay in foodstuffs. War was an entirely new endeavor. And no one ever expected that—by the end of the interminable three years—over 620,000 men would be killed, bodies piled all over the farms, the hillsides, the outskirts of cities, the forests, where real citizens, well-meaning citizens, who were just as ignorant as the soldiers were, were trying to lead normal lives.

The years Whitman had dreamed of as being his years as a New York poet had long since passed. In his 1856 letter to Emerson he had said confidently and enthusiastically,

> I much enjoy making poems ... the
> work of my life is making poems.[1]

He echoed that in one of the new 1860 poems, "Out of the Cradle Endlessly Rocking":

---

[1] Whitman, "Letter to Ralph Waldo Emerson," Library, 1327.

L. Wagner-Martin, *Walt Whitman*, Literary Lives, https://doi.org/10.1007/978-3-030-77665-7_8

Now in a moment I know what I am for—I awake,
And already a thousand singers—a thousand songs, clearer, louder,
    more sorrowful than yours,
A thousand warbling echoes have started to life within me,
Never to die …[2]

Whitman's excitement carried him through the third printing of *Leaves of Grass* in 1860 but maintaining the continuous energy—especially while feeling that he had failed—was difficult. All the new poems that appeared in the 1860 book spoke of *newness*, of reaching an *American* destiny of promise, as well as *personal* promise: but did that mean one more night of fellowship at Pfaff's bar? As his biographer phrased it, Whitman was mired in a period of transition, "looking for relief in his past on Long Island. His enthusiasm for Pfaff's and the bohemian life of late-night drinking was probably more than beginning to wane."[3]

To leave this limited personal view, to think only of Walt Whitman's state of mind, focused as it was on the 1860 printing of *Leaves of Grass*, provides us with the wider, and more threatening, comprehension of the decades of American history and politics that were leading to the American civil war. As Nicholas Cull said, it was not all the force of physical events: "the foundations of the Civil War lay not merely in sectional difference over slavery but in the ability of the contending sides to articulate their position in abstract terms. The abolitionist camp had its rhetoricians like William Lloyd Garrison and memoirists like Frederick Douglass."[4]

What was to become the Civil War was brewing for decades. In 1820 the Missouri Compromise brought federal law into the mix of slave versus non-slave settlements. It was followed in 1836 by the Gag Rule and then in 1850 by the Compromise that included the Fugitive Slave law. As the principle of states' rights fought to dominate a philosophical argument, made by many religious groups as well as churches—that slavery was *not* evil because these dark-skinned people were *not* human beings, the potential for bloodshed grew. Nat Turner's 1831 rebellion prompted increased militarism throughout the United States, as well as increased prohibitions against slaves being taught to read and write.

The mysterious death in 1830 of David Walker, a North Carolina free black, exacerbated tensions in what was not a slave-holding state in the way that Virginia and South Carolina were. *Walker's Appeal: in four articles together*

---

[2] Whitman, "Out of the Cradle Endlessly Rocking," Library, 392.

[3] Loving, *Walt Whitman*, 260.

[4] Nicholas J. Cull, "Propaganda for War from the Revolution to the Vietnam War," *War and American Literature*, ed. Jennifer Haytock. New York: Cambridge University Press, 2021: 28.

with a preamble to the coloured citizens of the world had been published in 1829, while Walker lived in Boston. The Southern states resented this publication; the state of Georgia, for example, offered a high bounty for Walker's death.

There was no question that the South's "peculiar institution" was going to lead to immense moral and physical conflict—we see foreshadowing of this in Whitman's "The Eighteenth Presidency!" an essay which appeared in 1856. In 1857, the Dred Scott decision held that Negroes were *not* citizens of the United States, a statement that removed all legal protection from their lives. It also decreed that slaveholding could *not* be excluded from any of the states or territories. As the invention of the cotton gin and other devices helpful to the production and manufacturing of cotton—a crop long dependent on slave labor—increased profits from this staple of Southern farming (as well as hemp and rice), the Southern states grew more adamant in their legal positions. Nineteenth-century culture was dominated by the essay form: the magazines and journals that many Northern subscribers read were filled with arguments that either supported states' rights or lamented the existence of slavery.

In 1858 during the Lincoln-Douglas Debates as the men struggled to win a seat in the Illinois state legislature, the differences between Stephen Douglas and Lincoln were already clear. In 1859, on October 16, the John Brown Revolt occurred at Harper's Ferry, Virginia. Horrified by the bloodshed, and by Brown's later execution, abolitionists knew that their stance was likely to lead to war.

When Abraham Lincoln was elected President of the United States on November 6, 1860, it was only a month till South Carolina seceded from the union. In January and February of 1861, many other Southern states— Mississippi, Alabama, Florida, Georgia, Louisiana, and Texas—followed suit. Representatives from these seven states met in Montgomery, Alabama, wrote their "Articles of Confederation," and elected Jefferson Davis their president; he was inaugurated several weeks *before* Lincoln's Inauguration.

March 4, 1861, Lincoln was inaugurated. On April 12 the first shots were fired at Fort Sumter, South Carolina, and the next week Virginia seceded. In June, Lincoln proclaimed a naval blockage of these states and North Carolina, with the territory of West Virginia being named a state because that population would not leave the union. Tennessee, Arkansas, and—eventually—North Carolina secede. The next month on July 18 Confederate forces won the First Battle of Bull Run.

When Whitman wrote about the beginning of the war, he recalled the news reaching New York City as he was leaving an opera on Fourteenth Street. All the newsboys were calling out their extras, and he quickly bought the paper. Walking across the street to stand in front of the Metropolitan Hotel, so that he could see to read, he soon was surrounded by a crowd of thirty to forty listeners. He read. The crowd was quiet. Then "all stood a minute or two before they dispersed. I can almost see them there now, under the lamps at midnight."[5]

In that same series of reminiscences, Whitman recalled the disdain the Union felt toward the Confederacy. He recounted that "a couple of companies of the Thirteenth Brooklyn ... were all provided with pieces of rope, conspicuously tied to their musket-barrels, with which to bring back each man a prisoner from the audacious South, to be led in a noose, on our men's early and triumphant returns!"[6]

Believing that the conflict might last sixty days, or perhaps ninety days (the term for the Union draft subscription was set at ninety days}, the surprising defeat of the Union at the hands of the Confederacy on July 18 at the First Battle of Bull Run/Manassas shocked the country, particularly the Washingtonians who had traveled out to watch the battle, complete with picnic lunches. Whitman wrote about the thousands of scurrying would-be observers, mingling with the thousands of retreating soldiers. He uses the debacle of the defeat to begin what would be a running stream of praise for President Lincoln, here saying, "The President, recovering himself, begins that very night—sternly, rapidly sets about the task of reorganizing his forces ... he resolv'd to lift himself and the Union out of such defeat."[7]

Just thirty miles west-southwest of Washington, the battle scene of defeat at the placid waterway (Bull Run) proved to be indelible; it took another year for the Union forces to begin to hold their own. Whitman described the Northern army as finally coming down to "a primal hard-pan of national Union will."[8] Serious battles raged throughout the coming year. Augmented by news stories and photographs, by detailed maps and drawings, the American citizenry followed the bloody conflicts at the previously unknown names: the Allegheny Mountain battle, the Battle of Belmont (Missouri), the Second Battle of Bull Run (Manassas), the Battle of Ivy Mountain/Ivy Creek (Kentucky); in North Carolina, the Battle of Hatteras Inlet; in West Virginia, the Battle of Kessler's Cross Lanes; in Tennessee, the Battle of Fort Henry; the Battle of Williamsburg, which was part of the Peninsular campaign against Richmond, Virginia, now serving as the capital of the Confederacy; and

---

[5] Whitman, "Specimen Days," Library, 706.
[6] Ibid., Library, 708.
[7] Whitman, "Specimen Days," Library, 711.
[8] Ibid., Library, 707.

numerous skirmishes and battles on rivers, over railroads and their access, and naval battles on many rivers as well as the Atlantic coast.

By the time of the Battle of Shiloh/Pittsburg Landing in Tennessee (April 1862), the Union forces of 30,000 men under the command of General William T. Sherman and General Ulysses S. Grant met 45,000 Confederate men, led by General Albert S. Johnson, a commander who died there from blood loss of an untended wound and was then replaced by General Pierre Beauregard. Winning narrowly, the Union had more than 13,000 dead; the Confederates, retreating to Corinth, Mississippi, had nearly 11,000 casualties. By June, 1862, the Confederate army—under siege—was driven out of Corinth.

More regularly, however, especially once the Confederate troops were commanded by General Robert E. Lee, *those* Southern troops won. As in the Seven Days Campaign (June 1862) Lee attacked the larger Union Army of the Potomac, under George McClelland, near Richmond. During the week of battles, over 30,000 men died, and the visibility of this conflict—along with other such battles—was staring to persuade British and European observers that they should support the Southern forces. They wanted to protect their trading partner.

Momentum continued through the Confederate victory at Fredericksburg, Virginia, in December of 1862 when the Union armies lost over twelve thousand men, compared with only five thousand Confederate deaths. "Battle" had been redefined: lost lives and mangled survivors' bodies were the rule, not the exception. The war that Lincoln had thought might last 90 days, and that the Confederacy had predicted would not be fought at all, was leading to nothing but more and more destruction and death.

Whitman was quietly following the war but publishing very little; in fact, his biographers leave blank much of late 1861 and 1862, although it is clear he sometimes visited the wounded in New York and Brooklyn hospitals. On December 16, 1862, the Whitmans read in the *New York Herald* that "First Lieutenant G. W. Whitmore" was among the 13,000 Union troops killed or wounded at Fredericksburg. Surmising correctly that the misspelling was to have been "Whitman," George's older brother went by train southward. (George had enlisted in early April, 1861, for a hundred days and then re-enlisted in September. On May 28, 1862, Andrew enlisted but did not stay for his term because of debilitating reactions to battle.)[9]

In the poet's modest account of his quick December trip to Fredericksburg, which led to his living and working in "Washington City" for subsequent

---

[9] Loving, *Walt Whitman*, 3, 13.

years, he wrote, "I went down to the war fields in Virginia (end of 1862), lived thenceforward in camp—saw great battles and the days and nights afterward—partook of all the fluctuations, gloom, despair, hopes again arous'd, courage evoked—death readily risk'd—*the cause*, too,—filling those agonists and lurid following years, 1863—'64—'65—the real parturition years (more than 1776–1783) of this henceforth homogeneous Union. Without those three or four years and the experiences they gave, "Leaves of Grass" would not now be existing."[10]

Stunned and sickened as he was at the sights of the battlefield, even after he was reunited with his only slightly wounded brother, Whitman became *himself*—the poet who could absorb all things, and find a way to express whatever he saw. This was a man who had spent the last decade of his life writing about America as *a poet*, delighting in his admiration for a younger generation of promising and spirited men. Suddenly, which the fear he had that he had lost his brother prompted, he saw the horrific mire of the modern battlefield in this most technologically contemporary military action. As Ty Hawkins states, these killing methods "meant that soldiers would die in near-anonymity, unpredictably, with great speed and in great numbers, and via abhorrent contortions of the body."[11] It took until Drew Gilpin Faust's 2008 *The Republic of Suffering: Death and the American Civil War* for today's readers to understand the real carnage of those battlefields: "The Civil War's 600,000 combat deaths comprised a portion of the US population whose contemporary analog would be around six to seven million people … the texture of the experience, the warp and woof, was the presence of death."[12]

Whitman knew enough *not* to write about the carnage. He had been reading the war poems published all over the New York press, and he knew that conventional platitudes came nowhere near being accurate descriptions. Once in Virginia, living in those fields of battle, he felt privy to new kinds of knowledge, and he rejected easy descriptions of that information. Among his first poems written in the early months of 1863 were formalistic (and nearly

---

[10] Whitman, "A Backward Glance O'er Traveled Roads," Library, 666. Although it seemed as if Whitman began his trip immediately, he had the foresight to get letters of recommendation from important figures in Brooklyn—he knew he would need work of some kind. He was at the end of his own financial resources, and the 1860 *Leaves of Grass* had been, for the most part, reviewed badly—if at all.

[11] Ty Hawkins, "War and Morality," *War and American Literature*, ed. Jennifer Haytock. New York: Cambridge University Press, 2021: 17. Michael Zeitlin underscores the kinds of injuries these soldiers would receive when he instructs readers to add "graphic medical accounts from combat zones" to the usual "war literature" such as fiction, memoir, poetry and war journalism. Michael Zeitlin, "Bodies, Injury, Medicine," *War and American Literature*, 57.

[12] Drew Gilpin Faust. *The Republic of Suffering: Death and the American Civil War.* New York: Knopf, 2008: xiii.

conventional) poems. But he worked his way through his personal horrors to find a stasis that would be both physically and tonally accurate. Some of the best of Whitman's war poems, in fact, are very close to poetry's most famous dirges.

> By the bivouac's fitful flame,
> A procession winding around me, solemn and sweet and slow—
>   but first I note,
> The tents of the sleeping army, the fields' and woods' dim outline,
> The darkness lit by spots of kindled fire, the silence,
> Like a phantom far or near an occasional figure moving,
> The shrubs and trees (as I lift my eyes they seem to be
>   stealthily watching me,)
> While wind in procession thoughts, O tender and wondrous
>   thoughts,
> Of life and death, of home and the past and loved, and of those that
>   are far away;
> A solemn and slow procession there as I sit on the ground,
> By the bivouac's fitful flame.[13]

In his redefinition of the sonnet, Whitman used the two closing lines to balance the opening couplet, but not in exact symmetry. The core sestet borrows authenticity from news descriptions, haunting in their own right, reflecting attention onto the observer who does not sleep, there by the "fitful" flames. Ominous—like the watching eyes—and well aware that death is just as close as that fire, the poem laments both the scene and the existence of war.

Unlike the poems Whitman was writing before he traveled to Virginia, this work modulates what the poet feels about the losses of men so heedlessly—without expressing that loss verbally. Several of the poems Whitman collected in *Drum-Taps* are much more workmanlike, moving with very little sense of reality. In his poem "Eighteen Sixty-One," for example, he describes "a strong man erect, clothed in blue clothes, advancing, carrying a rifle ... With well-gristled body and sunburnt face and hands." The fact of war is not much enhanced by the description of the Union blues, the youth of the enlisted man. Somewhat ironically, Whitman was trying to write about the war before the war existed. In 1860 he had published both "Over the Carnage Rose Prophetic a Voice" and "As I Walk These Broad Majestic Days." Whereas the "Carnage" poem metaphorically suggests war, the latter poem has clear overtones of conflict. Interestingly, Whitman wrote as if the conflict

---

[13] Whitman, "By the Bivouac's Fitful Flame," Library, 436.

has finished although the poet fears a worse debacle lies ahead, but the lines are appropriately weary.

> As I walk these broad majestic days of peace,
> (For the war, the struggle of blood finish'd, wherein, O terrific Ideal,
> Against vast odds erewhile having gloriously won,
> Now thou stridest on, yet perhaps in time toward denser wars,
> Perhaps to engage in time in still more dreadful contest, dangers,
> Longer campaigns and crises ....)
> ....
> Then my realities;
> What else is so real as mine?
> Libertad and the divine average, freedom to every slave on
>   the face of the earth,
> The rapt promises and lumine of seers, the spiritual world,
>   these centuries-lasting songs,
> And our visions, the visions of poets, the most solid
>   announcements of any.[14]

One poem he wrote in 1861 became the title poem for his collection of war poems: "Drum-Taps." Seemingly a poem that encourages men's going to war, the tone of the many poems that follow in that collection immediately changes, taking on the somber recognition that bravery cannot stop dying, and that no person needs to be encouraged to die. Whitman does not publish his collection of war poems until 1865 so in most cases there is no way of knowing when any one of the poems was written, but the increasingly morose tone of his works suggests that the arrangement of the poems might follow the progression of his personal involvement as he worked in Washington, D. C. while spending his nights and weekends visiting the wounded soldiers in the more than *forty* local hospitals.

Drum-Taps opens with several long poems, as if Whitman sees his need to relinquish the by-now familiar effects of his earlier, often exuberant, long-lined poems. "First O Songs for a Prelude" describes enlistment and leave-taking in New York; his dialogue poem (as "Poet" argues with "Pennant" and "Banner," flying above troops) features a wise "Child" questioning "Father"; "The Centenarian's Story" relates an earlier war. Perhaps because it reminds readers of poems by the popular William Cullen Bryant, Whitman's "Come Up from the Fields Father" was one of his most read poems. Not a usual theme for Whitman, the poem eulogizes the son shot in battle. Blank verse recounts the family members' dialogue—father, mother, sisters—but readers

---

[14] Whitman, "As I Walk These Broad Majestic Days," Library, 595–96.

recognize that traditional rhythm. Even as the official letter encourages them, saying that Pete will "soon be better," his mother knows:

Alas poor boy, he will never be better, (nor may-be need to be
    better, that brave and simple soul,)
While they stand at home at the door, he is dead already,
The only son is dead ...[15]

As Whitman gained control of the effects he realized that poems of war should maintain, he reworked some of the "bivouac" poems to include details of actual bloodshed. In "A March in the Ranks, Hard-Prest, and the Road Unknown," for example, he wrote,

... 'Tis a large old church at the crossing roads, now an
    impromptu hospital ....
Shadows of deepest, deepest black, just lit by
    moving candles and lamps,
... By these, crowds, groups of forms ...
At my feet more distinctly a soldier, a mere lad, in
    danger of bleeding to death, (he is shot in the abdomen,)
I staunch the blood temporarily, (the youngster's face is while as a lily,)
Then before I depart I sweep my eyes o'er
    the scene fain to absorb it all,
Faces, varieties, postures beyond description, most in
    obscurity, some of them dead,
Surgeons operating, attendants holding lights, the smell of
    ether, the odor of blood,
The crowd, O the crowd of bloody forms, the yard
    outside also fill'd,
Some on the bare ground, some on planks or stretchers
    some in the death-spasm sweating,
An occasional scream or cry ....
... I see again the forms, I smell the odor ....[16]

Whitman wrote "Vigil Strange I Kept on the Field One Night" as a true *vigil*: in its slow pace, the poem reflects the sorrow of the observer who tries to bring comfort. Caring for a young wounded boy, the poet leaves the scene. When he returns, the boy has died but he continues his watch. The closing three lines are memorable:

---

[15] Whitman, "Come Up from the Fields Father," Library, 438.
[16] Whitman, "A March in the Ranks, Hard-Prest," Library, 439–40.

> Vigil for comrade swiftly slain, vigil I never forget, how as
>   day brighten'd,
> I rose from the chill ground and folded my soldier well in
>   his blanket,
> And buried him where he fell.[17]

One of the powerful emotions in any person's life is mourning. Poets have through time written laments, eulogies, elegies, and free verse strategies for mourning, or at least describing the process of doing so, but faced with the "shocking carnage of the war," in Haytock's phrase, poets trying to evoke emotion toward the participants of the Civil War felt far removed from conventional poetic forms. Readers found comfort in Emerson's abstract sentiments. They understood that Herman Melville pegged his descriptions to specific battle scenes. And they also, once *Drum-Taps* appeared in 1865, saw that Whitman was reasonably courageous about describing the actual wounding and death of soldiers. But it was usually clear that Whitman wrote as an observer to the catastrophes of war, perhaps because his role for the first twenty years of his career had been as a newspaperman. It became more and more clear as the battles raged on that *no one* knew how to write plausibly or effectively about contemporary war.

One of the most introspective of Whitman's poems in *Drum-Taps* is placed near the poems discussed above. "Year That Trembled and Reel'd Beneath Me" refers to either 1862 or 1863, a reader surmises, because in it the poet deals with the enormity of a war that defies understanding. While not all the 620,000 deaths have already occurred, it is clear that *slaughter* is the operative mode. Whitman wrote,

> Year that trembled and reel'd beneath me!
> Your summer wind was warm enough, yet the air I breathed
>   froze me,
> A thick gloom fell through the sunshine and darken'd me,
> Must I change my triumphant songs? said I to myself,
> Must I indeed learn to chant the cold dirges of the baffled?
> And sullen hymns of defeat?"[18]

---

[17] Whitman, "Vigil Strange I Kept on the Field One Night," Library, 439.
[18] Whitman, "Year That Trembled and Reel'd Beneath Me," Library, 442.

In the same voice that closed "Eighteen Sixty-One," Whitman himself reels from the impact of thousands of casualties in a brutal war. That poem closed,

> Year that suddenly sang by the mouths of the round-lipp'd cannon,
> I respect you, hurrying, crashing, sad, distracted year.

9

Still More War

In her overview of both mass media and literature about the Civil War, Eliza Richards recently commented that the former may have been more influential. War news had become "a central cultural force." We have seen that Whitman's shorter poems from *Drum-Taps* showed the influence of the photograph as he chose a single event, and then often described that scene through his poet's *lens*. Richards, of course, appreciates the horrible newness of any writing about this war, and she concludes, "the more catastrophic the events, seemingly the more important literary inheritance becomes." It was poetry by John Greenleaf Whittier, Ralph Waldo Emerson, and Julia Ward Howe that gained popular acclaim. In the cases of Emily Dickinson (about whom readers knew next to nothing), Herman Melville (still considered a writer of exotic places), and Whitman, the general reader missed the fact that what *they* wrote about the Civil War was, and would remain, important because they shaped their poetry in innovative ways.[1]

For M. L. Rosenthal and Sally M. Gall, viewing Whitman's *Drum-Taps* as a major sequence, they call the book "the acknowledged poetic masterpiece of the war".[2] For J. D. McClatchy, editing *Poets of the Civil War*, the two great poets of the Civil War are "Walt Whitman in *Drum-Taps* (1865) and Herman

---

[1] Eliza Richards, *Battle Lines: Poetry and Mass Media in the United States Civil War*. Philadelphia: University of Pennsylvania Press, 2019: 1, 13. See Alice Fahs, *The Imagined Civil War: Popular Literature of the North and the South* . Chapel Hill: University of North Carolina Press, 2001. Fahs is accurate about the drug addiction that resulted from this war in particular.

[2] M. L. Rosenthal and Sally M. Gall, *The Modern Poetic Sequence*, 91.

© The Author(s), under exclusive license to Springer Nature Switzerland AG 2021
L. Wagner-Martin, *Walt Whitman*, Literary Lives,
https://doi.org/10.1007/978-3-030-77665-7_9

Melville in *Battle-Pieces and Aspects of the War* (1866).[3] Less hyperbolic is the assessment of Richard Marius, editing *The Columbia Book of Civil War Poetry*, who places "Vigil Strange I Kept on the Field One Night," "Dirge for Two Veterans," "A March in the Ranks Hard-Prest, and the Road Unknown," and "The Wound-Dresser" as key works in describing the horrors of war. Marius emphasizes this theme—that nobody had the skill to even attempt writing about this war, which "was too big to be a sign of something else—of divine providence or any other religious value: it was its own eternity." And for its survivors, "the war was the most intense experience of their lives. Nothing afterward was the same.... Those who lived through the perils were forever changed and removed from the civilians who stayed at home".[4]

James E. Miller, Jr. sees nearly all the poems in *Drum-Taps* as superior to much of the poetry of even the 1860 edition of *Leaves of Grass*, marking Whitman's writing in the 1865 war collection an important extension of many of the "Calamus" poems. He notes, "The war proved to be for Whitman a crucial national experience in which the social theories of 'Calamus,' untried on any large scale, could be tested and, as it turned out and as he recorded in *Drum-Taps*, confirmed under fire".[5] In agreement would be Randall Fuller, who uses the phrase "light-years ahead of" as well as "different in tone and intention from the earlier poetry of *Leaves of Grass*. Gone are the expansive catalogs,... the unbounded optimism, and the overbearing insistence on union and harmony. The speaker of 'A Sight in Camp' is more concerned with the human toll of a disastrous battle.... Stepping away from the row of the dead, Whitman encountered something even more disturbing: a pile of refuse stacked as high as his shoulders. The tang of blood was in the air, mixed with wood smoke and gunpowder, and upon closer inspection the pile of offal turned out to be 'a heap of feet, legs, arms, and human fragments....'"[6]

Jennifer Haytock critiques both the Melville and the Whitman war poems of 1865 and 1866, adding in Ted Genoways' approach, that Whitman had moved to the shorter poem because of the reliance in war journalism on the telegraph. Not only the speed, but the brevity of transmission, made only essential information compelling. Such an emphasis parallels Angus Fletcher's seeing the influence of Matthew Brady's photographs on Whitman's ability to

---

[3] J. D. McClatchy, "Introduction," *Poets of the Civil War*. New York: Library of America, 2005: xxiii.

[4] Richard Marius, "Introduction," *The Columbia Book of Civil War Poetry*. New York: Columbia University Press, 1994: xxvii, xxx.

[5] James E. Miller, Jr. *A Critical Guide to Leaves of Grass*. Chicago: University of Chicago Press, 1957: 63, 158–59.

[6] Randall Fuller, *From Battlefields Rising*. New York: Oxford University Press, 2011: 139.

single out, to create not only one specific scene but one specific character, as he writes poems about elements of the Civil War.[7]

Ed Folsom analyzes poetic styles from Whitman's pre-war compilations of *Leaves of Grass* and then his writing in *Drum-Taps*; Richard Gray sees one key to the change in poetry through Whitman's use of the "I" persona. That speaker centers all perception and provides a human consciousness—whether or not it is Whitman's—to guide perceptions. He finds Whitman to be in the "American Adam" mode in that he absorbed everything into the self.[8]

Walter Lowenfels recounts Whitman's pride in *Drum-Taps*, saying he was "mostly satisfied" with the book, commenting that he had told the stories of the "divine average".[9] He quotes Whitman's accounts of his "little notebooks for impromptu jottings in pencil to refresh my memory of names and circumstances and what was especially wanted, etc. In these I briefed cases, persons, sights, occurrences in camp, by the bedside and not seldom by the corpses of the dead." Some of Lowenfel's lines from Whitman, of course, are from "Specimen Days," but other segments are from reminiscences about the Civil War (what Whitman called "the distinguishing event of my time") during a period when archival materials were difficult to access.

The quality of Lowenfels' materials is impeccable. For instance, Whitman wrote in "Specimen Days" about his first week after finding George and then living amid the army tents ("After First Fredericksburg," December 23–31, 1862).

> The results of the late battle are exhibited everywhere about here in thousands of cases, (hundreds die every day,) in the camps, brigade, and division hospitals. These are merely tents, and sometimes very poor ones, the wounded lying on the ground, lucky if their blankets are spread on layers of pine or hemlock twigs, or small leaves. No cots, seldom even a mattress. It is pretty cold. The ground is frozen hard, and there is occasional snow. I go around from one case to another. I do not see that I do much good to these wounded dying; but I cannot leave them. Once in a while some youngster holds on to me convulsively, and I do what I can for him; at any rate, stop with him and sit near him for hours, if he wishes it...[10]

---

[7] Jennifer Haytock. *The Routledge Introduction to American War Literature*. New York: Routledge, 2018. Angus Fletcher, "Book of a Lifetime," Marcus and Sollors, 311.

[8] Ed Folsom, "Lucifer and Ethiopia: Whitman, Race, and Poetics Before the Civil War and After," *A Historical Guide to Walt Whitman*, ed. David S. Reynolds. New York: Oxford University Press, 2000: 45–95. Richard Gray, *A Brief History of American Literature*. Chichester: Wiley, 2011.

[9] Walter Lowenfels. *Walt Whitman's Civil War*. New York: Knopf, 1961: vii, x ff.

[10] Whitman, "Specimen Days," Library, 712–13.

As Whitman describes his learning to give comfort—become a care-giver by accident, out of a kind of desperation on his part, since he obviously had never expected to see so many wounded and dying men, or to be faced with the piles of corpses that every battle created. His poem "The Wound-Dresser" also explains that his role fell to him because he looked so *old* (too old to have enlisted, being now in his mid-forties, "My face droop'd and I resign'd myself,/ To sit by the wounded and soothe them, or silently watch the dead").

Whitman's poem is a brilliantly arranged set of descriptions of his acts, of the soldiers he was able to care for, of the gruesome details of the wounds and the amputations—and of the horror of it all. Some of his long poem is stridently objective:

> Bearing the bandages, water and sponge,
> Straight and swift to my wounded I go,
> Where they lie on the ground after the battle brought in,
> Where their priceless blood reddens the grass the ground...

And where "an attendant" holds a tray as well as "a refuse pail/Soon to be filled again with clotted rags and blood, emptied, and filled again."

Reminiscent of Whitman's poem "A March in the Ranks, Hard-Prest, and the Road Unknown," referred to previously, here too the poet makes readers understand the catastrophic injuries:

> The crush'd head I dress, (poor crazed hand tear not the bandage away,)
> The neck of the cavalry-man with the bullet through and through I examine,
> Hard the breathing rattles, quite glazed already the eye,
>   yet life struggles hard...
>
> From the stump of the arm, the amputated hand,
> I undo the clotted lint, remove the slough, wash off the
>   matter and blood,
> Back on his pillow the soldier bends with curv'd neck
>   and side-falling head,
> His eyes are closed, his face is pale, he dares not look on the
>   bloody stump,
> And has not yet look'd on it.
>
> I dress a wound in the side, deep, deep,
> But a day or two more, for see the frame all wasted and sinking,
> And the yellow-blue countenance see,
>
> I dress the perforated shoulder, the foot with the bullet-wound,

Cleanse the one with a gnawing and putrid gangrene, so
    sickening, so offensive,
While the attendant stands behind aside me holding the tray and pail."

Whitman has divided "The Wound-Dresser" into four sections; most of the graphic descriptions above are from part three. His point, need it be repeated, is that war is a horrifying experience, even if one is only a watcher. The dying are like the amputee above—afraid to even *see* what is surely a mortal wound. Unprepared for such injuries, excited at joining the ranks coming from their own cities beside their boyhood friends, these young soldiers cannot even imagine what war will be like: and for most of them, every battle can—and may—mean death.

The last stanza of part three leads into the sonnet-like part four as if to resolve this panorama of hell that began somewhat hesitantly. One of Whitman's most polished poems, "The Wound-Dresser" epitomizes his feeling that all people are *one,* that the war that existed between 1861 and 1865 was *not* a victory for either side, and that his role was only to alleviate pain. He could not, however, alleviate his own pain.

I am faithful, I do not give out,
The fractur'd thigh, the knee, the wound in the abdomen,
These and more I dress with impassive hand, (yet deep in
    my breast a fire, a burning flame.)

        4.

Thus in silence is dreams' projections,
Returning, resuming, I thread my way through the hospitals,
The hurt and wounded I pacify with soothing hand,
I sit by the restless all the dark night, some are so young,
Some suffer so much, I recall the experience sweet and sad,
(Many a soldier's loving arms about this neck have cross'd
    and rested,
Many a soldier's kiss dwells on these bearded lips.)[11]

Evidently torn by a need to both explain the soldiers' woundings and deaths, and commemorate their young lives, Whitman worked through clear experiments in poetry—there were no precedents for a poem like "The Wound-Dresser" or "A March in the Ranks, Hard-Prest." Except for Whitman's poems, there is still no precedent for an elegy that gives such unexpectedly disturbing details: elegies are meant to calm, to pose solace, to be reflective.

---

[11] Whitman, "The Wound-Dresser," Library, 443–45.

The fact that Whitman chose to remain in Washington in early January, 1963, after accompanying a group of wounded Fredericksburg survivors there, also reflects how devastated he had been by those days following the battle. He then asked friends, including Emerson, for letters of recommendation in finding a job. Most of his efforts failed but finally Charlie Eldridge, his Boston publisher, found him work as a copyist in the Army Paymaster's Office. He could live on that pay. His brother Jeff had sent him $6 to use for his hospital work, and subsequently Jeff collected money from his co-workers at the Brooklyn Water Works and sent that along. People began thinking of Whitman's hospital work as a kind of ministry.[12]

Whitman's decision to live in Washington City was less pragmatic than this description may sound. He was surely acting from an immediacy of grief, partly because so much of his anguish caring for and being surrounded by the Union survivors of the Fredricksburg debacle were from the New York Fifty-First unit, to which his brother George belonged. He knew some of those wounded and dying men, or George certainly did. It had become a family experience as well as a human one. As he wrote to friends in March of 1863, "These Hospitals, so different from all others—these thousands, and tens and twenties of thousands of American young men, badly wounded... open a new world somehow to me, giving closer insights, new things, exploring deeper mines than any yet".[13]

At the start, much of the mournful record-keeping Whitman wrote was in prose. But eventually, being a man who had been thinking in poetry for at least the past decade, he put his anguish into poems, and many of those eventually appeared in *Drum-Taps*. Writing a poem was a state of mind, a state of being, that—once life settled back into some kind of normalcy—Whitman could not repress. He prioritized. The "work" he did to cover his living expenses was *not* his real work. Comforting soldiers—not only Union soldiers and not only New York soldiers, but all the wounded—became his *work*, and he devoted his prime hours to planning for his hospital visits, making those hospital visits (sometimes staying overnight at a dying man's bedside), and then taking care of whatever promises he had made the following day. Being a care-giver in Washington's hospitals had become Whitman's primary work.

It was enervating. It was demanding. It drained Whitman's emotional capacity.

He seldom wrote his mother or his friends because he had little energy left for anything but this hospital work. Yet every day that he visited soldiers

---

[12] Loving, *Walt Whitman,* 17–18.
[13] Letter of March 19, 1863, to Nathanial Bloom and John F. S. Gray, quoted in Loving, *Walt Whitman,* 1.

led to other visits—and he found ways to move on public transportation to reach yet another hospital, another group of the wounded and dying men. Whitman lost weight, he sometimes had trouble sleeping when he did return to his room at night.

Eventually, Whitman showed his emotional exposure to the same traumatic effects as any soldier physically mired in the frightening battles of any war. As Philip Beidler recently explained, now that PTSD has become a psychiatric condition, listed since 1980 in the American Psychological Association's *Diagnostic and Statistical Manual*, the illnesses connected with "return and readjustment" after the trauma of war experiences are legitimate. They are real not only for the soldiers fighting—they would have been real for the medical workers, for the hospital personnel, and for the care-givers like Whitman.[14] While "combat trauma" is the most pertinent state—particularly during these incredibly mortal Civil War battles—any experience that creates "a form of enforced fear and suffering" (he mentions here domestic abuse) should correctly be categorized as *post traumatic stress disorder*.

Beidler goes on to note how scarce are the writings about the Civil War battles (not only in poetry—in all forms of literature). "War" as a designation had belonged to the earlier ages. It was cloaked in the shapes of "manly endurance." In the supposed rules of good Christian living, the *good* will survive. Any soldier who did not survive a battle was labeled a coward, weak, effeminate—yet here in the 1860s, nobody had even dreamed what would occur in any kind of modern war. The tools of contemporary war were not yet imagined. So a vocabulary that gave legitimacy to fear or stress or enervation had not yet been invented.

In Beidler's words, "a war of newly violent, endlessly destructive weaponry, and of mass woundings and slaughter" was something out of fantasy worlds. Without language, without any understanding of the *psychic* effects (seemingly remote even though the *physical* effects were omnipresent, inescapable), leaving the war meant only shame.[15] It made sense that writing about the Civil War would replicate eons of writing about earlier wars historically.

Beidler writes about all wars in this essay, a range which allows him to point out that in the twentieth century, replete with both its world wars, Korea, Vietnam and subsequent mass conflicts, the military has done years and years of studies about "battle fatigue" or "combat exhaustion." What these twentieth-century studies show is that "the average line soldier might

---

[14] Philip Beidler, "Veterans, Trauma, Afterwar," *War and American Literature*, 71–86. He also usefully extends PTSD into many other causative life experiences. Trauma is trauma; the term can be used in many areas of medicine and culture.

[15] Beidler, "Veterans, Trauma, Afterwar," *War and American Literature*, 72–75.

be stable and effective in the first 180 days, but almost as certainly *combat ineffective* by around 240".[16] There was no relief for Civil War combatants after this half year of service; the low figures are surprising. Also surprising is the fact that Walt Whitman spent years of giving the best of his days to hospital visits, going twice daily to many hospitals. (His paying job dwindled to part-time so that he had hours to give to this hospital service.) It must be pointed out, however, that he was forced back to his mother's home in Brooklyn in early November, 1863, diagnosed with something a doctor called"hospital malaria" or "hospital fever".[17]

Whitman's routine was inexorable. He visited hospitals from noon to late afternoon and then returned for the evening. The spring and summer had been particularly enervating. He worked three weeks straight after the battle of Chancellorsville, because the woundings and casualties were so heavy. When the survivors flowed in after Gettysburg, it was the same ceaseless nightmare. All this time he lived meagerly in his single room at 394 L. Street, going to his clerical work mornings.

One piece of evidence of Whitman's own mental state after he had done his hospital visits far past the 240 day endurance mark that Beidler references is his poem "The Artilleryman's Vision." Not admitting to the account as being personal, Whitman includes some jarring details as he describes the nightmare, long after the soldier has returned home:

> ... There in the room as I wake from sleep this vision presses upon me;
> The engagement opens there and then in fantasy unreal,
> The skirmishers begin, they crawl cautiously ahead, I hear
>   the irregular snap! snap!
> I hear the sounds of the different missiles, the short *t-h-t! t-h-t!*
>   of the rifle-balls,
> I see the shells exploding leaving small white clouds, I hear
>   the great shells shrieking as they pass,
> The grape like the hum and whirr of wind through the trees,
>   (tumultuous now the contest rages,)
> All the scenes at the batteries rise in detail before me again,
> The crashing and smoking, the pride of the men in their pieces,
> The chief-gunner ranges and sights his piece and selects a fuse
>   of the right time,
> After firing I see him lean aside and look eagerly off to note
>   the effect;...
> Then resumed the chaos louder than ever, with eager calls

---

[16] Ibid., 78. After 240 days, the military then would use established protocols of "rest, rotation, and reassignment to rear area places of relative safety".

[17] Loving, *Walt Whitman*, 266–75.

and orders of officers,
While from some distant part of the field the wind wafts to my ears
    a shout of applause, (some special success,)
And ever the sound of the cannon far or near, (rousing even
    in dreams a devilish exultation and all the old mad joy
    in the depths of my soul,)
And ever the hastening of infantry shifting positions,
    batteries, cavalry, moving hither and thither,
(The falling, dying, I heed not, the wounded dripping and red
    I heed not, some to the rear are hobbling,)
Grime, heat, rush, aide-de-camps galloping by or on a full run,
With the patter of small arms, the warning *s–s-t* of the rifles,
    (these in my vision I hear or see,)
And bombs bursting in air, and at night the vari-color'd rockets.[18]

A rarity here, given that so many of Whitman's war poems focus on the wounded and dying man, carried to whatever climax he plans with physical details of pallor, stoic conversations, or general acceptance, this internal dream monologue might well represent an experience the poet has either had or recognizes.

A similar near-confessional poem is "Not Youth Pertains to Me," and here Whitman also speaks introspectively.

      Not Youth Pertains to Me
Not youth pertains to me,
Nor delicatesse, I cannot beguile the time with talk,
Awkward in the parlor, neither a dancer nor elegant,
In the learn'd coterie sitting constrain'd and still, for learning.
    inures not to me,
Beauty, knowledge, inure not to me—yet there are two or three
    things inure to me,
I have nourish'd the wounded and sooth'd many a dying
    soldier,
And at intervals waiting or in the midst of camp,
Composed these songs.[19]

Walt Whitman became seriously involved in participating in the Civil War in late December, 1862; by the time he had traveled to Washington, the year had changed. According to historians, January 1, 1863, marked the beginning

---

[18] Whitman, "The Artilleryman's Vision," Library, 450–51.
[19] Whitman, "Not Youth Pertains to Me," Library, 452. A pair poem is "Look Down Fair Moon," in that it reveals Whitman's role in the dying men's reconciliations.

of the turn toward Union success. On January 1, President Lincoln issued the *Emancipation Proclamation.* His emphasis on the human issues of slavery made the war into a moral conflict—so that the participation of outsiders could no longer be justified. It was clear that slavery should be considered a sin. No matter how profitable crops raised with slave labor might be, the issues of human freedom outweighed any such profit. Lincoln had circulated a preliminary version of the document in September of 1862, soon after the Union victory at Antietam, but even though the document called for Confederate surrender—lest all slaves in those states and territories become free—people paid less attention to the document than expected: the Confederate states did not consider surrendering. Former slaves began fighting for the Union, though they received lower pay than did the white soldiers. By March, 1863, the Confederacy had turned to impressment (as the Union forces were using conscription), inflation was astronomical, and Southern women were waging "bread protests." The South had lost over 175,000 men.

There are more devastating losses to come: in May, 1863, the battle of Chancellorsville costs 30,000 lives from both armies; in July, the battle of Gettysburg—stretching over several days to include Pickett's Charge, Cemetery Ridge, and Little Round Top–gave the North a victory, but nearly 45,000 men died in those three days. Much of the combat in restricted spaces was hand-to-hand.

While both armies were more and more depleted, key battles such as the mid-September Battle of Chickamauga in Tennessee were shocking markers—18,000 men died there.

On November 19, 1863, the commemoration of the Gettysburg cemetery was held: Lincoln's short "Gettysburg Address" was a preliminary statement to the main oratory of the occasion, by Edward Everett of Massachusetts. In Lincoln's remarks, however, he changed the accepted definition of national purpose, calling for a "new birth of freedom" so that "government of the people, by the people, for the people, shall not perish from the earth." Lincoln's address was more significant in that it stated clearly, "all men are created equal."

During the last years of the Civil War—with Whitman still visiting hospitals in Washington—Lincoln may have insured the Union win by appointing Ulysses S. Grant the commander of the remaining 550,000 Union soldiers. May 3–4, 1864, the Union Army of the Potomac began its scourge of Virginia—the Wilderness, Spotsylvania Court House, Mechanicsville, Cold Harbor and eventually, a year later, Fort Stedman. (In the last battle alone, the Confederacy lost nearly 5,000 men.) When William T. Sherman marched his 60,000 Union troops from Chattanooga to Atlanta, capturing that city at the end of his hundred-mile conquest and then continuing "to the Sea," he gave Lincoln his reelection on November 8, 1864.

Whitman returned to Washington in early December of 1863 and then continued his hospital visits, his clerkship, and his living in his L. Street room. It was almost exactly another year till Lincoln's reelection. The aging poet had taken true leave during his weeks back home in November of 1863, going to Pfaff's, going to plays and operas, visiting with old friends. It was as if he unconsciously knew how to reinvigorate his mind and body—and his war-sickened spirit. A poem like "Give Me the Splendid Silent Sun" attests to a vestige of the earlier Walt Whitman, experiencing his beloved cosmos. The poem closes,

> ... O such for me! O an intense life, full to repletion and varied!
> The life of the theatre, bar-room, huge hotel, for me!
> .... People, endless, streaming, with strong voices, passions, pageants....
> Manhattan faces and eyes forever for me.[20]

The poet's work continues, however, suggesting that he cannot ever forget, or escape, his images of war:

> The swarming ranks press on and on, the dense brigades press on,
> Glittering dimly, toiling under the sun—the dust-cover'd men,
> In columns rise and fall to me undulations of the ground....[21]

His poems show that his memory of war will be omnipresent:

> How solemn as one by one,
> As the ranks returning worn and sweaty, as the men file by
>   where I stand,
> As the faces the masks appear, as I glance at the
>   faces studying the masks, ...[22]

Whitman's poem "Lo, Victress on the Peeks" concludes with some of his saddest images,

---

[20] Whitman, "Give Me the Splendid Silent Sun," Library, 447.
[21] Whitman, "An Army Corps on the March," Library, 435.
[22] Whitman, "How Solemn as One by One," Library, 455.

... No poem proud, I chanting bring to thee, nor mastery's
   rapturous verse,
But a cluster containing night's darkness and blood-dripping
   wounds,
And psalms of the dead.[23]

---

[23] Whitman, "Lo, Victress on the Peeks," Library, 455.

10

Whitman and Lincoln

He wrote about President Lincoln many times. In fact, Whitman seemed to think they somehow knew each other.... "I see the President almost every day, as I happen to live where he passes to or from his lodgings out of town. He never sleeps at the White House during the hot season.... He always has a company of twenty-five or thirty cavalry, with sabres drawn and held upright over their shoulders. 'They say this guard was against his personal wish, but he let his counselors have their way. The party makes no great show in uniform or horses. Mr. Lincoln on the saddle generally rides a good-sized, easy-going gray horse, is dress'd in plain black, somewhat rusty and dusty, wears a black stiff hat, and looks about as ordinary in attire as the commonest man."[1] In Whitman's mind, they were two commoners—with great achievement and talent—living lives of mostly obscure recognition.

It happened so quickly it was almost like a dream. In March, 1865, Lincoln took his second oath of office. On April 9, 1865, General Robert E. Lee surrendered at Appomattox Court House in Virginia, with only 15,000 men remaining in arms. On April 14, Lincoln was assassinated at Ford Theatre by John Wilkes Booth, a Maryland actor who was a Southern sympathizer. With the advent of Andrew Johnson as President of the United States, the Civil War ended and the turmoil of Reconstruction began. On May 10, 1865, Jefferson Davis was captured—during the 1500 mile funeral procession of

---

[1] Whitman, "Abraham Lincoln," "Specimen Days," Library 732–33.

© The Author(s), under exclusive license to Springer Nature
Switzerland AG 2021
L. Wagner-Martin, *Walt Whitman*, Literary Lives,
https://doi.org/10.1007/978-3-030-77665-7_10

Lincoln's casket from Washington, D. C. to the middle states. The journey was through "continued lines of people" as the country itself seemed to grieve.

Whitman had returned to Brooklyn again during late June and July of 1864, once more suffering from dizziness and bad headaches. He then went back to Washington, to a somewhat better job in the Indian Affairs offices, and so had saved enough money to have his collection of war poems published. In March of 1865 he traveled back to Brooklyn to have *Drum-Taps* printed. He was still at his mother's when the news of Lincoln's death, one day after his shooting, spread. Louisa was as deeply grieved as her son. The family had also been deeply saddened at the capture of George Whitman, who was placed into Libby Prison after the Poplar Grove Church battle. He had nearly died of illnesses there but finally, with luck, he became part of a prisoner exchange on February 22, 1865.[2]

Walt Whitman was just plain exhausted. He was experiencing some of the duration of battle effects that Paul Fussell described in his history of modern war.

There he questioned "the likelihood that peace would ever come again was often in serious doubt during the war. One did not have to be a lunatic or a particularly despondent visionary to conceive quite seriously that the war would literally never end and would become the permanent condition of mankind. The stalemate and the attrition would go on infinitely, becoming... a part of the accepted atmosphere of the modern experience."[3]

Not even watching his *Drum-Taps* go through the printing processes was exciting, but Whitman was pleased with his war collection. The last few poems in the book were less experimental and, somehow, less effective, he thought. Even the two closing poems which he had marked "(Washington City, 1865)"—"How Solemn as One by One" and "Spirit Whose Work Is Done"—seemed flat and predictable. It was as if even winning the war could not lead to celebration: the depletion of the Union ranks shadowed any possible joy.

> How solemn as one by one,
> As the ranks returning worn and sweaty,
>   as the men file by where I stand....[4]

---

[2] Loving, *Walt Whitman*, 280–85. Very few of the 1000 soldiers who had left New York at the start of the conflict had survived—George Whitman had gone through many of the worst battles, but being a prisoner of war nearly cost him his life.

[3] Paul Fussell, *The Great War and Modern Memory*. New York: Oxford University Press, 1975: 71.

[4] Whitman, "How Solemn as One by One," Library, 453.

Whitman couches the long-lined "Spirit Whose Work Is Done" with a quali-
fying "spirit of dreadful hours!" The enormity of the war's disasters, the losses
of hundreds of thousands of lives, property, household possessions, stifles any
mood of happy survival. Whitman speaks to what he knows the *soldiers* will
carry home after their emaciating ordeals:

> Leave me your pulses of rage—bequeath them to me—fill me
>   with currents convulsive;
> Let them scorch and blister out of my chants....[5]

"Adieu to a Soldier" and the very last poem, "Turn O Libertad," similarly
might have been written by any one of the many poets of the Civil War.
They are predictable and acceptable: they say what readers expect. Of his
group of closing poems in *Drum-Taps*, only "To a Certain Civilian" has the
sharp bite of classic Whitman expression, as he here complains of what he
has—at times—been forced to write—and he muses about the poems he did
not try to write at all.

True to his earlier form, here Whitman rails against the expected attitudes American poems must take. Even while he sometimes forced his readers
to face the bloody deaths of their cherished sons and lovers, he knew he
could not keep publishing such lines of affront. Here he acknowledges that
he should have given readers "dulcet rhymes," "the civilians' peaceful and
languishing" panaceas. Instead, Whitman the poet admits, he presents the
"slow wail and convulsive throb leading the officer's funeral."

His silence admits that he does not here mention descriptions of amputated limbs, of blood loss from deep wounds in the abdomens. But he has
put *all* his knowledge about the war into his poems. He angrily closes this
work with a reminder that he, Walt Whitman, *poet,* tells the truth:

> What to such as you anyhow such a poet as I? therefore
>   leave my words,
> And go lull yourself with what you can understand, and
>   with piano-tunes,
> For I lull *nobody*, and *you* will never understand me.[6]

After more than two years in Washington, D. C., Whitman realized that he
had relinquished his life as a poet in order to make what he felt were valuable contributions to the Union war efforts. He had worked at bottom-rung
jobs in the Capitol so as to spend these years visiting and caring for wounded

---

[5] Whitman, "Spirit Whose Work Is Done," Library, 456.
[6] Whitman, "To a Certain Civilian," Library, 455.

and dying soldiers throughout the Washington hospitals, more than forty of such institutions, making his trips usually twice a day, with no regard for his own health. In these years of his living away from his family, he had written comparatively little. His brother Andrew had died at home; his brother George had been a prisoner of war, and as a result was in perilous health. Once in a while he had been able to send his mother a dollar, but much of this time she and Eddy lived in great need. He had fallen ill for two long sieges of "hospital malaria" or exhaustion; he would experience the dizziness and headaches for the rest of his life. And he lived as he did, trying to bring some small comfort to the wounded soldiers—no matter their allegiances, no matter their skin color, no matter their religious beliefs.

And just on the edge of success—*Drum-Taps* about to be published, the war moving toward an end, the Union about to be victorious—comes one of the greatest losses of his life, Lincoln's death. He sees this as the greatest loss possible to the Union itself, and to the American nation.

As if the poet in Whitman had been close to dormant during his years of isolation in Washington City, this attack of sorrow created a kind of culminating pain. Surrounded back in Brooklyn by slowly emerging spring flowers, finally forced by his own health and the business of seeing his book into print, Whitman's incapacitating anguish throws open his reserves of language. Somehow, he chooses a rhythm that evokes such ranges of sorrow that all readers can experience the grief. The poem opens,

> When lilacs last in the dooryard bloom'd,
> And the great star early dropp'd in the Western sky in
>   the night,
> I mourn'd, and yet shall mourn with ever-returning spring...[7]

With the effectiveness of his familiar long line, Whitman allows himself the comfort of the devices of alliteration and accented rhythms, but he creates as well the abrupt *stop*—as if his grief halts his heart: "*I mourned*, and yet shall mourn...."

The poem moves on in tears. It speaks of "him I love". It anthropomorphizes the unnamed President with "O great star disappeared." His grief makes the poet's soul "helpless".

When Whitman writes the third section (of the sixteen parts of this eulogy), he claims not only his immense grief but his common roots, roots familiar to both himself the poet and to his President.

---

[7] Whitman, "When Lilacs Last in the Dooryard Bloom'd," Library, 459–67.

3

In the dooryard fronting an old farm-house near the white-
    wash'd palings,
Stands the lilac-bush tall-growing with heart-shaped leaves of
    rich green,
With many a pointed blossom rising delicate, with the
    perfume strong I love,
With every leaf a miracle—and from this bush in the dooryard,
With delicate-color'd blossoms and heart-shaped leaves of
    rich green,
A sprig with its flower I break.

The reader has seen Whitman break these commemorative twigs before; it is his most poignant symbol of a reunion with nature. But he quickly adds to this resonant placement a fourth part, the solitary (and all too common) thrush, "a shy and hidden bird," a singer who lovingly sings alone because he *must*, "for well dear brother I know,/ If thou wast not granted to sing thou would'st surely die." Whitman knows the loss of a gift—he seems himself as modest as the President or the thrush, a bird who creates his sounds despite his "bleeding throat".

The poem, remarkable for its easy rhythms, never uses the name *Abraham Lincoln,* but its story is of the President's coffin as it journeys through the country, a country itself so bereft it is filled with "dirges through the night, with the thousand voices rising strong and solemn." And when the coffin passes Whitman, he makes a wordless gesture there in the dark: "I give you my sprig of lilac".

This gesture closes the eighth part of the poem, though there are longer segments to come while the reader reaches part sixteen. Some of its lines rehearse the unforgettable war, some return again to the events of the natural world, often giving the poem a necessary pause as the reader re-connects with the star, the bird, the lilac bush. (Lincoln's "trinity" comes appropriately from nature, not from a religious source; but the effects of the symbols as he has created them are, finally, religious as well as mournful.)

The poem charts the poet's journey as well as the coffin's. In fact, the poem has two closing sections, and the earlier one of these ends with Whitman's passage:

Passing, I leave thee lilac with heart-shaped leaves, I leave thee there in the door-yard, blooming, returning with spring.

The last section of the poem draws together all the mourning elements, united in their sorrow but calmly at rest, surrounded by the natural world:

> With the holders holding my hand nearing the call of the
>   bird,
> Comrades mine and I in the midst, and their memory ever
>   to keep, for the dead I loved so well,
> For the sweetest, wisest soul of all my days and lands—and
>   this for his dear sake,
> Lilac and star and bird twined with the chant of my soul,
> There in the fragrant pines and the cedars dusk and dim.

J. D. McClatchy refers to this poem as perhaps the last great wound that Whitman addressed—Lincoln's death—as a "threnody". Randall Fuller said the poem became "the voice of an entire nation, a communal expression of mourning for the slain president and, through association, for the hundreds of thousands killed in the war." Alfred Habegger saw it in tandem with Emily Dickinson's war poems, describing the effects of these masterpieces as "elegiac meditations." "Some songs propose to release us from loneliness; this song merely enlarges it.... It is the chant of acceptance, not Christian but Druid, leaving behind a keener sense of nature and solitude, a recognition that every-thing is different from what one thought and hoped, and that one has already begun to live with that".[8]

Sixty years later, when William Carlos Williams published his mixed-form biographies about figures from the country's history, titled *In the American Grain*, he closed the book with a brief prose poem about Abraham Lincoln. Here he described Lincoln as "a woman. He babies them. He leans over and floods them with his insistences.... The least private would find a woman to caress him, a woman in an old shawl—with a great bearded face and a towering black hat above it, to give unearthly reality."[9]

Although Whitman knew that "Lilacs" was a very fine poem, he kept writing about Lincoln. And when he picked up the copies of *Drum-Taps* from the printer, he arranged that there would also be a shorter book, ready to be published in early fall. "When Lilacs Last in the Dooryard Bloom'd" would be the keystone of that work. Meanwhile, as he had written in his "Specimen Days" essay, "He leaves for America's history and biography, so far, not only its most dramatic reminiscence—he leaves, in my opinion, the greatest, best,

---

[8] J. D. McClatchy, "Introduction," *Poets of the Civil War*, xxvi; Randall Fuller, *From Battlefields Rising*, 217; Alfred Habegger, *"My Wars Are Laid Away in Books"*, 491, 93.

[9] William Carlos Williams, "Abraham Lincoln," *In the American Grain*. New York: New Directions, 1925: 234–35. More recently, George Saunders' *Lincoln in the Bardo*, winner of the British Man Booker Prize in 2017, gives expression, both linguistically and vocally in its recording of more than two hundred voices, to the evocative power of the Lincoln story.

most characteristic, artistic, moral personality. Not but that he had faults...
but honesty, goodness, shrewdness, conscience, and (a new virtue, unknown
to other lands, and hardly yet really known here... UNIONISM, in its truest
and amplest sense.... These he seal'd with his life."

11

The Wages of Class

Jerome Loving correctly emphasizes the rigidity of the US Army not allowing Colonel George Whitman to continue his service after the war ended. Retrieved from the prison camp he had spent several months in, during the prisoner exchange in February, 1865, Whitman was given a long furlough so that he could recuperate. And then the war ended. He was then promoted to major. At the end of the summer, when his unit, the Fifty-First Regiment of New York Volunteers, disbanded, he was promoted once more, to the rank of breveted lieutenant colonel. Loving states that all permanent soldiers were to be graduates of a military academy. Whitman, a cabinetmaker, had no choice but to return to Brooklyn and resume his previous occupation from 1861. He had tried for "a regular or permanent commission," which would have paid a salary and benefits, but he was refused.[1]

The economics of life had changed little. Betsy Erkkila discusses the fact that it looked as if the United States was undergoing great change, but to the Whitmans—and others of the lower-middle-class in the North and the West—making any kind of living was still hard. "The gravitation of power from the periphery to the center during the Civil War represented a radical shift from the state-centered union of the past: America was no longer a union of states but a national union. Without the opposition of the South during the war years, government power was exercised increasingly in the interests of the urban and industrial North: economic legislation of the period—a

---

[1] Loving, *Walt Whitman*, 294.

L. Wagner-Martin, *Walt Whitman*, Literary Lives, https://doi.org/10.1007/978-3-030-77665-7_11

protective tariff, a national banking system, railroad subsidies, and the release of national resources—reflected the new nationalism and the entrepreneurial interests of an industrial, capitalist class."[2]

These economic shifts were of little use to Walt Whitman as he tried to find a position so that he could continue to live in Washington. The hospitals were just as full after the war as they had been during the conflict, and he had found a rhythm to his life—working, caring for his wounded, writing— in the large and politically aware city. Unfortunately, his job in the Indian Affairs office was gone, said to be a casualty of downsizing. He was dismissed as of June 30, 1865. Some of his powerful friends decided Whitman had been let go because of his *Leaves of Grass* poems. His closest friend in the city, William O'Connor, became so incensed over this job loss that he ended up writing a book about Whitman, *The Good Gray Poet* (there are suggestions in the manuscript pages that Whitman may have helped O'Connor with the project).

Eventually it worked out that Whitman was given a post in the Attorney General's Office, filling a spot just vacated by Edmund Clarence Stedman. While this work was more time-consuming, it also was more interesting. It also paid him $1200 annually. Whitman interviewed Confederate officers and others who had requested presidential pardons. These men were applying under a new policy created by President Andrew Johnson, who thought most men who had served the Confederacy should not be charged with treason. Only the most involved and those Southerners with property valued at over $20,000 could *not* apply. By the time Whitman began his work, the files held four to five thousand applications.[3]

Whitman was, of course, glad to have both the work and the pay. He enjoyed his meals with the O'Connors, and he was eager to be able to have the means to take small gifts to the wounded men he continued to visit. He reveled in the two May days of the troops being reviewed in Washington City: all members of the Union Army marched on Pennsylvania Avenue and then were retired from service forever. (He would write in "Specimen Days" that his best memories from the Civil War were, at the start, "the general, voluntary arm'd upheaval, and then the peaceful and harmonious disbanding of the armies in the summer of 1865.")[4]

As he wrote to his mother about those marching troops, "it was too much and too impressive, to be described.... Imagine a great wide avenue like Flat-bush avenue... quite flat, & stretching as far as you can see, with a great white

---

[2] Betsy Erkkila, *Whitman the Political Poet*. New York: Oxford University Press, 1989: 246.
[3] Loving, *Walt Whitman*, 291–93.
[4] Whitman, "Specimen Days," Library, 707.

building half as big as fort Greene at the commencement of the avenue, &
then through this avenue marching solid ranks of soldiers, 20 or 25 abreast,
just marching steady all day long for two days, without intermission, one
regiment after another, real war-worn *soldiers*, that have been marching &
fighting for years.... the *rank & file* was the greatest sight of all".[5]

There may have been some important ceremonies but no one could ever
forget the immense toll the war had taken—all the dead, all the wounded, all
the destroyed property. As Theodor Ropp pointed out, the Civil War was the
first in the world to be fought by really large numbers of *literate* men, fighting
as common soldiers. There was no hierarchy of the educated or the wealthy
holding leadership positions. The carnage, therefore, was a different kind of
decimation, a more intense kind of loss.[6] For Alice Fahs, people could not
forget the terrible loss of lives. How could anyone forget "the bodily sacrifices
of soldiers within an explicitly Christian framework." And then there was "the
shocking anonymity of suffering and death undergone by ordinary soldiers far
from home. This was an aspect of war that many Americans found unbearable: They simply could not accept that soldiers' suffering and death would
go unsung and unmourned." She quotes from one of Whitman's letters to
his mother, as he tells her that the identity of a soldier could not be learned:
"The worst of it is too there was nothing on his clothes, or any one with him,
to identify him—& he is altogether unknown—Mother, it is enough to rack
one's heart, such things—very likely his folks will never know in the world
what has become of him."[7]

For what little he could do for the wounded soldiers, Whitman knew any
care was worth his efforts. Again, the immensity of the losses drives home
the particularization of each loss. When Whitman wrote a poem about a
single casualty, it stood for many other lives and deaths that he could not
describe. What is important to remember, as Whitman's art shows, is that for
all the thousands who died, even more thousands were racked with their own
mourning.

Here at the start of the panoply that was to be *modern* war, Whitman
could handle only his own immersion in death. He did not write about the
weapons of war; he wrote about the results of those weapons. And so long
as the Civil War was considered some kind of artifact dealing with "the slave
situation," its prophetic power may be lost. Today's historians see this war
as a telling debacle that provides information about the effects of monstrous
tactical machines, machines new to history. More importantly, they see it as a

---

[5] Quoted by Loving, *Walt Whitman*, 294.
[6] Theodor Ropp, *War in the Modern World*. Durham, NC: Duke University Press, 1959: 162.
[7] Alice Fahs, *Popular Literature*, 96.

reflection of still-ongoing patterns of economic health or disease, of class and caste.

Recent historians have stated clearly that the polarization between the South—whose soldiers considered themselves elite in that they were in the company of slave-holders, even if they themselves did not own slaves—and the Union forces accrued in part from what the men perceived as *class* differences. As historian Nancy Isenberg explains, many in the South thought that people in the North and West were little better than slaves: they owned no property, they did their own work, they lived in small dwellings, and if they were not "squatters" or "clay-eaters" themselves, they neighbored with such. If this description marked those who believed in "Jacksonian democracy," many Southerners wanted nothing to do with such a belief, Isenberg states. The animosity many Southerners felt for all Northern "democrats" was less about the ownership of slaves than it was about winning back their national leadership.[8]

Jefferson Davis promoted this understanding—that Southerners were the aristocrats, they had a "positive pedigree". Northerners, in contrast, were rag-tag, heirs to "a homeless race". All Yankees were "degenerate," and the Southern soldiers wanted to be rid of those "mudsill" human beings.

The Civil War was a class war. The Northern army was seen to be "a foul collection of urban roughs, prairie dirt farmers, greasy mechanics, unwashed immigrants... the off-scourings of the earth." Worse, soldiers fighting for the Union were said to believe in "class mixing, race mixing, and the redistribution of wealth." Isenberg points out that even though the haughty Southern soldiers considered themselves—and their cause—much superior to the Union, in actuality, the educated men fighting on the Union side outnumbered those in the Confederate army *six to one.*[9]

When the fighting began, wealthy Southerners were exempt from serving. Conscription took only whites between the ages of 17 and 50. Blacks were not allowed to serve. But casualties mounted and soon nearly everyone, even the white aristocrats, joined the army. But even after Lincoln's 1863 *Emancipation Proclamation*, no African Americans were accepted into the Confederate ranks. (Many of the freed slaves, however, joined the Union forces.)

Walt Whitman's *Leaves of Grass* poems were unknown to most Southerners, but if his work had reached the South before the war, readers would have felt confirmed in their opinions of the urban North, the mindless industrialized and relatively classless populace. In his poems they would have read

---

[8] Nancy Isenberg, *White Trash*, 135–59.
[9] Nancy Isenberg, *White Trash*, 154–61.

about New York crowds, "mechanics" going to work and being neighborly with "immigrants," traveling by ferry—no Southern aristocrat would think this kind of life desirable. Even if most Southerners knew they were not, themselves, from the aristocracy, they championed the prestige inherent in class stratification in the South. "Refinement" was the measuring rod.

Isenberg states, "For anxious social commentators, 'pride of caste' and 'pride of race' were under attack." In the Southern hierarchy of social values, wealthy Southern whites were at the top of the pyramid; middle level wealthy Southerners came next; poor whites—i.e., *trash*, similar to Northern and Western poorer whites—were next; and some of this class might well fall below the social position of slaves. But finally, Isenberg notes, "race could never be de-coupled from class".[10]

These attitudes didn't begin just before the Civil War, of course; they were inherited from the British as they watched many of their poorest (not to mention their most adventurous) subjects sail across an ocean to find various kinds of freedoms. It was the British who created some of the most insulting names for the colonial settlers: "lubbers," "rubbish," "crackers," "human waste." The lower classes in the new country were seen as "incurable, irreparable 'breeds,'"—they became what Isenberg calls "persistently mongrelized".[11]

The Southern slave-holders, trying to create their own patrician lives, gradually erased that social condemnation, which is one reason England was considering offering support to the *Confederacy* as the war continued.

As the Western United States was developed, these attitudes toward the poor not only continued but were exaggerated. The poor in the American West were "criminals" in that they stole land; they trespassed; they cut timber and took animals. In the East they may have been categorized as "working people" but in the Southern view, they were "a semi-criminal class of men." During the 1840s and the 1850s, in fact, the states of South Carolina, Virginia, Louisiana, and North Carolina were obsessed with land ownership, and they made owning land a prerequisite to voting. In the South, social standing depended on pedigree, and when Jefferson Davis wanted to unify the Confederate troops, he talked about the Union soldiers as "miscreants," fighting for a government that was "rotten to the core." Supposedly, Abraham Lincoln was plotting to lead a class revolution that would destroy the South—his term for Lincoln, "Black Republican".[12]

---

[10] Nancy Isenberg, *White Trash*, 183–84.
[11] Nancy Isenberg, *White Trash*, 2.
[12] Nancy Isenberg, *White Trash*, 102–9; 155–58.

In 2021, Philip Beidler shames the current United States military policy by explaining, with clear irony, that the draft is no longer needed: "regarding the vast American body of the poor, the unemployed, the undereducated, the frequently blue-collar and minority enlistees, the convenient fiction of an all-volunteer military has clouded the hard facts of its operation as conscription by other means".[13]

Isabel Wilkerson works from similar understandings of recruitment policies for war. She sees the American Civil War as the means for Irish and Polish immigrants to realize their standings in relation to the African American slaves. With some acerbity, she writes, "It would take a civil war, the deaths of three quarters of a million soldiers and civilians, the assassination of a president, Abraham Lincoln, and the passage of the Thirteenth Amendment to bring the institution of slavery in the United States of America to an end".[14]

She begins with the knowledge that any white immigrant who reached the States would easily learn that the bottom rung of the social scale was guaranteed to blacks. Any white person was easily ranked above the black. Although most immigrants had never thought of themselves as "white"—since their national origin was their cognomen—they quickly learned to be white. "Thus Irish immigrants who would not have had anything against any one group upon arrival and were escaping famine and persecution of their own under the British, were pitted against black residents when they were drafted to fight a war over slavery from which they did not benefit and that they did not cause".

> Unable to attack the white elites who were sending them to war and who had prohibited black men from enlisting, Irish immigrants turned their frustration and rage against the scapegoats who they by now knew were beneath them … {During Reconstruction} they hung black men from lamp poles and burned to the ground anything associated with black people—homes, businesses, churches, a black orphanage—in the Draft Riots of 1863, considered to be the largest race riot in American history.[15]

Wilkerson knows the fault lies not with these immigrants but rather with the social power of those who believe in caste. "The dominant caste devised a labyrinth of laws to hold the newly freed people on the bottom rung even more tightly.... People on the bottom rung could be beaten or killed with

---

[13] Philip Beidler, "Veterans, Trauma, Afterwar," *War and American Literature*, 84.
[14] Isabel Wilkerson, *Caste*, 48.
[15] Ibid., 49–50.

impunity for any breach of the caste system, like not stepping off the sidewalk fast enough or trying to vote."[16]

Throughout her comprehensive study, Wilkerson reminds her reader that "class" is not synonymous with "caste." The concept of class may change. Caste, however, (calling it "casteism") "is the investment in keeping the hierarchy as it is in order to maintain your own ranking, advantage, privilege….Caste is the granting or withholding of respect, status, honor, attention, privileges, resources, benefit of the doubt, a human kindness to someone on the basis of their perceived rank or standing in the hierarchy…. Caste is insidious because it is *not* hatred, it is not necessarily personal".[17] As she had earlier stated, "The dominant caste lived under the illusion of an innate superiority over all other groups of humans…"

Beliefs in the caste system influenced both the Confederacy's and the Union's conscription rules. The South created their draft to use their poor white underclass, those who did not own slaves. The slave-owning class was, for quite a while, exempt. The saying traveled quickly, that the Civil War was the "rich man's war and the poor man's fight." The draft also exempted the educated, office holders at all levels of politics, slave owners, and men employed at "valuable trades".

The Confederacy also allowed the practice of substitution, so that a drafted man could pay someone else—usually a person from a lower social class—to take his spot. It came as little surprise that, as battles continued, thousands of Southern soldiers deserted. Yet, back home, the Southern planters would not give up planting cotton in order to grow more food. Women raided stores and factories; the Confederacy was facing battles from both outside and inside.[18]

In the North, the practice of substitution was also in full swing. (Members of neither culture evinced much disapproval of this practice.) When Austin Dickinson (Emily Dickinson's brother) was finally drafted on May 13, 1864, payment was made—by either the town or by the family, facts are unclear—that he not go to war. His place was taken by an Irish immigrant, "Chauncey 'Julius' Pierce of Sunderland" for $500. The rate for this service ranged from $300 to $500, and many of the substitute soldiers were African Americans. Since January 1, 1863, communities had been using a sentence in Lincoln's *Emancipation Proclamation* that stated that slaves freed under this edict would "be received into the armed service of the United States to garrison forts,

---

[16] Isabel Wilkerson, *Caste*, 48. She adds in her description of the 1951 Cicero, Illinois, race riots—including some 4000 Italian and Polish immigrants—to protest a black family's moving into the Chicago suburb: "Hostility toward the lowest caste became part of the initiation rite into citizenship in America" (50).

[17] Isabel Wilkerson, *Caste,* 70, 180.

[18] Nancy Isenberg, *White Trash*, 159–66.

positions, stations, and other places, and to man vessels of all sorts in said service".[19]

Whitman consistently sees the wounded soldiers that he visits, from both sides of the war, as his brothers and his neighbors. Given the assumptions of the class of most of these men, he is probably accurate—and his gifts to the wounded of an envelope and a postage stamp would have been happily received. Even if the substitute soldier was killed during his military service, the hundreds of dollars of substitute soldier payment would keep his family afloat for years after the war had ended. (Payment in the South was not so high, but then the class structure shaped economics in this as in many areas of life.)

From his poems dated 1865, one of Whitman's most acerbic and financially oriented is "Ah Poverties, Wincings, and Sulky Retreats," using the war imagery of battle to analyze his behaviors—and it could be, of course, that this is written while he waits to see if he will find new employment in Washington, after his Indian Affairs job has been lost:

> Ah poverties, wincings, and sulky retreats,
> Ah you foes that in conflict have overcome me,
> (For what is my life or any man's life but a conflict with foes,
>   the old, the incessant war?).
> You degradations, you tussle with passions and appetites,...
> You shallow tongue-talks at tables, (my tongue the
>   shallowest of any;)....[20]

But more characteristic is, again from 1865, one of his meditative war-focused memorials for those dead in battle.

> Ashes of Soldiers
> Ashes of soldiers South or North,
> As I muse retrospective murmuring a chant in thought,
> The war resumes, again to my sense your shapes,
> And again the advance of the armies.
>
> Noiseless as mists and vapors,
> From their graves in the trenches ascending,
> From cemeteries all through Virginia and Tennessee,

---

[19] Aife Murray, *Maid as Muse: How Servants Changed Emily Dickinson's Life and Language*. Durham: University of New Hampshire Press, 2009: 53.

[20] Whitman, "Ah Poverties, Wincings, and Sulky Retreats," Library, 589.

From every point of the compass out of the countless
    graves,
In wafted clouds, in myriads large, or squads of twos or
    threes or single ones they come,
And silently gather round me.

Now sound no note O trumpeters,
Not at the head of my cavalry parading on spirited horses,
With sabres drawn and glistening, and carbines by their
    thighs, (ah my brave horsemen!
My handsome tan-faced horsemen! What life, what joy and
    pride,
With all the perils were yours.)....

    Moving from the descriptive, Whitman announces his aim, saying "I chant this chant of my silent soul in the name of all dead soldiers," and then the center of his mourning begins:

Faces so pale with wondrous eyes, very dear, gather closer yet,
Draw close, but speak not.

Phantoms of countless lost,
Invisible to the rest henceforth become my companions,
Follow me ever—desert me not while I live.

Sweet are the blooming cheeks of the living—sweet are the
    musical voices sounding,
But sweet, ah sweet, are the dead with their silent eyes.

Dearest comrades, all is over and long gone,
But love is not over—and what love, O comrades!
Perfume from battle-fields rising, up from the foetor arising,
Perfume therefore my chant, O love, immortal love,
Give me to bathe the memories of all dead soldiers,
Shroud them, embalm them, cover them all over with tender
    pride.

Perfume all—make all wholesome,
Make these ashes to nourish and blossom,
O love, solve all, fructify all with the last chemistry.

Give me exhaustless, make me a fountain,
That I exhale love from me wherever I go like a moist
   perennial dew,
For the ashes of all dead soldiers South or North.[21]

Back in the same commemorative vein as when he wrote "O Captain! My Captain!" and "Spirit Whose Work Is Done," Whitman seldom strayed from his intense mourning about the lost young soldiers. His poems became their own kind of memorial to both the war and his personal grief. And he kept writing poems in that tenor—along with his masterful, stately prose—for the rest of his years.

---

[21] Whitman, "Ashes of Soldiers," Library, 598–600.

12

Afterwar

Philip Beidler uses the term here in 2021 but he sees it as an extension of the older "PTSD." One means of defining the impermeable effects of the slaughter of war, or of any personal wounding, "afterwar" attempts to describe "the psychological and spiritual problems experienced by returnees, as well as their families and loved ones." For everyone touched by war trauma, "life has somehow become profoundly different." Walt Whitman and his post-war writings give a poignant picture of those effects, particularly since he involved so much of his emotional self in the caring for wounded men. It was an unusual role, and he felt its urgency in ways that most people would have ignored.

Writing about graves of the dead may have been one of the simplest explorations of his feelings. Literature is replete with mourning songs, and even though Whitman was never one who copied traditional forms, he knew how to create the dirge-like movement, the slowness of realization, that an awareness of death should evoke. He had written the masterful lament for Lincoln in his "When Lilacs Last in the Dooryard Bloom'd" but that was his poem for a beloved leader, as well as for his nation. He would not ever again copy that form or that rhythm.

Beidler recognizes the impossibly difficult subject matter in dealing with war experiences. He describes the trauma as "the endless, mindless, pointless killing, with the nameless, faceless, unclaimed dead, littering the ruined streets...." In retrospect, however, even more difficult to describe may be what

© The Author(s), under exclusive license to Springer Nature
Switzerland AG 2021
L. Wagner-Martin, *Walt Whitman*, Literary Lives,
https://doi.org/10.1007/978-3-030-77665-7_12

happens to soldiers involved in these atrocities: "a uniform malaise of alienation, strangeness, mind-numbing fear, and exhaustion, coupled in most cases to an afterwar life of shocked silence."[1]

The critic acknowledges that attempts are regularly made to save these shells of returning soldiers (time in a "secure base camp, R & R, an anti-psychotic drug like Thorazine," which serves the same cause as does the writing of history, the stabilization of war, so that other people can understand it.) Sometimes, however, there is no understanding. Finally, says Beidler, "every war, for the combatant, has its own etiology of trauma."

Where did Walt Whitman go, mentally, as he worked at his new job, lived at a new address, and tried to write the poems for that second edition of *Drum-Taps*? Was it during those months that he realized he was still *in* war, still seeing daily the torn remains of soldiers so promising in their youth and—as he always said—their beauty? How long could he write works that should have appeared in the spring of 1865 in *Drum-Taps*? Perhaps the almost organized confusion that led to the often unpredictable order of Whitman's poems starts here, in his personal bewilderment. What is *his* life and where does "the war" end? He was never *in* the war. He seems to be caught in the somber confusion that he has witnessed in some of the hospital patients. And now the hospitals are still full to bursting with not only the wounded but the sick, battlefield sick, malaria sick, typhoid sick, exhaustion sick. Years later, when he wrote in "Specimen Days" about the immediate post-war years, he said only, "I continued at Washington working in the Attorney-General's department through '66 and '67, and some time afterward." Titled "An Interregnum Paragraph," the account resumes, "In February '73 I was stricken down by paralysis, gave up my desk, and migrated to Camden, New Jersey, where I lived during '74 and '75, quite unwell—but after that began to grow better."[2]

Whitman's poems written in the late 1860s and the early 1870s tell one part of his life story. Somehow, the prose that later was written and published as "Specimen Days" seems to more fully evoke the war years and the following, disappointing Reconstruction. (He had published "Democratic Vistas" in 1872 and "Memoranda During the War" in 1873—the latter he reworked and supplemented for the 1882 "Specimen Days.") But to isolate the poems he dated as coming from 1865, 1866, and 1867 mirrors some replication of his Civil War work that he collected and published in *Drum-Taps*. There is a kind of stasis here. To read "Vigil Strange I Kept on the Fields One Night" moves the reader toward "Hush'd Be the Camps To-day,"

---

[1] Philip Beidler, "Veterans, Trauma, Afterwar," *War and American Literature*, 80–81, 84.
[2] Whitman, "Specimen Days," Library, 779–80.

"As I Lay with My Head in Your Lap Camerado," and "A Sight in Camp in the Daybreak Gray and Dim." We are isolated with the wounded and fearful soldiers—with some of the dead—and with the poet-observer who cannot get past the grief that swamps him. All are effective poems. What more could a poet say?

In 1867 when Whitman wrote "The Return of the Heroes," he was surely thinking that this would be an omnibus poem, a work as inclusive as the ever-expanding "Song of Myself." In its opening stanza, the poet implores,

> "O earth that hast no voice, confide to me a voice."

What the poet aims to write, that stanza concludes, is

> "A song to narrate thee."

It is not until Part 4 that the poet returns in memory to the war:

> "When late I sang sad was my voice,
> Sad were the shows around me with the deafening noises of
>   hatred and smoke of war;
> In the midst of the conflict, the heroes, I stood.
> Or pass'd with slow step through the wounded and dying.
>
> But now I sing *not* war,
> Nor the measur'd march of soldiers, nor the tents of camps,
> Nor the regiments hastily coming up deploying in line of
>   battle;
> No more the sad, unnatural shows of war.
>
> Ask'd room those flush'd immortal ranks, the first forth-
>   stepping armies?
> Ask room alas the ghastly ranks, the armies dread that follow'd.
>
> (Pass, pass, ye proud brigades, with your tramping sinewy legs,
> With your shoulders young and strong, with your knapsacks
>   and your muskets;
> How elate I stood and watch'd you, where starting off you march'd....[3]

The reader recognizes the bodies and the details—we have seen these young soldiers before. But as the poem continues, Whitman turns it into a kind of fusion with nature, the warm sunlight changing the sorrow, reminding

---

[3] Whitman, "The Return of the Heroes," Library, 486–91.

readers that it was first titled "A Carol of Harvest for 1867." *The Galaxy* published the poem, paying $60 for its use. It is a poem that meanders, as if Whitman was trying to decide how the war had affected both his *life* and his role as American *poet*. He is no longer the poet of "Song of Myself" or the crowded New York streets; he is now the poet of airless and morbid hospitals, aging rapidly under the worries and concerns *for*—and *of*—his soldier patients. Although he has written "When Lilacs Last in the Dooryard Bloom'd," he has not yet fully come to terms with the assassination of Lincoln. What he knows is that he needs to stay in Washington because that city is the place of the memories he will draw from to keep writing about the Civil War—as well as his making continuing visits to men who are still hospitalized.

For Vivian Pollack, at this time in Whitman's life, he was searching to write the story of *his* life. He had been a healthy man, much envied by his friends. The war, however, had injured his health and it was all he could do to funnel his energy into the writing he felt compelled to do—about the war and its aftermath. She points out that even before the war, Whitman was visiting the disabled in New York hospitals; he considered himself a "wound healer" during those earlier years. Disabilities fascinated Whitman.[4]

E. Fred Carlisle views the war years and after as the consolidation of Whitman's autobiographical search for story. Whereas he will later turn to prose, while he writes his unique poetry he disdains the conventions of both literary form and social opinion. Beginning with "Song of the Open Road," Carlisle traces the journey Whitman makes to create a profile of himself through "the open, unfinished quality of a concrete person in living dialogue." He describes Whitman's progressive stances, beginning with 1850, moving to what he calls "the famous, mysterious crises of 1858–59" and then to the Civil War, followed by a "similar mystery in the early 1870s." Carlisle echoes the pattern Roger Asselineau had earlier drawn, "the movement from crisis or despair to equilibrium," referring to the last stages of "*Drum-Taps*, in which Whitman recognizes the war's destructiveness (which he now repudiates) to find equilibrium in the final poems of *Drum-Taps*.[5]

---

[4] Vivian Pollack, "'Bringing Help for the Sick': Whitman and Prophetic Biography," *Leaves of Grass: The Sesquicentennial Essays*, ed. Susan Belasco, Ed Fulsom, and Kenneth M. Price. Lincoln: University of Nebraska Press, 2007: 244–65.

[5] E. Fred Carlisle, *The Uncertain Self: Whitman's Drama of Identity*. East Lansing: Michigan State University Press, 1973: 6, 30, 31–35.

For Martin Buinicke, too, the early post-war years must be seen as reflecting Whitman's long process of coming to terms with all the death and subsequent grieving he had both seen and known.[6]

Some of Whitman's *Drum-Taps* poems were already marking a new mode of reflection, We have seen the power evoked by his "Ashes of Soldiers South or North" in the previous chapter. So too is the moderating tone of "Long, Too Long America," in which he calls on people who had been accustomed to "traveling roads all even and peaceful,

> But now, ah now, to learn from crises of anguish, advancing, grappling
>   with direct fate and resisting not,"[7]

the survivors of war must re-think every vestige of their normal lives. One of the most eloquent of Whitman's calls to his readers to face a new existence with bravery is "As Toilsome I Wander'd Virginia's Woods," a praise poem for burial rites as well as nature's beauty.

> As toilsome I wander'd Virginia's woods,
> To the music of rustling leaves kick'd by my feet, (for 'twas
>   autumn,)
> I mark'd at the foot of a tree the grave of a soldier;
> Mortally wounded he and buried on the retreat, (easily all
>   could I understand,)
> The halt of a mid-day hour, when up! No time to lose—yet
>   this sign left,
> On a tablet scrawl'd and nail'd on the tree by the grave,
> Bold, Cautious, True, and My Loving Comrade.
>
> Long, long I muse, then on my way go wandering,
> Many a changeful season to follow, and many a scene of life,
> Yet at times through changeful season and scene, abrupt,
>   alone, or in the crowded street,
> Comes before me the unknown soldier's grave, comes the
>   inscription rude in Virginia's woods,
> *Bold, cautious, true, and my loving comrade.*[8]

---

[6] Martin T. Buinicke, *Walt Whitman's Reconstruction, Poetry and Publishing Between Memory and History*. Iowa City: University of Iowa Press, 2011: 3. See also Kathleen Diffley. *Where My Heart Is Turning Ever: Civil War Stories and Constitutional Reform, 1861–1876*. Athens: University of Georgia Press, 1992.

[7] Whitman, "Long, Too Long America," Library, 445.

[8] Whitman, "As Toilsome I Wander'd Virginia's Woods," Library, 441–42.

Replicating a kind of informal sonnet, this poem creates the rhythm that evokes reader sympathy. There is a consciousness here of the elegiac words left on the tree trunk. Using italics calls our attention to what those words truly signify.

As he had with "Ashes of Soldiers," here Whitman expects his readers to understand the common rituals of burying the dead—leaving a marker of words, in this case; in "Ashes," he asks the reader to recall physical burial—cleansing the body, preparing it, perfuming it. As Whitman wrote toward the closing of "Ashes of Soldiers,"

> Give me to bathe the memories of all dead soldiers,
> Shroud them, embalm them, cover them all over with tender
>   pride.

His shift to the metaphor of "memories" as replacement for bodies is an apt resolution. He keeps readers from revisiting Biblical passages about death, and he even allows them the ritual without envisioning the whole of war. In effect, Whitman creates his own *ritual of memory* in a poem unlike most war elegies.

Steven Trout has recently written about the importance of war memorials—of any army, any conflict, any nationality. In his "Mourning, Elegy, Memorialization from the Civil War to Vietnam," he describes the effectiveness of particularly government efforts to give the common soldier lasting burial. Considering the aftermath of the Civil War, which he calls leading to "a scale of carnage unheard of since Europe's Napoleonic War a half century earlier," the quantity of federal cemeteries reaches near a hundred, fulfilling Lincoln's promise to those soldiers, and to later men who served, from the *Emancipation Proclamation*. Within those cemeteries, the common soldiers receive "perpetual graves and markers." Trout also notes that "In the late nineteenth century, the commemoration of the war dead expanded even further to include former enemies."[9]

It goes without saying that many of Whitman's Civil War poems, and those he wrote subsequently, were about young soldiers killed in the conflict. But in the poet's mind, he seemed to choose more traditional structures for poems that were, in fact, commemorative, as if the elegies of his youth were coming back into view. Stanza patterns are more recognizable; forms like the sonnet or the quatrain repeat. There is some line repetition though seldom does Whitman use end rhyme. With "Dirge for Two Veterans," one of his 1865

---

[9] Steven Trout, "Mourning, Elegy, Memorialization from the Civil War to Vietnam," *War and American Literature*, ed. Jennifer Haytock: 87–102.

poems that is clearly an elegy, Whitman creates a line arrangement, repeated stanza by stanza, unlike any of his other poems. In this work he mourns the son and his father, "In the foremost ranks of the fierce assault they fell,/Two veterans son and father dropt together,/and the double grave awaits them."

> The last sunbeam.
> Lightly falls from the finish'd Sabbath,
> On the pavement here, and there beyond it is looking,
> Down a new-made double grave.
>
> Lo, the moon ascending,
> Up from the east the silvery round moon,
> Beautiful over the house-tops; ghastly, phantom moon,
> Immense and silent moon.
>
> I see a sad procession,
> And I hear the sound of coming full-key of bugles,
> All the channels of the city streets they 're flooding,
> As with voices and with tears....[10]

Whitman wrote a number of short, compact poems in the mid to later 1860s, similar to those that were scattered throughout the 1860 printing of *Leaves of Grass*. This 1865 poem, titled "Pensive and Faltering," seems to be a mourning poem for the poet himself:

> Pensive and faltering,
> The words *the Dead* I write,
> For living are the Dead,
> (Haply the only living, only real,
> And I the apparition, I the spectre.).[11]

There are some tonal similarities with other of Whitman's poems ("The Last Invocation," "Thick-Sprinkled Bunting,", "Quicksand Years" (which continues its title "that whirl me I know not whither,/ Your schemes, politics, fail, lines give way, substances mock and elude me." The closing to that six-lined poem is, "When shows break up what but One's-Self is sure?".[12]

---

[10] Whitman, "Dirge for Two Veterans," Library, 447–48.
[11] Whitman, "Pensive and Faltering," Library, 568.
[12] Whitman, "Quicksand Years," Library, 563.

Following this cluster comes Whitman's "Old War-Dreams," which replicates the substance of "The Artilleryman's Vision" in creating the horror of war and battle memory. Here, however, the dream seems to belong to the poet:

> In midnight sleep of many a face of anguish,
> Of the look at first of the mortally wounded, (of that
>   indescribable look,)
> Of the dead on their backs with arms extended wide,
>   I dream, I dream, I dream.[13]

There are two other stanzas, but both end with the same refrain line, "I dream, I dream, I dream" while the speaker shares his sad memories. The stanzas share the same line arrangement.

"Camps of Green," one of Whitman's best 1865 poems, begins by picturing "those camps of white, old comrades of the wars," but leaving the heart of the poem of prophecy to explore a different, verdant, camp of green. Here is the peaceful remaining four stanzas, a kind of idyll that Whitman hypothesizes as his coming peace.

> . . .
> Lo, the camps of the tents of green,
> Which the days of peace keep filling, and the days of war
>   keep filling,
> With a mystic army, (is it too order'd forward? Is it too only
>   halting awhile,
> Till night and sleep pass over?}.
>
> Now in those camps of green, in their tents dotting the world,
> In the parents, children, husbands, wives, in them, in the old
>   and young,
> Sleeping under the sunlight, sleeping under the moonlight,
>   content and silent there at last,
> Behold the mighty bivouac-field and waiting camp of all,
> Of the corps and generals all, and the President over the
>   corps and generals all,
> And of each of us O soldiers, and of each and all in the
>   ranks we fought,
> (There without hatred we all, all meet.)

---

[13] Whitman, "Old War-Dreams," Library, 593.

For presently O soldiers, we too camp in our place in the
　　bivouac-camps of green,
But we need not provide for outposts, nor word for the.
　　countersign,
Nor drummer to beat the morning drum.[14]

Not a simple poem, "Camps of Green" shows the indelible mixture of feelings in everyone who had lasted to the end of the Civil War. The mournfulness in many of Whitman's post-war poems gives several critics the sense of his relative despair, even in the midst of the Union's victory. As the poet imagines his healthful—and health-giving—"camps of green," he envisions entire families, safe together in myriad tents "dotting the *world*." Yet as the family members sleep easily "under the sunlight" as well as "under the moonlight," they are not alone. Whitman cannot avoid seeing "a mystic army" haunting the perceived happiness of victory.

The positioning of this ghostly army near the start of the poem reminds the reader of what the war has given—eons of memories of death, of loss that becomes tactile—and accordingly, just as the present "days of peace keep filling," the poet hears a parallel echo: the "days of war keep filling with a mystic army."

Whitman as poet has the power to write the seemingly happy ending: "There without hatred we all, all meet." Adding the repetition of the word *all* speaks volumes for Whitman's personal willingness to forgive the Confederacy. In some respects, he followed the thinking of both Abraham Lincoln and Andrew Johnson, seeing the Southern revolution as something *less* than treason. Whitman does not express that sentiment. What he does create is a reassuring voice to close the poem, reminding the imagined figures happily sleeping there in "the bivouac-camps of green" that war is done: the sleepers need no "outposts," or "countersign," or "drummer." The trappings of war are now unnecessary.

Throughout many of Whitman's 1865 and 1866 poems runs this undercurrent of sorrow. In even the most celebratory poems, someone is haunted by the relentless scene of outright war. In this most pacific poem of green nature, Whitman plants more than a few suggestions that the calm he envisions may not come to be. Among the most direct of Whitman's observers has been M. Wynn Thomas, who has long pointed out that even poems of victory are not unmixed. Shadows, doubts, hover. In this period especially, Thomas thought

---

[14] Whitman, "Camps of Green," Library, 606–7.

that not only the war but Lincoln's death may have "threatened his mental equilibrium." Simultaneously, however, he believed Whitman when he stated that he had to work to preserve his own painful memories so as to create the national history he yearned to write, becoming "the prophet of the past" able to inform the future.[15] Martin Buinicki, too, dwells on the fact that Whitman spent years coming to terms with his own "memorials of war," both in his countless small notebooks, his pieces of cloth, and petals of flowers.[16] Roy P. Basler catches something of this tone in his important introduction to the *Memoranda During the War*, speaking about Whitman as a "sensitive, almost feminine, spirit" as he labored hard to give the world his "unique" memories of the war. He quotes Whitman's phrase that he gave the world his recollections of war, "full of the blood and vitality of the American people."[17] Very recently, Ty Hawkins has proposed that even Whitman's magisterial "When Lilacs Last in the Dooryard Bloom'd" is shrouded in sorrow. Elegaic as it is, the poem still encompasses angry sorrow, a kind of impetuous breaking of the supposed mood of lament. Hawkins comments on its mixed tones, pointing to the questions the poet asks, along with the poem's false starts. But Whitman not only questions the direction of the poem itself, he includes the brutality of Sect. 15:

> I saw battle-corpses, myriads of them.
> And the white skeletons of young men, I saw them,
> I saw the debris and debris of all the slain soldiers of the war,
> But I saw they were not as was thought,
> They themselves were fully at rest, they suffer'd not,
> The living remain'd and suffer'd, the mother suffer'd,
> And the wife and the child and the musing comrade suffer'd,
> And the armies that remained suffer'd."

For Hawkins, this great poem memorializes not just Lincoln's death but "all the death, maiming, and heartbreak common to Americans' war experiences, including Whitman's own.[18]

---

[15] M. Wynn Thomas, *The Lunar Light of Whitman's Poetry*. Cambridge, MA: Harvard University Press, 1987: 278.

[16] Martin Buinicke, *Walt Whitman's Reconstruction*, 3.

[17] Roy P. Basler, "Introduction," *Walt Whitman's Memoranda During the War and The Death of Abraham Lincoln*. Bloomington: Indiana University Press, 1962: 1–2.

[18] Ty Hawkins, "War and Morality," *War and American Literature*, 18–20.

The reader has Whitman's own careful statements about his experiences during the war being the wellspring of his poetry; and we have his relatively cheerful letters home as he grows more pleased with the work that has replaced what he formerly did in the Indian Affairs office. But he also ages almost visibly. In fact, a few years later, he writes this modest poem, called, helpfully, "My Legacy". The first stanza, not given here, describes a wealthy businessman who has a large estate to bequeath to his family. The second stanza is in Whitman's voice, and it speaks with much less detail:

> But I, my life surveying, closing,
> With nothing to show to devise from its idle years,
> Not houses nor lands, nor tokens of gems or gold for my
>   friends,
> Yet certain remembrances of the war *for* you, and *after* you,
> And little souvenirs of camps and soldiers, with my love,
> I bind together and bequeath in this bundle of songs.[19]

---

[19] Whitman, "My Legacy," Library, 605.

13

Reconstruction

One historian of acerbic bent states, "The Civil War provided real ruins, the ruins of Atlanta, the ruins of Richmond, the ruins of the old South. It sealed off and preserved the entire South, its speech, its customs, as a ruin. The North became the *nation,* the South a *region,* and as the North, progressive, modernizing, expensive, turned westward in 1866 to build its transcontinental railroads, it left the South behind as something of a cultural appendix."[1] For Whitman and his family, as well as for all the families devastated by the losses of sons, fathers, and brothers during the war, the conflict "changed American dreams forever."[2]

The death of Abraham Lincoln complicated the transition from war to peace without question—an intuitive and cagey man, Lincoln might have foreseen the political problems although, in many ways, Andrew Johnson believed in some Lincolnesque principles himself. But as Whitman watched from his cat-bird seat in the Capitol, he vowed to leave politics behind and tend to his own writing—as well as his visiting in the still-full hospitals. Within the first year of Andrew Johnson's term of office, he was impeached (and acquitted), but it was to take years before the franchise was given to African American men. Whatever movement there was in the wheels of government had been slowed appreciably during 1865, 1866, and 1867.

---

[1] Neil Schmitz, "Forms of Regional Humor," *Columbia Literary History of the United States,* ed. Emory Elliott. New York: Columbia University Press, 1988: 306.

[2] Angus Fletcher, "Book of a Lifetime," Marcus and Sollors, 311.

© The Author(s), under exclusive license to Springer Nature Switzerland AG 2021
L. Wagner-Martin, *Walt Whitman,* Literary Lives,
https://doi.org/10.1007/978-3-030-77665-7_13

On April 6, 1866, Congress passed the first Civil Rights Act over Johnson's veto. Johnson was like Lincoln, not believing that the Confederacy had left the Union. Congress, however, did not accept that belief. The former "Union" party was now represented by the Radical Republicans—they did not want the South to gain anything from the war. They had agreed with Sherman as he marched from Atlanta, Georgia, to the Atlantic, destroying much the army passed so as to leave that area of the South virtually devastated.

Thaddeus Stevens of Pennsylvania led the opposition to Johnson. Even though in the Fourteenth Amendment full suffrage was given to all black men (even former slaves), the act made Johnson only a figurehead. Then on March 7, 1867, Congress passed the Military Reconstruction Act which destroyed all the state governments installed by the Southern rebel government so as to create five military districts, each under the charge of a Union general who commanded twenty thousand troops. This situation panicked the Ku Klux Klan: Union troops were providing federal surveillance south of the Mason-Dixon line. Quickly the KKK spread north and west, and within a few years would be lynching whatever blacks they could scour the earth to find.[3]

In 1870 the Fifteenth Amendment "gave black males the national right to vote." The Congress was so worried that the Southern states would rescind the right to vote for men of color that they took this extra precaution, which was finally ratified in 1871.[4] The spread of the Ku Klux Klan may have been one of the most pernicious and uncontrollable results of Reconstruction.

Through these stormy political years, Whitman kept visiting his soldiers, doing his clerical work, and writing the poems that might begin to convey all the scenes and emotions the war had given him. As he told Horace Traubel at that time, "There were years in my life—years there in New York—when I wondered if all was not going to be bad with America—the tendency downwards—but the war saved me: what I saw in the war set me up for all time—the days in the hospitals."[5] In his own prose accounts of the war years, he said even more emphatically: "These three years I consider the greatest privilege and satisfaction... and, of course, the most profound lesson of my life. I can say that in my ministerings I comprehended all, whoever came in my way, Northern or Southern, and slighted none. It aroused and brought out and decided undreamed-of depths of emotion. It had given me my most fervent view of the true ensemble and extent of these States." Calling his

[3] Luke Mancuso. *The Strange Sad War Revolving: Walt Whitman, Reconstruction and the Emergence of Black Citizenship, 1865–1876*. Columbia, SC: Camden House, 1997: 70.

[4] Loving, *Walt Whitman*, 300–02. See also Martin Buinicke, *Walt Whitman*, 3.

[5] Horace Traubel, *With Walt Whitman in Camden*, 9 volumes. New York: Appleton, 1908. Vol. 1: 130–33.

accounts "stories of the 'divine average,'"[6] Whitman found the dissension immediately after the war disturbing but the main thrust of his own work, giving him his continuing insight, kept going.

Just as he was resuming his life in Washington, Whitman was writing some of his most poignant "war" profiles. One prose account, dated April 30, 1866, is titled "Left-Handed Writing By Soldiers." Framed as a new event, the story works more like poetry:

> Here is a single significant fact, from which one may judge of the character of the American soldier in this just concluded war: A gentleman in New York City, a while since, took it into his head to collect specimens of writing from soldiers who had lost their right hands in battle, and afterwards learn'd to use the left. He gave public notice of his desire, and offer'd prizes for the best of these specimens. Pretty soon they began to come in, and by the time specified for awarding the prizes three hundred samples of such left-handed writing by maimed soldiers had arrived.
>
> I have just been looking over some of the writing. A great many of the specimens are written in a beautiful manner. All are good. The writing in nearly all cases slants backward instead of forward. One piece of writing, from a soldier who had lost both arms, was made by holding the pen in his mouth.[7]

A few months earlier, Whitman had written one of the first of his "Mother of All" poems, where the capacious mother figure stands guard for her dead sons. Sometimes the herald of death, sometimes the herald of life, this poetic "Mother" had come to epitomize the earthly care all human souls need. Dated 1865, "Pensive on Her Dead Gazing," expresses an unusual post-war sentiment, its tone far from victorious. The poem begins,

> Pensive on her dead gazing, I heard the Mother of All,
> Desperate on the torn bodies, on the forms covering the
>   battle-fields gazing,
> (As the last gun ceased, but the scent of the powder-smoke
>   linger'd,)
> As she call'd to her earth with mournful voice while she stalk'd.
> Absorb them well O my earth, she cried, I charge you lose
>   not my sons, lose not an atom....
> And you mountain sides, and the woods where my dear
>   children's blood trickling redden'd,
> And you trees down in your roots to bequeath to all future
>   trees,

---

[6] Whitman, "Specimen Days," Library, 776.
[7] Whitman, "November Boughs," Library, 1179–80.

My dead absorb or South or North—my young men's
    bodies absorb, and their precious precious blood,....
Exhale me them centuries hence, breathe me their breath, let
    not an atom be lost,
O years and graves! O air and soil! O my dead, an aroma
    sweet!
Exhale them perennial sweet death, years, centuries hence.[8]

As easy as Whitman appeared to be in picturing himself as a comforting *father*, and fluid as the mid-nineteenth century was about changing acceptable or unacceptable patterns of masculine behavior, from this point on in his poetry he seems to think this benevolent Mother figure is closer to reader sentiments. Giving her both mystic and mythic qualities, he began to move more regularly back to "religious" answers; but the progression, given his own increasing age, seemed reasonable. Alice Fahs considers Whitman's war and post-war poetry far above the most sentimental work appearing in newspapers, but she does explain:

> During the war the concept of manliness included feminized components that late in the century would be excised from new concepts of masculinity. On appropriate occasions it was considered manly to show emotion, even to cry.... At the same time, within a culture of domesticity that tightly bound not just women but also men to their homes, the solder's imagined longing for home were also deemed highly appropriate and represented not only in poems and songs, but also in numerous popular engravings.[9]

Financially more at ease, Whitman did not worry about his accommodations in Washington—and he gratefully accepted meals and hospitality from not only the O'Connors but other friends in that city. What he did worry about were the circumstances of both his mother and Eddy, neither of whom could earn wages. They were currently living with Jeff, Mat, and their daughters. On May 1, 1866, the six of them moved from Portland Street to 840 Pacific Avenue. The next year Jeff would take a good permanent job in St.Louis but Mat and the girls would stay with Louisa and Eddy.[10]

Occasionally dispirited, even as he remained committed to working with the surviving soldiers in the Washington hospitals, Whitman said repeatedly that he no longer followed politics. As Randall Fuller explained, "A natural raconteur, he held forth to an expanding coterie of acolytes who transcribed

---

[8] Whitman, "Pensive on Her Dead Gazing," Library, 605–6.
[9] Alice Fahs, *Popular Literature*, 98.
[10] Loving, *Walt Whitman*, 302.

his every word. Despite the adulation, he never allowed himself to forget the fundamental experiences that had made him who and what he was. Reflecting in "Specimen Days" on guerilla tactics... he found the war characterized by "lurid passions, the wolfs,' the lions' lapping thirst for blood—the passionate volcanoes of human revenge for comrades, brothers, slain."[11]

Whitman loved to share his stories, and his ideas, and his emotions, with receptive people. He had usually found his greatest satisfaction in friendships with men, usually men younger than he. Particularly in the poems he had grouped under the "Children of Adam" heading in the 1860 expanded collection of *Leaves of Grass*, he chose to express his need for friendship in sexualized terms. "Calamus," the section of poems that followed "Children of Adam," has often been considered even more flagrant in that respect, but according to Jerome Loving, most of the social disapproval was aimed at poems in the "Children" section. Giving readers an historical perspective, Loving states that in the mid-1850s, the "Children of Adam" poems brought "outrage." Readers felt that "Whitman, apparently.... drew no distinction between the kinds of love" to be celebrated. Today the "Calamus" poems seem homosexual—at least to some readers.[12] Critic Andrew Lawson chooses to use the term "Adhesiveness," suggesting manly love and perhaps creating a kind of eighteenth-century poem cycle that allows the poet "passage to nowhere except the doubts and fears of personal—and very possibly homosexual—love."[13] Critic Betsy Erkkila offers a possible dynamic of change during the war years as Whitman grew less visibly masculine: she suggests that for Whitman the hospital may have become a metonymic figure for the nation at war.... It was precisely because the hospital "softened the aggressive masculinity associated with war that so many observers found their ideas of manhood in the hospital."[14]

Whitman's years of painful observation after he had moved to Washington to take up what he considered his war *mission,* visiting the wounded and sick in the city's hospitals, doing his small but helpful bit for the war effort, may well have changed the nature of his search for a "camerado," a friendpartner who shared his love of nature, the physical, long walks in both day and night, and the exuberance of any close friendship. During the war years, all Whitman wanted was that the soldiers he met would continue to stay alive.

---

[11] Randall Fuller, *From Battlefields Rising*, 218.

[12] Loving, *Walt Whitman*, 238. Loving points out that the word "homosexual" came into the language in 1892. Innuendo was the more likely process of reading sexual texts (270).

[13] Lawson, *Walt Whitman*, 455–56.

[14] Betsy Erkkila, *Whitman the Political Poet*. New York: Oxford University Press, 1989: 206.

His biographer discussed the fact that many of Whitman's friends never knew he wrote poetry, or that he had published a book. He had befriended a good many ferry pilots and stage drivers during his years in New York, but he was not mentioning literature to any of them. In fact, said Loving, "before the first edition of *Leaves of Grass*, Whitman had almost nothing to do with literary people."[15] And it is said that even though Whitman sometimes read poetry to his wounded soldiers in hospital, he never read his own poems.

In the years of Whitman's life before he moved to Washington, he had been visibly close to at least two young men that friends remember. Tom Sawyer and Lewy Brown were close to the then-journalist. But sometime soon after the war's end, Whitman met Peter Doyle, a trolley driver in Washington; the poet soon became a part of Doyle's young "conductor gang," and the terms of friendship seem to replicate the groups Whitman had befriended those years ago in Pfaff's.

Loving states it this way: "Doyle may or may not have been Whitman's lover, but it is certain he became Walt's dearest friend. Through Walt, he also became the fond acquaintance of Eldridge, Burroughs, and O'Connor."[16] Born to a recent immigrant family as large as the Walter Whitman's, Doyle was 18 in 1861 when he joined the Richmond Fayette Artillery crew on the Confederate side. One of his brothers fought for the Union. Wounded at Antietam, he reclaimed his status as a British citizen in order to leave the war but did not return to England—as he should have done. Later he crossed the Confederate lines to get to Washington, DC. For that offense he was briefly jailed. After he had promised not to aid the South, he was released. He was 24 years younger than Whitman, but they remained friends for the rest of Whitman's life.

There is no correspondence between the two before 1868 but Whitman earlier refers to Doyle in his diaries and in letters to others. For the gregarious Whitman, it was important to have friends, particularly those to go walking with. But the aging poet could see even clearer now that it would be important to have good critics as well. He had had some hope that *Drum-Taps* would get at least a few good reviews. If anything, critics seemed more hostile to his war poems than to his editions of *Leaves of Grass*. The New England literary establishment was slow to warm to Whitman's free-form poetry, an attitude which continued, but even the more welcoming William Dean Howells, who controlled opinion through *The Atlantic Monthly*, found *Drum-Taps* "too abstract." A very young Henry James also reviewed *Drum-Taps*, and used the occasion to complain about the provincialism of most

---

[15] Loving, *Walt Whitman*, 296.
[16] Loving, *Walt Whitman*, 297.

American writing. Never fond of what he called "self-expression," James at twenty-two would trace the elements of American writing that he disliked back to the fact that most Americans had not imbibed European cultures. Travel was his mandate. He had only disdain for Emerson's figure of self-sufficiency. Therefore, any connection between Emerson and Whitman would have been a negative one. As James wrote in 1865, "To be positive, one must have something to say; to be positive requires reason, labor, and art; and art requires, above all things, a suppression of one's self, a subordination of one's self to an idea."[17]

As if in a kind of answer to James—who later changed his mind about Whitman and probably influenced Edith Wharton to herself become very favorable toward the American poet and his work, Joel Porte discussed the self-revelatory stance at the heart of Whitman's art. "The aging Whitman believed his own book to be 'a candidate for the future' mainly because it was 'an attempt, from first to last, to put a PERSON, a human being (myself, in the latter half of the Nineteenth Century, in America), freely, fully and truly on record.' And he added, 'I could not find any similar personal record in current literature that satisfied me.'"[18]

Cultural change, in part, was going to influence later opinions about Whitman. The 1870s was to become the decade of the magazine—and magazines were in need of poetry and essays to publish. Martin Buinicke points out that in 1865 seven hundred magazines existed. By 1870, the number had doubled. There were many more rail lines (necessary for troop transport), so all levels of circulation for magazines improved. Accordingly, Whitman published more poems in these magazines than he ever had because magazines were now much more stable. When Whitman published in *Harper's Monthly*, he thought he had arrived at respectability. In February, 1874, his poem "Song of the Redwood Tree" was published. In March of 1874, "Prayer of Columbus" appeared. He considered the pay very high. Because he had to leave his government job in 1873, magazine publication could fill an immense need.[19]

"Song of the Redwood Tree" is a poem that looks ahead, not backward. It opens,

"A California song,
A prophecy and indirection, a thought impalpable to breathe
        as air,

---

[17] Henry James, *Literary Criticism: Essays on Literature, American Writers and English Writers*, 1984: 633.

[18] Joel Porte, *Representative Man*, 332–33.

[19] Martin Buinicke, *Walt Whitman's Reconstruction*, 5–6, 26.

A chorus of dryads, fading, departing, or hamadryads
     departing,
A murmuring, fateful, giant voice, out of the earth and sky,
Voice of a mighty dying tree in the redwood forest dense

Farewell My Brethren,
Farewell O Earth and Sky, Farewell Ye Neighboring Waters,
My Time Has Ended, My Term Has Come.

Along the northern coast,
Just back from the rock-bound shore and the caves...."

Much of the next three pages is in italics, the tree continuing to speak from this introductory passage, explaining its natural life and the history of California. Rhythmically, the poem is euphoric, copying the energy of many of Whitman's early *Leaves of Grass* long-lined works. As it comes to a conclusion, the tree returns the narrative to the poet, who spends some time praising California and then segues:

But more in you than these, lands of the Western shore,
(These but the means, the implements, the standing-ground,)
I see in you, certain to come, the promise of thousands of
     years, till now deferr'd,
Promis'd to be fulfill'd, our common kind, the race.
The new society at last, proportionate to Nature,
In man of you, more than your mountains peaks or stalwart
     trees imperial,
In woman more, far more, than all your gold or vines, or
     even vital air.
Fresh come, to a new world indeed, yet long prepared,
I see the genius of the modern, child of the real and ideal,
Clearing the ground for broad humanity, the true America,
     heir of the past so grand,
To build a grander future.[20]

Surely a poem of victory, Whitman here speaks to future eons of American life, pegging his particulars on the state to which he has never gone—California. With a tone of Eldorado, the poem yet speaks of successful women and men, in glorious health, but more importantly, of people in synch with a glowing natural world. One is reminded of Paul Fussell's scrutiny of the kind of poetry written after major wars, when he found that many writers turned instinctively to nature—either to put the tragedies of war behind them, or

---

[20] Whitman. "Song of the Redwood Tree," Library, 351–55.

to build a newly franchised world, one predicated on a healthy people, a healthful planet. Fussell calls this "recourse to the pastoral" and he sees writing about nature serving two purposes—"both fully gauging the calamities of war and imaginatively protecting against them."

He uncouples nature from the concept of a "pastoral poetry," noting that one would not need sheep or shepherds to create the latter. But he notes that there are a great many post-war poems that include flowers, especially orange and red flowers, as well as birds and their songs. Then, too, "pastoral has always been a favored mode for elegy, whether general or personal, because pastoral contains perennial flowers and perennials betoken immortality."[21]

In his matter-of-fact analysis, Fussell equates the fact that nature is alive out of doors, and most battles exist out of doors, so the natural world—like a person—has been so assaulted. "The opposite of war is peace, the opposite of experiencing moments of war is proposing moments of the pastoral. Since war takes place outdoors and always within nature, its symbolic status is that of the ultimate anti-pastoral."[22]

Whitman turned to pastoral scenes within his prose as well as his poetry. As he drafted what would eventually become his "Specimen Days," he often wrote descriptive passages about little but a natural scene. For instance, "Entering a Long Farm-Lane," dated 1876–1877:

> As every man has his hobby-liking, mine is for a real farm-lane fenced by old chestnut-rails gray and green with dabs of moss and lichen, copious weeds and briers growing in spots athwart the heaps of stray-picked stones at the fence bases—irregular paths worn between, and horse and cow tracks—all characteristic accompaniments marking and scanting the neighborhood in their seasons—apple-tree blossoms in forward April—pigs, poultry, a field of August buckwheat, and in another the long-flapping tassels of maize—and so to the pond, the expansion of the creek, the secluded—beautiful, with young and old trees, and such recesses and vistas.[23]

Paralleling this prose piece is this journal-type passage, dated from the same period, "1876–77":

> I find the woods in mid-May and early June my best places for composition. Seated on logs or stumps there, or resting on rails, nearly all the following Memoranda have been jotted down. Wherever I go, winter or summer, city or

---

[21] Paul Fussell, *The Great War*, 235, 253.
[22] Paul Fussell, *The Great War*, 231.
[23] Whitman, "Entering a Long Farm-Lane," "Specimen Days," Library, 781.

country, alone at home or traveling, I must take notes—(the ruling passion strong in age and disablement, and even the approach of it—but I must not say it yet.

Then underneath the following excerpts—crossing the *t*'s and dotting the *i*'s of certain moderate movements of late years—I am fain to fancy the foundations of quite a lesson learn'd. After you have exhausted what there is in business, politics, conviviality, love, and so on—have found that none of these finally satisfy, or permanently wear—what remains? *Nature* remains....[24]

Calm as these excerpts from Whitman's post-war writings are, his frenetic activity soon after the war's end tells a somewhat different story: he then was an anxious man, anxious about his source of income, anxious about the political strife between existing parties, anxious about the eventual outcome of life in the southern part of the country. Once his occupation in Washington had been decided, he took leave to return to Brooklyn and work toward creating the *fourth* edition of *Leaves of Grass*. He knew that both *Drum-Taps* and its addition should become a part of his ongoing book, which he would now accomplish. Although the fourth edition would include only six new poems, it added both the war poem collections. And, perhaps most significant, he started the thorough *re-arrangement* of all the poems beginning with the initial 1855 *Leaves of Grass*. His work of placing poems for their best effect would be continuous.

Because the house in which Jeff's family, Eddy, and his mother lived was small, he planned to rent a room near by, but Mrs. Abby Price, who was living in Manhattan, offered him the use of her extra room. Whitman was happy to have that accommodation for the next month, and the fourth edition was completed. When he returned to Washington, he found that his temporary appointment was now permanent, and his salary had been raised to $127 a month. As Loving confirmed, "From now until the end of the decade, he made more money than at any other time of his life (except for the landslide of cash he received upon the banning of the sixth edition of *Leaves of Grass* in Boston."[25] (There had been a sale of several hundred copies of earlier editions, and a sale of 2000 copies of the 1860 *Leaves of Grass*—but then that Boston publisher had gone bankrupt in the devastation of the war. Whitman needed income to continue to be the significant American poet he thought he was becoming.)

---

[24] Whitman, "New Themes Entered Upon," "Specimen Days," Library, 480–1.
[25] Loving, *Walt Whitman*, 306–8.

Whitman was never chary with his funds. On Sundays, he would take a cake to the hospital he visited; over the holidays, he supplied a full table of ham, turkey, desserts, and many smoking supplies, for all the patients. He regularly sent Louisa money, which he had never been able to do before: occasionally he sent funds to Jeff.

He began to sense some interest in the 1867 edition of *Leaves of Grass*. On December 1, 1866, *The Galaxy* (a New York magazine that was attempting to become for that city what *The Atlantic Monthly* had become for Boston) published John Burroughs's essay on *Drum-Taps*. On December 2, William O'Connor published a four-column review of the 1867 *Leaves of Grass* in the *New York Times*. Through O'Connor, Whitman had met Moncure Conway, a British rector who much admired Emerson, who then wrote enthusiastically about Whitman and his *Leaves of Grass* in the London *Fortnightly Review*. It was Conway who got William Michael Rossetti, brother of poets Christina and Dante Gabriel and a key British critic, interested in Whitman. Rossetti wrote about the poems in *The Chronicle* (London) and the following year, 1868, brought out *his* selection of Whitman's poems in several British editions. In 1872, Rossetti included a number of Whitman's poems in a collection titled *American Poems*, a book dedicated to Whitman.

As important as these scattered essays and reviews was the publication of the first part of Whitman's v long essay about America, the challenges to its democracy, and the direction the country should take. Whitman had begun working on this serious political essay early in 1867; eventually, the entire essay would be titled "Democratic Vistas." But in later 1867 *The Galaxy* published the first part, titled "Democracy." In it Whitman speaks of his experiences during the Civil War, his belief in the (common) People—especially the men who served in the war voluntarily, in his words, "the unnamed, unknown rank and file.... The People, of their own choice, fighting, dying for their own ideas." He waxes eloquent about what the soldiers faced, "the more fearful tests—the wound, the amputation, the shatter'd face or limb, the slow hot fever, long impatient anchorage in bed, and all the forms of maiming, operation and disease." In short, America has been "brought to hospital. There have we watch'd these soldiers and their decorum, their religious nature and fortitude, and their sweet affection."[26]

He places this section of memoir within larger discussion, but the center of his thinking stems, frequently, from his Civil War experiences. As Angus Fletcher noted, this essay became "a powerful prose polemic against political and financial corruption in the United States.... perhaps the most telling

---

[26] Whitman, *Democratic Vistas*, Library, 944–45.

of all Whitman's statements of his deep belief in, and his fears for, true democracy."[27]

Much of the first part of this essay gives the reader choices—doing this, means success; doing the opposite, means loss. While one should always think of Country in line with the all-inclusive force of Nature, each concept is difficult, if not amorphous. Whitman admits to being fearful while the country executes "universal suffrage," because of the dichotomy between success and failure. The essay operates on those polarities as it develops—and it is a long essay.

The following year, 1868, *The Galaxy* brought out another part of *Democratic Vistas*, with Whitman's attention on "Personalism," which was the title chosen for this second part. Urging each human being to find his or her own self became less a formula in Whitman's urging. He stated, "There is, in sanest hours, a consciousness, a thought that rises, independent, lifted out from all else, calm, like the stars, shining eternal. This is the thought of identity— yours for you, whoever you are, as mine for me.... The quality of BEING, in the object's self... is the lesson of Nature." Would each person try to find individuality, America might see "a copious rise of superb American men and women, cheerful, religious, ahead of any yet known."[28]

To find "personalism," Whitman directs: "To take expression, to incarnate, to endow a literature with grand and archetypal models—to fill with pride and love the utmost capacity, and to achieve spiritual means, and suggest the future—these, and these only, satisfy the soul. We must not say one word against real materials; but the wise know that they do not become real till touched by emotions, the mind."

Further on, Whitman picks up a theme he had used in his important poem from the 1865 *Leaves of Grass*, "Weave In, My Hardy Life." A tone poem with each section beginning with "Weave in," modulating the emphasis to merge through tactile insistence, he tries to reach physical merger through mysticism. As he admits, "Many will say it is a dream... but I confidently expect a time when there will be seen, running like a half-hid warp through all the myriad audible and visible worldly interests of America, threads of manly friendship, fond and loving, pure and sweet, strong and life-long.... not only giving tone to individual characters, and making it unprecedently emotional, muscular, heroic, and refined, but having the deepest relations to general politics...."[29]

---

[27] Angus Fletcher, "The Book of a Lifetime," Marcus and Sollors, 311.

[28] Whitman, *Democratic Vistas*, Library, 961–62. He adds that no one wants "a class of supercilious infidels, who believe in nothing."

[29] Whitman, *Democratic Vistas*, Library, 970, 982note.

He reminds his reader that all sentient human beings need "the image-making faculty" because each person must find his or her own "Conscience, moral soundness, Justice.... the moral conscientiousness, crystalline, without flaw, not Godlike only, entirely human, awes and enchants forever. Great is emotional love, even in the order of the rational universe." The great drive is to "express Nature, and the spirit of Nature, and to know and obey the standards. I say the question of Nature, largely consider'd, involves the questions of the esthetic, the emotional, and the religious—and involves happiness."[30]

Whitman published a booklet titled *Democratic Vistas* in 1871 but the essay sold poorly. To the two essays appearing in the *Galaxy*, he had added an introduction and a segment titled "Orbic Literature." Most critics find a lack of continuity in the composed book, and there seems to be a great amount of circling, of using different examples to illustrate ideas, of finding those ideas somewhat difficult to prove—or not attempting any proof that is relevant. Jerome Loving suggests that "Prose was too linear for Whitman's imagination."[31] In illustration, Whitman's poem about weaving seems in some respects a clearer evocation.

> Weave in, weave in, my hardy life,
> Weave yet a soldier strong and full for great campaigns to
>   come;
> Weave in red blood, weave sinews in like ropes, the senses,
>   sight weave in,
> Weave lasting sure, weave day and night the weft, the warp,
> incessant weave, tire not,
> (We know not what the use O life, nor know the aim, the
>   end, nor really aught we know;
> But know the work, the need goes on and shall go on, the
>   death-envelop'd march of peace as well as war goes on.)
> For great campaigns of peace the same wiry threads to
>   weave,
> We know not why or what, yet weave, forever weave.[32]

---

[30] Whitman, *Democratic Vistas*, Library, 982, 987.
[31] Loving, *Walt Whitman*, 332.
[32] Whitman, "Weave In, My Hardy Life," Library, 590–91.

14

Suggestions of Success

Along with Whitman's work on *Democratic Vistas*, he also wrote a shorter essay titled "Origins of Attempted Secession." In it he explained—something along the lines that Andrew Johnson, following Lincoln, might have approved—that,

> I consider the war of attempted secession, 1860–65, not as a struggle of two distinct and separate peoples, but a conflict (often happening, and very fierce) between the passions and paradoxes of one and the same identity....[1]

A century later, Edmund Wilson said Whitman created the term "Unionism."[2]

Part of a psychological pattern that historian Nina Silber has named "the romance of reunion,"[3] Whitman here re-unites the desperately warring factions, as if somehow to erase—or at least to blur—those hundreds of thousands of deaths the war had caused. Whitman adopts an argumentative strategy of blaming the war on marauding politicians, whose behavior at their party conventions seems most evil to him. As a peripheral benefit, he

---

[1] Whitman, "Origins of Attempted Secession," Library, 994.

[2] Edmund Wilson, *Patriotic Gore: Studies in the Literature of the American Civil War.* New York: Oxford University Press, 1962: 184.

[3] Nina Silber, *The Romance of Reunion: Northerners and the South, 1865–1900.* Chapel Hill: University of North Carolina Press, 1997.

© The Author(s), under exclusive license to Springer Nature Switzerland AG 2021
L. Wagner-Martin, *Walt Whitman*, Literary Lives,
https://doi.org/10.1007/978-3-030-77665-7_14

projects that "great imaginative efforts" (especially literature) will come from what he foresees will be the resolution of this conflict—"a great homogeneous Nation—free states all—a moral and political unity in variety, such as Nature shows in her grandest physical works, and as much greater than any mere work of Nature, as the moral and political, the work of man, his mind, his soul, are, in their loftiest sense, greater than the merely physical."[4]

The full confidence Whitman shows here places him squarely in the line of many other pseudo-apologists for the expected reintegration of the decimated South and the much more prosperous North. Whitman was not the only Northern writer who sounded Messianic. In David Davis's phrasing, "The emerging equation of post-Civil War nationalism involved reintegrating white Southerners into the social, political, and economic sectors of American life, usually at the expense of African Americans."[5] For the literate, dozens of novels published after the war portrayed interregional romances—a man from the North marrying a Southern woman, for instance. Such metaphoric imagery shows that true union is possible. Whereas Whitman had personal reasons for taking this stance—remembering that Peter Doyle had fought for the Confederacy, not the Union—he also had himself been relatively undecided when the war began.

Whitman's conciliatory attitude shifted as Reconstruction wore on and the ever-spreading Ku Klux Klan perpetuated more and more horrors on "freed" African Americans, many of whom had themselves fought in the war. He was also frustrated by the lack of federal legislation as Washington seemed more interested in impeaching Andrew Johnson than in resolving the nation's problems.

With his new job, Whitman had had to reduce his hospital visits to Sundays, but he remained faithful to his mission. More time-consuming had become his attention to the process of publicizing his own writing. With the attention of his friends William O'Connor and John Burroughs focused on his poems, he was learning to accept their somewhat exaggerated story of his having been ignored in his own country. By 1868 it was becoming harder to claim that few readers had ever found, or appreciated, *Leaves of Grass* or *Drum-Taps*.

Whitman was also learning that important critics could create networks of readers. The ripple effects from William Michael Rossetti's review and his books of Whitman's poems were surprising. Similarly, Charles Algernon Swinburne made a. favorable reference to Whitman in his book on William

---

[4] Whitman, "Origins of Attempted Secession," Library, 999.
[5] David A. Davis, "African American Literature, Citizenship, and War, 1863–1932," *War and American Literature*, 166–79.

Blake (1868). Then in 1871 Swinburne published a collection of his new poems, including a poem titled "To Walt Whitman." More significantly, he dedicated this book, *Songs Before Sunrise*, *to* Whitman. Through this publicity, Anne Gilchrist, widow of Blake biographer. Alexander Gilchrist, came to be an enthusiast of Whitman's poetry. She read a great deal of Whitman's work, discussed it, and eventually wrote a long essay about *Leaves of Grass* for the London *Radical*. Gilchrist also became infatuated with the poet and wrote him several letters—to which he did not reply. She told him that her marriage had been a typical Victorian union, even though she had borne four children. She talked about the passion she had never known, but that she realized now as she read his work: "I understand the divineness & sacredness of the Body." Her essay, "An English Woman's Estimate of Walt Whitman," made what she considered her love for the American no secret.[6]

Women's admiration was not new to Whitman, and he was always his courtly self. Women were his friends as well as men—he would have it no other way. In fact, during his fall, 1868, vacation he had accepted an invitation to visit Providence with the suffragette Pauline Wright Davis and her wealthy industrialist spouse. Again staying with Abby Price, he was learning to move within higher social circles than he had previously known. Invited by Dr. William F. Channing and his wife Mary Jane to stay with them for a while, he moved house. (Dr. Channing was the son of William Ellery Channing, Sr. and contributed a great deal to the study of electricity, spending more time in research than he did practicing medicine.) While there Whitman met with the Church brothers, who invited him to keep contributing to their new journal, *The Galaxy*. He liked the notion of being published regularly with such respected writers as Horace Greeley, Richard White Grant, and Rebecca Harding Davis. And from England, soon after the Rossetti edition of his poems had appeared, *Broadway Magazine* invited him to send poems: published there were "Whispers of Heavenly Death" and "A Noiseless, Patient Spider."[7]

Sometimes difficult to see what new poems are being written in the midst of Whitman's busier social life and his longer working hours, the latter poem is an almost perfect depiction of one of the themes becoming dominant in his writing.

---

[6] Loving, *Walt Whitman*, 328–30.

[7] Loving, *Walt Whitman*, 324–31; as Randall Fuller points out, it was because Whitman had known Theodore Winthrop from his Pfaff's drinking days, that he understood the power of personal acquaintance. Before Winthrop had been killed in the war, he regularly wrote for *The Atlantic Monthly*. (Fuller, *From Battlefields Rising*, 24–25.).

Along with his insistence on the greatness of the United States now that war is past, and the various parts of America are once again unified, is Whitman's long-existing belief in the individual wholeness of each person, in the way the physical becomes both the natural and the spiritual. In a brief ten lines of two balanced stanzas, "A Noiseless Patient Spider" becomes the active metaphor for the process of creation:

"A noiseless patient spider,
I mark'd where on a little promontory it stood isolated,
Mark'd how to explore the vacant vast surrounding,
It launch'd forth filament, filament, filament, out of itself,
Ever unreeling them, ever tirelessly speeding them.

And you O my soul where you stand,
Surrounded, detached, in measureless oceans of space,
Ceaselessly musing, venturing, throwing, seeking the spheres
    to connect them,
Till the bridge you need be form'd, till the ductile
    anchor hold,
Till the gossamer thread you fling catch somewhere, O
    my soul."[8]

Unusual in its concision, this poem also works through assonance, beginning with the sibilants, punctuated with the stops of –*d* and -*t*, but moving rhythmically throughout on all those –*s* and –*f* sounds. Nowhere in any other of his poetry does Whitman use a repetition such as "*filament, filament, filament*." It is as if he heard himself reading this poem to an audience. He was a strikingly sound-sensitive poet; conveying meaning through sounds was one base of his art.

By this time in Whitman's career as a poet, people may have thought they knew exactly what a Whitman poem would be. Yet throughout his life, he was always ready to experiment. His move to shorter and more traditional poems had shown itself after Lincoln's assassination, when Whitman, thoroughly satisfied with "When Lilacs Last in the Dooryard Bloom'd," had then written the seemingly traditional "O Captain! My Captain!" in its modernized ballad form, a poem that was recited for decades after its 1865 publication. Even then, Whitman changed the foundational rhythms of the ballad, making the paean to Lincoln its own, less-than-somber work. As if he were composing a trilogy of Lincoln poems, he added to these two the prayer-like "Hush'd Be the Camps To-day," dated May 4, 1865, to commemorate the actual burial,

---

[8] Whitman, "A Noiseless Patient Spider," Library, 564.

appropriately speaking from the soldiers' hearts because Lincoln was, and remained, "our dear commander." It was a rare poetic offering and Whitman knew he wanted those poems to be published as a group. Therefore he brought out the second part of the earlier collection, *Drum-Taps*.

A few years on, Whitman *would* be asked to read a poem at a ceremonial occasion. In the spring of 1872 he read for the Dartmouth College commencement, and his choice was both apt and oratorical. Continuing the message of his *Democratic Vistas*, "As a Strong Bird on Pinions Free" serves as a postscript to his earlier insistence that America is *one* country. (The poem is later re-titled "Thou Mother with Thy Equal Brood," "Mother" representing the country for the separate states which constitute her "brood"). This is the beginning stanza and then the second stanza is perhaps the beginning as the poem was read in 1872.

> "Thou Mother with thy equal brood,
> Thou varied chain of different States, yet one identity only,
> A special song before I go I'd sing o'er all the rest,
> For thee, the future.
>
> I'd sow a seed for thee of endless Nationality,
> I'd fashion the ensemble including body and soul,
> I'd show away ahead thy real Union, and how it may be
>   accomplish'd.
>
> The paths to the house I seek to make,
> But leave to those to come the house itself.
>
> Belief, I sing, and preparation;
> As Life and Nature are not great with reference to the
>   present only,
> But greater still from what is yet to come,
> Out of that formula for thee I sing
>
>
>   2
>
>
> As a strong bird on pinions free,
> To you, the amplest spaces heavenward, cleaving,
> Such be the thoughts I'd think of thee America,
> Such be the recitative I'd bring for thee.
>
> The conceits of the poets of other lands I'd bring thee not,
> Nor the compliments that have served their turn so long,
> Not rhyme, nor the classics, nor perfume of foreign court or

indoor library;
But an odor I'd bring as from forests of pine in Maine, or
      breath of an Illinois prairie,
With open airs of Virginia or Georgia or Tennessee, or from
      Texas uplands, or Florida's glades,
Or the Saguernay's black stream, or the wide blue spread
      of Huron,
With presentment of Yellowstone's scenes, or Yosemite,
And a murmuring under, pervading all, I'd bring the rustling
      sea-sound
That endlessly sounds from the two Great Seas of the world.....

And for thy subtler sense subtler refrains dread Mother,
Preludes of intellect tallying these and thee, mind-formulas fitted
      for thee, real and sane and large as these and thee,
Thou! mounting higher, diving deeper than we knew, thou
      transcendental Union!
By thee fact to be justified, blended with thought,
Thought of man justified, blended with God,
Through thy idea, lo, the immortal reality!
Through thy reality, lo, the immortal idea!".

Part three of the poem addresses the power of the modern brain and all its knowledge; part four apostrophizes the "ship of Democracy" and part five images the country "Like a limitless golden cloud filling the western sky." Part six, which is the lengthy closing, opens with this tercet of praise:

"Land tolerating all, accepting all, not for the good alone, all
      good for thee,
Land in the realms of God to be realm unto thyself,
Under the rule of God to be a rule unto thyself...."

The poem moves musically, each part creating a different pace. One of the most important is Part 2, where Whitman describes the various kinds of lands and occupations representing America—these lines are the longest of any in the six segments. Here, in the sixth, while the poet thinks of many positive elements of the rising and now-solidified country, he writes in his closing lines a kind of diminuendo: we can hear the poet's voice modulating to a close:

"Thou mental, moral orb—thou New, indeed new,
      Spiritual World!

The Present holds thee not—for such vast growth as thine,
For such unparallel'd flight as thine, such brood as thine,
The FUTURE only holds thee and can hold thee."[9]

It was as if success itself was fueling Whitman's actual writing. Being asked to give a poem at Dartmouth College seemed to prompt him toward one strain of thematic motion. Similarly, having *The Atlantic Monthly* take "Proud Music of the Storm," one of his own favorite poems—which Emerson had conveyed to that magazine—was serving as a catalyst for a trio of subsequent poems. The February 1, 1869, issue of the *Atlantic* included "Proud Music of the Sea-Storm," but subsequently the last word was replaced, probably because the poem's winds relate to land as well as water.

Another poem in segments, Whitman varies rhythms more emphatically here. The first part gives the literal rush of uncontrolled winds, some reinscribing the sounds of war. Part 2 begins the poet's personal cry:

"Come forward O my soul, and let the rest retire,"

as the catalog of sorrows—"the sobs of women, the wounded groaning in agony"—shakes the personal equilibrium. History, with its own myriad wars, intervenes and in this long segment, Whitman echoes a symphony, an organ base, a rush of cathartic sound.

Part 3 views history from a child's perspective until the music resumes. Part 4 modulates the symphony into opera and then to "dance-music of all nations through the past." Part 5 adds the greatest religious chords; that section ends:

"Give me to hold all sounds, (I madly struggling to cry,)
Fill me with all the voices of the universe,
Endow me with their throbbings, Nature's also,
The tempests, waters, winds, operas and chants, marches
     and dances,
Utter, pour in, for I would take them all!".

Part 6, the conclusion, begins in a whisper,

"Then I woke softly,
And pausing, questioning awhile the music of my dream... "

---

[9] Whitman, "Thou Mother with Thy Equal Brood," Library, 568–73.

through a rehearsal of those earlier stanzas. Here, Whitman's *story* is his success: he has found "the clew I sought so long" and then the following— and last—stanza explicating that clew:

"... a new rhythmus fitted for thee,
Poems bridging the way from Life to Death, vaguely wafted in
    night air, uncaught, unwritten,
Which let us go forth in the bold day and *write*."[10]

Perhaps mining the vein of the power of personal creation, the poet here— though he knows a great deal about music and grows calm thinking of many sounds/songs—circles back to "A Noiseless, Patient Spider." By the time he sets up what will be the fifth edition of *Leaves of Grass*, in 1871, the *Atlantic Monthly* poem, "Proud Music of the Storm" will have led to "Passage to India," but for now, it seemed to lead Whitman to a pause, a place of consolidation.

Whitman felt besieged. He enjoyed the visibility of his poems—and of himself as a poet. But his clerkship in Washington was demanding, as was his hospital work. His favorite sister-in-law had contracted tuberculosis; his mother had aged terribly, and she—like Whitman—lived with the vertigo that troubled many family members. In March, 1870, his older brother Jesse died, in his institution, of a ruptured aneurism.

Whitman himself felt a new fragility. After the reading at Dartmouth, he suffered a heat stroke (as he had during the summer of 1858) and told friends that he had been "very ill." The correspondence with Anne Gilchrist continued, as did overtures from various British admirers.

Nellie O'Connor, the wife of his good friend William, confessed that she too loved Whitman. This imbroglio—along with political differences— destroyed the long friendship that had been so central to Whitman's life in Washington. After the O'Connors' separation, they never lived together again.[11]

Whitman felt a clear urgency about getting his poetry written. And so he created one of his strongest long poems from this post-war period. "Passage to India" opens with a confident singer, no longer listening to various music but now making his own.

"Singing my days,
Singing the great achievements of the Present,
Singing the strong light works of engineers,

---

10 Whitman, "Proud Music of the Storm," Library, 525–30.
11 Loving, *Walt Whitman*, 330–31.

Our modern wonders, (the antique ponderous Seven outvied,)
In the Old World the east the Suez canal,
The New by its mighty railroad spann'd...."

In this nine-part poem, the rhythm of a chanting human voice connects various sequences—of memory, of history, of information. When Whitman adds in the soul, serving in its replacement role of the Deity, he pays less attention to information. But like "Proud Music of the Storm," this poem too is encyclopedic. The singing voice draws from the worlds of information available to the sentient person in the latter quarter of the nineteenth century. The union of disparate geographies is a given.

The brotherhood and sisterhood of human beings become an emotional possibility, no less difficult than such engineering feats as the Suez Canal.

Part 6 varies the opening chant. It instead begins.

"Year at whose wide-flung door I sing!
Year of the purpose accomplish'd!
Year of the marriage of continents, climates and oceans!
(No mere doge of Venice now wedding the Adriatic,)
I see O year in you the vast terraqueous globe given and
     giving all,
Europe to Asia, Africa join'd, and they to the New World,
The lands, geographies, dancing before you, holding a
     festival garland,
As brides and bridegrooms hand in hand.
Passage to India!
Cooling airs from Caucasus far, soothing cradle of man,
The river Euphrates flowing, the past lit up again."

Part 7 travels to include the soul; part 8 identifies the soul with God:

"Ah more than any priest O soul we too believe in God,
But with the mystery of God we dare not dally."

Part 9 is the poem's crescendo, opening with the often-quoted inclusive,

"Passage to more than India!"

A second stanza here opens,

"Passage to more than India!

O secret of the earth and sky!
Of you O waters of the sea! O winding creeks and rivers!
Of you O woods and fields! Or you strong mountains of my land!
Of you O prairies! Of you gray rocks!
O morning red! O clouds! O rain and snows!
O day and night, passage to you!...

Passage, immediate passage! The blood burns in my veins!
Away O soul! Hoist instantly the anchor!..."

For Whitman, as he pushes past the catalogs that had filled his earlier sweeping, inclusive poems, he seems to have arrived at a kind of portmanteau work. The reader sometimes has difficulty in breathing through these rhythms, even as the pace speeds the chants and seems to sweep hesitation away. The closing comes with a mood of decrescendo, triumph restoring calm:

"Sail forth—steer for the deep waters only,
Reckless O soul, exploring, I with thee, and thou with me,
For we are bound where mariner has not yet dared to go,
And we will risk the ship, ourselves and all.
O thy brave soul!
O farther farther sail!
O daring joy, but safe! Are they not all the seas of God?
O farther, farther, farther sail!"[12]

In 1871, the year he wrote "Passage to India," Whitman published three books: *Democratic Vistas*, the fifth edition of *Leaves of Grass*, with many new arrangements of poems, and a new book, *Passage to India*. Of that book's 73 poems, 23 were new, mixed with Whitman's selections from previous books. He placed his blessing on the poem for which the collection was titled: he felt that he had come through—once more—with "Passage to India."

---

[12] Whitman, "Passage to India," Library, 531–40.

15

The Hardiness of Fame

Whitman seldom turned down an invitation of any kind. But he was coming to realize that he was living in a world that was often nothing but work. His earlier robust health had diminished. He missed his friendship with the O'Connors; he felt regret that some of his Brooklyn friends had lost their jobs. He worried about a great many things.

On January 23, 1873, Whitman suffered a major stroke. He was at work when the first signs appeared but he managed to walk to his rooming house and rest. The next morning, his left side was paralyzed. Being immobilized meant that all his friends came to care for him, feed him, take him to their homes, and help him to avoid the terrible depression that was, naturally, occurring. His doctor arranged for electric shock treatments, which alleviated some of the paralysis. For many months, however, he could not walk.

Finally well enough to be taken to his brother's home in Camden, New Jersey, Whitman was eager to see his mother—who had moved in with George weeks before her own health failed rapidly. He arrived three days before Louisa died, and the mourning—along with the viewing held in the home—was further debilitating.

Abby Price and her daughter came for the service and saw that Whitman was clearly in anguish over the loss of his constant supporter, the mother who had been his benevolent spirit. When he wrote to the Prices, thanking them

L. Wagner-Martin, *Walt Whitman*, Literary Lives, https://doi.org/10.1007/978-3-030-77665-7_15

for coming, he said that Louisa's passing was a "staggering, staying blow....
My physical sickness, bad as it is, is nothing to it."[1]

Two weeks later he returned to Washington but it was clear he could not
work; he could not get to his office. Friends were worried at his acute depression—they brought meals, they talked with him. But he could not bear the
loneliness of his room. His friends the Ashtons invited him to live with them.
That too failed. After several weeks, he moved back to George and Lou's
Camden home.

Living in industrial New Jersey, close to the railroad depot, Whitman
had trouble visiting friends, walking anywhere, but he suffered most from
a lack of intellectual conversation. He wrote letters to friends, he worried,
he mourned the death of Henry Clapp, who owned the beloved Pfaff's bier-
garten, as he mourned the macabre death from rabies of the beautiful Ada
Clare, another friend from Pfaff days. Eventually he learned to take the ferry
to Philadelphia, where he read and wrote at the Mercantile Library—as if
he were doing regular work. During this return to Camden, he was asked
by David Goodman Croly, current editor of the *New York Daily Graphic*,
to submit whatever he wrote: he found that writing occasional poems about
daily happenings was useful—to him and to his writing process—so he sent
Croly many poems. He also tried writing prose sketches about events. Croly
took everything.

It was important work, even if some of the writing was inferior to
Whitman's usual standard: it kept him at his trade. It kept him alive. Even
crippled as he was, he helped George and Lou as they built a bigger house on
Stevens and West streets, a location closer to the ferry. He had also primed his
processes to write serious poetry by reconstructing his developing the 1869
Atlantic Monthly poem, "Proud Music of the Storm," the poem which had
led him, in 1871, to "Passage to India."

That meditative process led him now to a fine, if uncharacteristic, work,
"Prayer of Columbus." Unusually autobiographical in that the poem laments
both the loss of good health and the permanence of aging, it also took on
qualities more expected in a Robert Browning dramatic monolog. It also
reminds the reader of Shakespeare's Prospero in *The Tempest*—especially since
Columbus worries about his ships, a metonymic reminder of Whitman's
worrying about his poems. (When he has finally arranged all his poems into
thematic headings, a process that is close to being finished in the late 1870s,
Whitman places "Prayer of Columbus" directly after "Passage to India" and
"Proud Music of the Storm." Then following "Columbus" come three poems

---

[1] Loving, *Walt Whitman*, 347–48.

from the original 1855 *Leaves of Grass*—"The Sleepers," "Transpositions," and "To Think of Time." Whitman places these six poems, all of them among his best writing, together to close his new book "Autumn Rivulets." Not only are the three most recent poems from different years of his experience, but he links them with these original-book poems as if the thematic stream is all one.

In his second book on *Leaves of Grass*, James E. Miller, Jr., had explained the importance of Whitman's selection and *placement,* warning readers to attend to his choices. Miller was correct in his observations.[2])

Whitman's "Prayer of Columbus" opens in the explorer's voice of lament:

> "A batter'd, wreck'd old man,
> Thrown on this savage shore, far, far from home,
> Pent by the sea and dark rebellious brows, twelve dreary
>   months,
> Sore, stiff with many toils, sicken'd and nigh to death,
> I take my way along the island's edge,
> Venting a heavy heart.
>
> I am too full of woe!
> Haply I may not live another day;
> I cannot rest O God, I cannot eat or drink or sleep,
> Till I put forth myself, my prayer, once more to Thee,
> Breathe, bathe myself once more in Thee, commune with
>   Thee,
> Report myself once more to Thee.
>
> Thou knowest my years entire, my life,
> My long and crowded life of active work, not adoration
>   merely;
> Thou knowest the prayers and vigils of my youth....

Emphatically personal, Whitman uses the details of his own convalescence to explore Columbus's broken and aging body—the sleeplessness, the inability to eat, the twelve months living as a castaway. We remember that Whitman made out his will shortly before his stroke: he was already thinking of debility or death. This opening holds all those weary fears. But this turn to God, his

---

2 James E. Miller, Jr. *Leaves of Grass: America's Lyric-Epic of Self and Democracy.* New York: Twayne, 1992: 113. Somewhat earlier than Miller, Roger Asselineau had made the point that nothing Whitman did, particularly toward the end of his writing life, was accidental. He had become "a more and more conscious craftsman." *The Evolution of Walt Whitman.* Cambridge, MA: Harvard University Press, 1960: 252.

remembering his childhood years, relates to the thought, the actuality, of his mother and her dying. Worried as he was about his own health, he seems not to have believed Louisa would ever leave him.

After the main part of the poem, which focuses on Columbus's devotion to God's work, Whitman returns to the acute and accurate physical details of his debility:

> "My hands, my limbs grow nerveless,
> My brain feels rack'd, bewilder'd,
> Let the old timbers part, I will not part,
> I will cling fast to Thee, O God, though the waves buffet me,
> Thee, Thee at least I know.
>
> Is it the prophet's thought I speak, or am I raving?
> What do I know of life? What of myself?
> I know not even my own work past or present,
> Dim ever-shifting guesses of it spread before me,
> Of newer better worlds, their mighty parturition,
> Mocking, perplexing me.
>
> And these things I see suddenly, what mean they?
> As if some miracle, some hand divine unseal'd my eyes,
> Shadowy vast shapes smile through the air and sky,
> And on the distant waves sail countless ships,
> And anthems in new tongues I hear saluting me."[3]

For the readers of *Harper's Magazine*, the juxtaposition of this poem with "Song of the Redwood Tree" (see Chapter 12) showed Whitman's great versatility—although from the comments "Prayer of Columbus" received, readers' attention was focused more often on the way this character's aging body might parallel the poet's own health. To have poems published in *Harper's Magazine* allowed Whitman to resume that path to fame that he thought had been developing. This visibility made him less focused on his dragging left foot.

In 1874, too, Whitman was discharged from his Washington position, again the victim of downsizing. Even though he had, a year earlier, hired a replacement worker—which was then allowed—and even though he argued to keep the post, his life in Washington ended. (His arguing won him two months salary more in compensation.)

He kept up his writing, often working on more of the prose passages in a war memoir fashion that would eventually comprise *Memoranda During the*

---

[3] Whitman, "Prayer of Columbus," Library, 540–42.

War. He became good friends with young Harry Stafford from the printing shop, and together they would visit the Staffords' family farm, Timber Creek, where Whitman wrote many of the nature passages for his later *Specimen Days*.

If some readers wondered at Whitman's increasing use of religious themes—or at least of the figure of God, or the mention of not only death but of a person's soul—he did not explain. For some critics, among them Angus Fletcher, religion had been a staple in much of Whitman's poetry. Particularly in the poems of *Drum-Taps,* religion was omnipresent. With war or without, Whitman had lived all his years benefiting from his mother's complacent reliance on her family's Quaker acceptance of life's eventual goodness. As a younger poet he had sometimes expressed the belief that mysticism provided surprising answers, that, finally, death was "the mother of us all." He wrote about that recognition with very little apprehension then—but by the 1870s, when life was more and more threatening, the possibility of death was drawn as less cordial.

In 1871, he had written "Gods," a true praise poem of belief:

"Lover divine and perfect Comrade,
Waiting content, invisible yet, but certain,
Be thou my God.

Thou, thou, the Ideal Man,
Fair, able, beautiful, content, and loving,
Complete in body and dilate in spirit,
Be thou my God.

O Death, (for Life has served its turn,)
Opener and usher to the heavenly mansion,
Be thou my God.

Aught, aught of mightiest, best I see, conceive, or know,
(To break the stagnant tie—thee, thee to free, O soul,)
Be thou my God.

All great ideas, the races' aspirations,
All heroisms, deeds of rapt enthusiasts,
Be ye my Gods.

Or Time and Space,
Or shape of Earth divine and wondrous,
Or some fair shape I viewing, worship,

> Or lustrous orb of sun or star by night,
> Be ye my God."[4]

By Whitman's own organization, he places this poem in the midst of a set of much earlier works—short, exploratory, his early "statement" poems, such as "Perfections":

> "Only themselves understand themselves and the like of
>   themselves,
> As souls only understand souls."

Alongside "Answer,"

> "That you are here—that life exists and identity,
> That the powerful play goes on, and you may contribute a verse."[5]

Within this cluster are two of Whitman's best-liked poems, one ostensibly about religious belief, one not: "When I Heard the Learn'd Astronomer" is the former:

> "When I heard the learn'd astronomer,
> When the proofs, the figures, were ranged in columns before
>   me,
> When I was shown the charts and diagrams, to add, divide,
>   and measure them,
> When I sitting heard the astronomer where he lectured with
>   much applause in the lecture-room,
> How soon unaccountable I became tired and sick,
> Till rising and gliding out I wander'd off by myself,
> In the mystical moist night air, and from time to time,
> Look'd up in perfect silence at the stars.[6]

"I Sit and Look Out" captures the stasis of a belief turned to confusion. Here the poet remains in the listing-and categorizing mode rather than providing answers. These poems, except for "Gods," all date from either 1860 or 1865. Again, Whitman's arrangement within a collection shows the thematic relationship.

> "I Sit and Look Out"

---

4 Whitman, ""Gods," Library, 408–09.
5 Whitman, "Perfections" and "Answer," Library, 410.
6 Whitman, "When I Heard the Learn'd Astronomer," Library, 409.

"I sit and look out upon all the sorrows of the world, and
  upon all oppression and shame,
I hear secret convulsive sobs from young men at anguish
  with themselves, remorseful after deeds done,
I see in low life the mother misused by her children, dying,
  neglected, gaunt, desperate,
I see the wife misused by her husband, I see the treacherous
  seducer of young women,
I mark the ranklings of jealousy and unrequited love
  attempted to be hid, I see these sights on the earth,
I see the workings of battle, pestilence, tyranny, I see martyrs
  and prisoners,
I observe a famine at sea, I observe the sailors casting lots
  who shall be kill'd to preserve the lives of the rest,
I observe the slights and degradations cast by arrogant persons
  upon laborers, the poor, and upon negroes, and the like;
All these—all the meanness and agony without end I sitting
  look out upon,
See, hear, and am silent."[7]

Somewhat ironically, at the close of this cluster, Whitman placed "To Old Age," a poem from 1860. It is a two-line metaphor, but it was accurate:

"I see in you the estuary that enlarges and spreads itself
  grandly as it pours in the great sea."[8]

Still truly handicapped by his instability of movement, Whitman visited people less and traveled by ferry or train, usually with another person. He did not trust his leg to carry him and acknowledged, sadly, that he is a cripple. The poet once so proud of his perfect health would rather not face the actuality of old age.

In 1875 he worked hard to re-arrange his poems into yet more books. He wrote the prose "Memoranda" from the war, and assembled new and related poems into the new "Two Rivulets." These are published in 1876, as well as an "Author's" or "Centennial" edition of *Leaves of Grass,* reprinting the 1871 edition of that collection.

A hundred copies of each of the three titles were published. Making the most money was his essay "Walt Whitman's Actual American Position," from West Jersey Press in Camden. (This unsigned article generated international controversy, as well as bringing in cash gifts.) Whitman here complained

---

[7] Whitman, "I Sit and Look Out," Library, 411.
[8] Whitman, "To Old Age," Library, 414.

about his standing among American readers and publishers, lamenting his poverty now as a retiree. Unfortunately, his complaint fed into a running battle in England about the propriety of the Rossetti poets—Christina and Dante Gabriel, whose poetry had been called "The Fleshly School of Poetry" by young critic Robert Buchanan. He included Whitman's "Children of Adam" poems in that category. In the States, poet Bayard Taylor got into the argument, as well as, on the opposing side, John Burroughs and William O'Connor. Eventually there was a subscription drive to benefit Whitman's finances, much to his distaste. As the arguments raged, Philadelphia opened its Centennial Exhibition and Taylor was chosen the Exhibition poet, an honorific which Whitman envied.[9]

His work progressed and the three titles were being sold out of George's home because distribution had been a problem with earlier books. (Later another 600 copies were printed.) George Eliot was said to admire his poems; Tennyson sent regards. Anne Gilchrist with several of her children arrived in Philadelphia and rented a large house, giving Whitman a permanent room in her establishment. She may have made the trip because he had sent her a ring soon after Louisa's death, but she also wanted her daughter to be educated in the States. Whitman not only spent much time in that room, complete with a rocking chair; he also invited family and friends to visit him there, at 1929 North Twenty-Second Street, Philadelphia. Edward Carpenter visited, so did Joaquin Miller, and Whitman enjoyed being included in the family life of the Gilchrists.[10]

Whitman gave a poetry reading at Swarthmore in 1877, and then lectured at Lincoln Hall in Philadelphia on "The Memory of Thomas Paine." He came to know such well-placed New Yorkers as John H. Johnson, with whom he stayed several weeks on one occasion. The role of house guest suited Whitman well.

He was sorry to see the Gilchrists leave their Philadelphia address as their daughter progressed through medical studies though they would visit again after extensive travels, before returning to England. But he was busily working on a lecture on Lincoln that he proposed giving—and he had his prose and poetry to keep writing.

Memoranda During the War was one of many such publications: many people with any historical or literary bent had collected such notes during those long four years. Whitman the newsman had written well, and he felt his paragraphs deeply, though the sale of this book disappointed him. (In 1882, he incorporated these passages into the much longer *Specimen Days*.)

[9] Loving, *Walt Whitman*, 361–71.
[10] Loving, *Walt Whitman*, 377–79.

He began with his days spent looking for his brother George after the Battle of Fredericksberg, an entry dated December 21, 1862. Here he describes one of the countless field hospitals, this one a mansion: "quite crowded upstairs and down, everything impromptu, no system... all the wounds pretty bad, some frightful, the men in their old clothes, unclean and bloody. Some of the wounded are rebel soldiers and officers, prisoners. One, a Mississippian, a captain, hit badly in leg, I talk'd with some time; he ask'd me for papers, which I gave him. (I saw him three months afterward in Washington, with his leg amputated, doing well.) I went through the rooms, downstairs and up. Some of the men were dying. I had nothing to give at that visit but wrote a few letters to folks at home, mothers, etc. Also talk'd to 3 or 4, who seem'd most susceptible to it, and needing it."[11]

He then compressed entries for the week between December 23 to 31, intent on providing well-detailed information so his readers can visualize his work:

> Besides the hospitals, I also go occasionally on long tours through the camps, talking with the men. Sometimes at night among the groups around the fires, in their shebang enclosures of bushes.... I soon get acquainted anywhere in camps, with officers or men, and am always well used. Sometimes I go down on picket with the regiments I know best. As to rations, the army here at present seems to be tolerably well supplied, and the men have enough, such as it is, mainly, salt pork and hard tack.

More detail comes from this entry dated simply "January, 1863," "I am now remaining in and around Washington, daily visiting the hospitals.... Am now able to do a little good, having money (as almoner of others home,) and getting experience. To-day, Sunday afternoon and till nine in the evening, visited Campbell hospital; attended specially to one case in ward 1, very sick with pleurisy and typhoid fever, young man, farmer's son, D. F. Russell, company E, Sixtieth New York, downhearted and feeble; a long time before he would take any interest, wrote a letter home to his mother, in Malone, Franklin county, N. Y. at his request; gave him some fruit and one or two other gifts, envelop'd and directed his letter. Then went thoroughly through ward 6, observ'd every case in the ward, without, I think, missing one, gave perhaps from twenty to thirty persons, each one some little gift, such as oranges, apples, sweet crackers, figs, etc."[12]

---

[11] Whitman, "December 21, 1862," "Specimen Days," Library, 712.
[12] Whitman, "December 23–31" and "January, 63," Specimen Days, Library, 713–15.

As a journalist, Whitman gave readers a base of specifics; in later entries, he might focus on one figure or one episode. At times he wrote a cumulative account, as when he titled his notes "The Wounded from Chancellorsville" or, somewhat later, "Soldiers and Talks." Dated "May, '63," "As I write this, the wounded have begun to arrive from Hooker's command from bloody Chancellorsville. I was down among the first arrivals. The men in charge told me the bad cases were yet to come. If that is so pity them, for these are bad enough. You ought to see the scene of the wounded arriving at the landing here at the foot of Sixth street, at night. Two boat loads came about half-past seven last night. A little after eight it rain'd a long and violent shower. The pale, helpless soldiers had been debark'd, and lay around on the wharf and neighborhood anywhere. The rain was, probably, grateful to them; at any rate they were exposed to it. The few torches light up the spectacle. All around—on the wharf, on the ground, out on side places—the men are lying on blankets, old quilts, etc., with bloody rags bound round heads, arms, and legs. The attendants are few, and at night few outsiders also—only a few hard-work'd transportation men and drivers. (The wounded are getting to be common, and people grow callous.)… The men generally make little or no ado, whatever their sufferings. A few groans that cannot be suppress'd, and occasionally a scream of pain as they lift a man into the ambulance. To-day, as I write, hundreds more are expected, and to-morrow and the next day more, and so on for many days. Quite often they arrive at the rate of 1000 a day."[13]

"Soldiers and Talks" is undated. "Soldiers, soldiers, soldiers, you meet everywhere about the city, often superb-looking men, though invalids dress'd in worn uniforms, and carrying canes or crutches. I often have talks with them, occasionally quite long and interesting. One, for instance, will have been all through the peninsula under McClellan-narrates to me the fights, the marches, the strange, quick changes of that eventful campaign, and gives glimpses of many things untold in any official reports or books or journals. These, indeed, are the things that are genuine and precious. The man was there, has been out two years, has been through a dozen fights, the super-fluous flesh of talking is long work'd off him, and he gives me little but the hard meat and sinew. I find it refreshing, these hardy, bright, intuitive, American young men, (experience'd soldiers with all their youth.)[14]

Many of Whitman's accounts of single soldiers are sadly moving; many of his treks through various crowded hospitals lead to myriad conclusions about the good he is, modestly, able to do. Some of his notes have been often reprinted. One of these is "A Glimpse of War's Hell Scenes;" another, "Boys

---

[13] Whitman, "May, '63," "Specimen Days," Library, 720–21.

[14] Whitman, "Soldiers and Talks," "Specimen Days," 714–15.

in the Army." Among the best known are "Three Years Summ'd Up" and "The Million Dead, Too, Summ'd Up."

The latter opens, "The dead in this war—there they lie, strewing the fields and woods and valleys and battle-fields of the south—Virginia, the Peninsula—Malvern hill and Fair Oaks—the banks of the Chickahominy—the terraces of Fredericksburgh—Antietam bridge—the grisly ravines of Manassas—the bloody promenade of the Wilderness—the varieties of the *strayed* dead, (the estimate of the War department is 25,000 national soldiers kill'd in battle and never buried at all, 5,000 drown'd, 15,000 inhumed by strangers, or on the march in haste, in hitherto unfound localities—2,000 graves cover'd by sand and mud by Mississippi freshets, 3,000 carried away by caving-in of banks, etc.)—Gettysburgh, the West Southwest—Vicksburgh—Chattanooga—the trenches of Petersburgh—the numberless battles, camps, hospitals, everywhere—the crop reap'd by the mighty reapers, typhoid, dysentery, inflammations—and blackest and loathesomest of all, the dead and living burial-pits, the prison-pens of Andersonville, Salisbury, Belle-Isle, etc., (not Dante's pictured hell and all its woes, its degradations, filthy torments, excell'd those prisons)—the dead, the dead, the dead—*our* dead—or South or North, ours all, (all, all, all, finally dear to me)...."

"And everywhere among these countless graves—everywhere in the many soldier Cemeteries of the Nation, (there are now, I believe, over seventy of them)—as at the time in the vast trenches, the depositories of slain, Northern and Southern, after the great battles—not only where the scathing trail passed those years, but radiating since in all the peaceful quarters of the land—we see, and ages yet may see, on monuments and gravestones, singly or in masses, to thousands or tens of thousands, the significant word *Unknown*."

"(In some of the cemeteries nearly *all* the dead are unknown. At Salisbury, N. C., for instance, the known are only 81, while the unknown are 12,027, and 11,700 of these are buried in trenches."[15]

Another note made famous through repeated quotation is "The Real War Will Never Get in the Books," Whitman's ending segment for his Civil War accounts. It opens, "And so good-bye to the war. I know not how it may have been, or may be, to others—to me the main interest I found, (and still, on recollection, find,)in the rank and file of the armies, both sides, and in those specimens amid the hospitals, and even the dead on the field. To me the points illustrating the latent personal character and eligibilities of these States, in the two or three millions of American young and middle-aged

---

15 Whitman, "The Million Dead, Too, Summ'd Up," "Specimen Days," Library, 776–78.

men, North and South, embodied in those armies—and especially the one-third or one-fourth of their number, stricken by wounds or disease at some time in the course of the contest—was of more significance even than the political interests involved. (As so much of a race depends on how it faces death, and how it stands personal anguish and sickness. As, in tne glints of emotions under emergencies, and the indirect traits and asides in Plutarch, we get far profounder clues to the antique world than all its more formal history.) Future years will never know the seething hell and the black infernal background of countless minor scenes and interiors . . . of the Secession war; and it is best they should not—the real war will never get in the books ....[16]

A century after Whitman published his notes from his war, Paul Fussell in his study of world wars stated, "Everyone who remembers a war first-hand knows that its images remain in the memory with special vividness... The very enormity of the proceedings, their absurd remove from the usages of the normal world, will guarantee that a structure of irony sufficient for ready narrative will attach to them."[17]

---

[16] Whitman, "The Real War Will Never Get in the Books," "Specimen Days," Library, 778–79.
[17] Paul Fussell. *The Great War*, 326.

16

To Travel, II

The 1870s rushed past. Whitman gave his Lincoln lecture for the first time, he re-arranged the poems within *Leaves of Grass* again, and he felt strong enough to go by train to do what he had promised himself for decades—to see the American West.

He had praised Westerners, he had written poems to California, he had criticized established Eastern cultures—the West had beckoned him for years. His careful notes on the journey comprise a long section of his 1882 *Specimen Days*; he begins the journey with this description: "The following three or four months (Sept. to Dec.'79) I made quite a western journey, fetching up at Denver, Colorado, and penetrating the Rocky Mountain region enough to get a good notion of it all. Left West Philadelphia after 9 o'clock one night, middle of September, in a comfortable sleeper." This entry was titled "Begin a Long Jaunt West." As the train covers those hundreds of miles, some locations get more description than others. Whitman loved Missouri; he also enjoyed Kansas, both Lawrence and Topeka—where he was scheduled to read a poem at a conference. He did not do the latter, but he was excited to train the next six hundred miles to Denver, a city he described as "all unmistakably prolific, western, American, and on the largest scale." It is clear that he loved Denver and the Rocky Mountains. This was what he wrote as he toured the river within the Platte canon:

© The Author(s), under exclusive license to Springer Nature Switzerland AG 2021
L. Wagner-Martin, *Walt Whitman*, Literary Lives,
https://doi.org/10.1007/978-3-030-77665-7_16

We follow the stream of amber and bronze brawling along its bed, with its frequent cascades and snow-white foam. Through the canon we fly—mountains not only each side, but seemingly, till we get near, right in front of us—every rood a new view flashing, and each flash defying description—on the almost perpendicular sides, clinging pines, cedars, spruces, crimson sumach bushes, spots of wild grass—but dominating all, those towering rocks, rocks, rocks, bathed in delicate vari-colors, with the clear sky of autumn overhead. New senses, new joys, seem develop'd. Talk as you like, a typical Rocky Mountain canon, or a limitless sea-like stretch of the great Kansas or Colorado plains, under favoring circumstances, tallies, perhaps expresses, certainly awakes, those grandest and subtlest element emotions in the human soul, that all the marble temples and sculptures from Phidias to Thorwaldsen—all paintings, poems, reminiscences, or even music, probably never can.[1]

In case the import of his last sentence was not clear, several entries on he said more clearly: "Talk, I say again, of going to Europe, of visiting the ruins of feudal castles, or Coliseum remains, or kings' palaces—when you can come *here*. The alternations one gets, too; after the Illinois and Kansas prairies of a thousand miles—smooth and easy acres of the corn and wheat of ten million democratic farms in the future—here start up in every conceivable presentation of shape, these non-utilitarian piles, coping the skies, emanating a beauty, terror, power, more than Dante or Angelo ever knew."[2]

Whitman spends several days in Denver, claiming that he "loves" the city. Then he turns South, and then east. He leaves Denver by the Rio Grande Railroad going to Pueblo. Then his trip takes him east on the Atchison, Topeka, and Santa Fe line, coming back over the Great Plains and crossing the Mississippi River. He spends more days in St. Louis, about which city he rhapsodizes: "The points of St. Louis are its position, its absolute wealth, (the long accumulations of time and trade, solid riches, probably a higher average thereof than any city,) the unrivall'd amplitude of its well-laid out environage of broad plateaus, for future expansion—and the great State of which it is the head. It fuses northern and southern qualities, perhaps native and foreign ones, to perfection, rendezvous the whole stretch of the Mississippi and Missouri rivers, and its American electricity goes well with its German phlegm. Fourth, Fifth and Third streets are store-streets, showy, modern, metropolitan, with hurrying crowds, vehicles, horse-cars, hubbub, plenty of people, rich goods, plate-glass windows, iron fronts often five or six stories high. You can purchase anything in St. Louis (in most of the big

---

[1] Whitman, "New Senses—New Joys," "Specimen Days," Library, 856; see also 850–55.
[2] Whitman, "Art Features," "Specimen Days," Library, 858.

western cities for the matter of that) just as readily and cheaply as in the Atlantic marts."[3]

Whitman admits he cannot stay away from the Mississippi River. In this less-factually oriented note, titled "Nights on the Mississippi," his love of water comes through clearly:

Oct. 29th, 30th, and 31st—Wonderfully fine, with the full harvest moon, dazzling and silvery. I have haunted the river every night lately, where I could get a look at the bridge by moonlight. It is indeed a structure of perfection and beauty unsurpassable, and I never tire of it. The river at present is very low; I noticed to-day it had much more of a blue-clear look than usual. I hear the slight ripples, the air is fresh and cool, and the view, up or down, wonderfully clear, in the moonlight. I am out pretty late: it is so fascinating, dreamy. The cool night-air, all the influences, the silence, with those far-off eternal stars, do me good. I have been quite ill of late. And so, well-near the centre of our national demesne, these night views of the Mississippi.[4]

Although Whitman spoke of an illness, it was only three years earlier that he described himself as a "half-paralytic." His system had at least partly recovered from the crippling 1873 stroke, though he knew he was still somewhat fragile. His decision to make this trip appeared to indicate the old, adventurous, Whitman, a man relatively unencumbered now that his mother had died and his immediate family responsibilities were in the hands of his brothers. By staying so long in St. Louis, he had more time with Jeff than any other of his brothers—so they became close again. The last entry in this segment of *Specimen Days* read: "I return'd home, east, Jan. 5, 1880, having travers'd, to and from and across, 10,000 miles and more. I soon resumed my seclusions down in the woods, or by the creek, or gaddings about cities ...."[5]

As his notes in this segment of "Specimen Days," Whitman was taking in whatever activities New Jersey and Philadelphia offered. He took the Fulton ferry and the Camden. He trekked up the Hudson River on the *Mary Powell*. He visited his long-time friend John Burroughs and stayed at his cottage for some time. He walked often in Central Park, one of his favorite places. He took a river trip out of West Philly. He traveled into New York to attend the funeral of poet William Collen Bryant, a man he had long admired; and at that gathering, talked with the man who would become his biographer, Dr.

---

[3] Whitman, "St. Louis Memoranda," "Specimen Days," Library, 870.
[4] Whitman, "Nights on the Mississippi," "Specimen Days," Library, 871.
[5] Whitman, "Upon Our Own Land," "Specimen Days," Library, 872.

Richard M. Bucke, a psychiatrist who ran a mental hospital in Canada—
he had read Whitman's poetry since 1855. Living in London, Ontario, the
Buckes had made one visit to Whitman in the States but now Dr. Bucke
invited him to travel to Canada and spend as much time together as he
could.Whitman was happy to accept: he had found some good news when he
returned from Colorado—a professor was writing a book about him, a musi-
cian had arranged his poem "Dirge for Two Veterans" for piano, his second
Lincoln lecture, in Philadelphia's Association Hall, would be well attended.
But life with George did not excite him, whereas going to Canada—his first
"foreign" country—did.[6]

On June 3 of 1880, the party stopped to see Niagara Falls, a new adventure
in its own right; it had been thirty years since Whitman and Jeff had seen the
Falls on their way back from New Orleans. Arriving in London, Whitman
grew fascinated with the full operation of the asylum—which held a variety
of patients, some deaf and dumb, some barely functional, some at different
stages of recovery. The grounds and buildings were modern and, as always,
Whitman was interested in whatever technology was innovative.

Bucke was pleased to have Whitman as his guest but his wife worried that
the poet's reputation (as an obscene writer) would damage her social position. When Bucke suggested that he take Whitman to Montreal and Quebec,
Whitman was pleased—and so was Mrs. Bucke. July 16 the two left by train
for Toronto, then they traveled across Lake Ontario to Kingston and then up
the St. Lawrence, stopping for several days in Montreal and then briefly in
Quebec. Whitman wrote very little about the travel, but he wrote to friends
and Jerome Loving details the trip.

They reached the Saguenay River on August 6 and traveled up and down
the river for two days. Comparing this Canadian river to the Hudson,
Whitman described it in *Specimen Days:*

> Up these black waters, over a hundred miles—always strong, deep, (hundreds
> of feet, sometimes thousands,) ever with high, rocky hills for banks, green
> and gray—at times a little like some parts of the Hudson, but much
> more pronounc'd and defiant. The hills rise higher—deep their ranks more
> unbroken. The river is straighter and of more resolute flow, and its hue, though
> dark as ink, exquisitely polish'd and sheeny under the August sun. Different,
> indeed, this Saguenay from all other rivers—different effects—a bolder, more
> vehement play of lights and shades. Of a rare charm of singleness and simplicity
> ....

---

[6] Loving, *Walt Whitman*, 194–95.

He follows this description with a similarly evocative passage headed "Capes Eternity and Trinity," evidently finding in the surprisingly huge distances he has experienced throughout Canada a parallel excitement in that country's strange natural effects. Whitman had thought he was learning about different terrain when he visited Colorado, but now he was seeing how vast these stretches of Canada were.

Whitman wrote about the Canadian people, "a simple, hardy population, lumbering, trapping furs, boating, fishing, berry-picking and a little farming. I was watching a group of young boatmen eating their early dinner— nothing but an immense loaf of bread, had apparently been the size of a bushel measure, from which they cut chunks with a jack-knife. Must be a tremendous winter country this, when the solid frost and ice fully set in.."[7]

With his attention focused now on completing *Specimen Days* (which he explained, as a title, indicated "authentic glints, specimen-days of my life,") Whitman made one of his last journeys. He did not travel to Holland to explore the Van Velsor family beginnings, nor did he go to England to search out the Whitmans. As we have seen, Whitman believed in the *American* roots of his family, surrounded by all the glories of the *American* nation. Instead, appropriately, he went into the Long Island territory where both his parents had grown up. He also visited each family graveyard. Then he wrote those visits into a kind of historical opening, and that is the way *Specimen Days* presented the Whitman hegira to readers.

Whitman's first passage explained the amalgamation of these topics[8]— beginning with the family history (leading off with "Genealogy—Van Velsor and Whitman" and then presenting both the Cemeteries and the "Maternal Homestead," followed by "Two Old Family Interiors"). At that point Whitman described his boyhood. But the initial passage created the joy he found in putting this book together. He exulted in going home, where he would "untie the bundle, reel out diary-scraps and memoranda, just as they are, large or small, one after another, into print-pages, and let the melange's lackings and wants of connection take care of themselves."

Whitman recognized that he had created a new kind of writing in *Specimen Days*. This is no poem. This is not even an essay. It is a "bundle." And once more, Whitman was in search of a publisher. But first, working through a number of new arrangements for the poems in *Leaves of Grass*, Whitman

---

[7] Whitman, "The Savage Saguenay," "The Inhabitants—Good Living," "Specimen.
    Days," Library, 881–84. Loving, *Walt Whitman*, 196–400.

[8] Whitman, "Specimen Days, "Library 689: "Incongruous and full of skips and jumps as is that huddle of diary-jottings, war-memoranda of 1862-'65, Nature notes of 1877-'81, with Western and Canadian observations afterwards, all bundled up and tied by a big string.".

had found a Boston house to bring out the next edition. James R. Osgood and Company would publish the book, and so Whitman traveled yet again, to Boston, to oversee that work. He was in that city from August through October of 1881. Whitman was hopeful that Osgood would also bring out "Specimen Days," once it had been carefully presented during early 1882.

There was activity around Whitman's sixth edition—and around Whitman. British writer Oscar Wilde called on Whitman in Camden. He learned of the enthusiasm other English writers, George Eliot and John Aldington Symonds, had for his poetry. He had already met Edward Carpenter, who had visited him in the States several times. But in early spring, Osgood was warned by Boston District Attorney that certain poems in *Leaves of Grass* fell within provisions of "Public Statutes respecting obscene literature." Osgood knew that Whitman would not delete any of the objectionable poems—they had been included in the collection for years. So he withdrew the book from distribution.

Whitman's royalties from 1881 had totaled $25. He clearly was eager for *Leaves of Grass* to bring him income. But having Boston "ban" his book was not without favorable consequences. He made $1430.30 in 1882, a sum sufficient for him to buy a house for himself, taking out only a small mortgage.

Seeing a profitable opportunity, Rees Welsh and Company of Philadelphia had bought the rights and plates from Osgood and Company; later that company became David McKay Publishers. After *Leaves of Grass*, McKay issued *Specimen Days and Collect*, as well as R. M. Bucke's biography, *Walt Whitman*.[9]

In spring of 1884 Whitman moved to 328 Mickle Street in Camden, calling it "a little old shanty of my own." A two-story house, he could barely get to the upper floor but he hired a couple to do the work and the cooking. When that arrangement failed, he was fortunate to hire Mrs. Mary Davis, a sailor's widow, who moved into the house and did everything that needed doing, including the cooking. (Whitman never relinquished his hearty breakfasts, fish and eggs or meat and eggs, even when doctors advised him to cut out red meat if possible.) Completely without a family now, Whitman learned to take care of himself—Jeff was still in St. Louis, Eddy boarded out at a local farm, and George had moved to Burlington, Vermont.

By the summer of 1885, Whitman was experiencing more vertigo. His mobility was compromised because of a sprained ankle; he seemed content to stay within the confines of Camden. Sometimes a neighbor would drive

---

[9] Loving, *Walt Whitman*, 414–16.

him out with his aging horse and buggy; his days of visiting friends as a houseguest were done. He was living on the income from occasional writings and from his Lincoln lectures, most of which brought in small amounts– $30 here, $60 there. He had developed the practice of ending his lectures by reading "O Captain! My Captain!" It was if he had written that simple poem for such occasions. People filled the lecture halls whenever he spoke: he read sitting in a comfortable chair, talking beforehand, then reading his talk, and finishing with the Lincoln poem. On the twenty-fifth anniversary of Lincoln's assassination, he was asked to give the lecture at the Opera House in Philadelphia, the audience by subscription: for that reading, he received nearly $700. Such windfalls were rare.[10]

There were signs that Whitman's long-held hope of literary fame might come to fruition. In the summer of 1886 a first edition of *Leaves of Grass* sold for $18; book dealers became aware and started collecting. A signed Whitman letter went at auction for $80. Some permission requests arrived—usually for British publications—so that a Whitman poem would be published more widely. While he often re-cycled earlier publications, he was still careful about the presentation of his work: the perfectionist in him would never diminish. The important essay that closed the 1888 edition of *Leaves of Grass*, "A Backward Glance O'er Travel'd Roads," perhaps his most significant late prose piece, was an assemblage of two other writings, "My Book and I" (published first in *Lippincott's Monthly Magazine*, January, 1887) and the earlier "How I Made a Book," published in *Philadelphia Press*, July 11, 1886.[11]

Whitman uses his comforting voice to start: "So here I sit gossiping in the early candle-light of old age—I and my book—casting backward glances over our travel'd road …. After completing my poems, I am curious to review them in the light of their own thirty years." He describes the seven or eight stages he thinks his work has gone through in that time; he admits then "that I have not gain'd the acceptance of my own time." He goes on to say that "from a worldly and business point of view *Leaves of Grass* has been worse than a failure."

He gives his reader retrospective passages, beginning with his providing a calendar: "as I nigh my three-score-and-ten I live largely in memory …." He then admits that in his ongoing *Leaves of Grass*, he had had his say as he wanted it, which meant abandoning poetry's conventional themes. He surveys some of America's history, describing himself as the poet of his country.[12]

---

[10] Loving, *Walt Whitman*, 439–41.
[11] Loving, *Walt Whitman*, 442–43.
[12] Whitman, "A Backward Glance O'er Travel'd Roads," Library, 656–58.

Whitman pauses as he describes what he learned during the Civil War, "the Secession War, and what it show'd me as by flashes of lighting with the emotional depths it sounded and aroused (of course, I don't mean in my own heart only, I saw it just as plainly in others, in millions)—that only from the strong flare and provocation of that war's sights and scenes and final reasons-for-being of an autochthonic and passionate song definitely came forth."

> I went down to the war fields in Virginia (end of 1862), lived thenceforward in camp—saw great battles and the days and nights afterward—partook of all the fluctuations, gloom, despair, hopes again arouns'd, courage evoked—death readily risk'd … . Without those three or four years and the experiences they gave, *Leaves of Grass* would not now be existing.[13]

What any perusal of Whitman's ever-growing body of poetry within the covers of *Leaves of Grass* (which includes *Drum-Taps* and its annex) makes clear is that through his involvement with history, he recognized that his poetry had to grow and change to mimic the times. Even in the last decade of his writing life, Whitman was creating new poems, generally shorter and more traditional. But as Roger Asselineau stated in the midst of the revival of interest in Whitman (in the mid-twentieth century), the poet of the endless, rhapsodic, catalogs "became increasingly mindful of form …. Whitman slowly became a more and more conscious artist, a more and more subtle craftsman, more and more master of himself and his means of expression."[14]

His readers had come to understand the way he organized poems into thematic clusters. In these three poems, all dated 1891, some sense of his still optimistic spirit comes through. Drawing on metaphor rather than an explicit statement, Whitman writes a trio of thoroughly promising poems. In "Unseen Buds," the catalog is modified to describe the way buds unfold into flowers:

> Unseen buds, infinite, hidden well,
> Under the snow and ice, under the darkness, in every square
>   or cubic inch,
> Germinal, exquisite, in delicate lace, microscopic, unborn,
> Like babes in wombs, latent, folded, compact, sleeping;
> Billions of billions, and trillions of trillions of them waiting,
> (On earth and in the sea—the universe—the stars there in
>   the heavens,)

---

[13] Whitman, "A Backward Glance O'er Travel'd Roads," Library, 666.

[14] Roger Asselineau, *The Evolution of Walt Whitman* (Cambridge, MA: Harvard University Press, 1960): 252.

Urging slowly, surely forward, forming endless,
And waiting ever more, forever more behind.[15]

Moving from the dark buried scene, Whitman draws from a spiritual vocabulary—"infinite" and "germinal" are unexpected adjectives. By the time the reader reaches the ecstatic "billions of billions, and trillions and trillions," the realization that life exists even if invisibly has come home. And these buds—bursts of life and joy—cover not only the earth but the sea and the heavens, and what is best of all, there will always be "more behind." We have a poem of exuberance at Whitman's best.

Relying on a somewhat different metaphor, within the same cluster is "Grand Is the Seen," a poem that makes double use of "seen" and the implied "scene." The aura here is completely *light*-filled.

Grand is the seen, the light, to me—grand are the sky and stars,
Grand is the earth, and grand are lasting time and space,
And grand their laws, so multiform, puzzling, evolutionary;
But grander far the unseen soul of me, comprehending, endowing
    all these,
Lighting the light, the sky and stars, delving the earth, sailing the sea,
(What were all those, indeed, without thee, unseen soul? Of
    what amount without thee?)
More evolutionary, vast, puzzling, O my soul!
More multiform far—more lasting thou than they.[16]

With the mention of the soul, the tenor of the poem changes and becomes much less metaphoric. It seems to be a poem praising all the forces that could possibly lead to eternal life. Yet the poet's reliance on the sheer light—paralleling the growth of the unseen buds—makes the progression of the poem plausible. The initial irony of the title gives way to a poem of praise.

The most businesslike of the three poems in this group is "L. of G.'s Purport," reminding his readers that Whitman's whole writing life had fed into the creation of his *Leaves of Grass*. Beginning in 1855 with only a dozen poems, here in the final edition, Whitman has included four hundred poems. (There are some poems not included in the last compilation.) Stanzas three and four are reproduced here:

"Begun in ripen'd youth and steadily pursued,
Wandering, peering, dallying with all—war, peace, day and

---

[15] Whitman, "Unseen Buds," Library, 654.
[16] Whitman, "Grand Is the Seen," Library, 653–54.

> night absorbing,
> Never even for one brief hour abandoning my task,
> I end it here in sickness, poverty, and old age.
>
> I sing of life, yet mind me well of death:
> To-day shadowy Death clogs my steps, my seated shape, and
>   has for years—
> Draws sometimes close to me, as face to face."[17]

Balancing his characteristic joyful responses to life, the poet here admits the factual conflicts—he is terribly frail, incapacitated, yet his purpose—to keep bettering the life-giving book—has never flagged. He sings of life but such song does not erase the eventualities of his—or any person's—waning existence. Simpler than some of Whitman's "treatise" poems about his writing, this 1891 work cannot be improved upon.

It is in this vein that he created a cluster of similarly joyous poems twenty years earlier, and within those short poems, embedded the work that closed each edition of *Leaves of Grass*—"So Long!" Dated from 1871 is "Joy, Shipmate, Joy!".

> Joy, shipmate, joy!
> (Pleas'd to my soul at death I cry,)
> Our life is closed, our life begins,
> The long, long anchorage we leave,
> The ship is clear at last, she leaps!
> She swiftly courses from the shore,
> Joy, shipmate, joy.[18]

Clustered with several short poems, the group leads to what became his valedictory poem, "So Long!" The short poems include "The Untold Want" and "Now Finale to the Shore."

> The untold want by life and land ne'er granted,
> Now voyages sail thou forth to seek and find.
>
> Now finale to the shore,
> Now land and life finale and farewell.[19]

---

[17] Whitman, "L. of G.'s Purport," Library, 612–13.

[18] Whitman, "Joy, Shipmate, Joy!," Library, 608.

[19] Whitman, "The Untold Want," "Now Finale to the Shore," Library, 608.

In "So Long!" Whitman shapes what appears to be a farewell poem into a framed picture of his country, America. The catalogs are shorter and the poem's rhythms are more varied, but this is in many ways a poem of culmination. He beings with his early history:

> "To conclude, I announce what comes after me.
>
> I remember I said before my leaves sprang at all,
> I would raise my voice jocund and strong with reference to consummations.
>
> When America does what was promis'd,
> When through these States walk a hundred millions of
>   superb persons,
> When the rest part away for superb persons and contribute
>   to them,
> Then to me and mine our due fruition.
>
> I have press'd through in my own right,
> I have sung the body and the soul, war and peace have I
>   sung, and the songs of life and death,
> And the songs of birth, and shown that there are many births.
>
> I have offer'd my style to every one, I have journey'd with
>   confident step;
> While my pleasure is yet at the full I whisper *So Long!* …

Whitman used the italicized title, as here, throughout his listing poem—two full pages of typical coverage of the most affirmative traits of his country. Just as the opening provided history, the beginning of the poem's frame, the closing provides the impending demise. That section begins,

> Camerado, this is no book,
> Who touches this touches a man,
> (Is it night? Are we here together alone?)
> It is I you hold and who holds you,
> I spring from the pages into your arms—decease call me forth. … .
>
> I receive now again of my many translations, from my
>   avataras ascending, while others doubless await me,
> An unknown sphere more real than I dream'd, more direct,
>   darts awakening rays about me, *So long*!

> Remember my words, I may again return,
> I love you, I depart from materials,
> I am as one disembodied, triumphant, dead.[20]

There has always been critical commentary about this poem, partly because Whitman used it to close each edition from the third on of *Leaves of Grass*. His use of the clearly American phrase, complete with its bravado, often receives comment, as does the mystical blend of living energy brought to that quick stop with "dead" in the last line. As Anton Vander Zee comments in a 2018 essay, the poem indicates "Whitman's national, democratic longing as the promise of America, always, awaits. Such longing, such leave-taking—alongside the elegiac tenor of lasting and lateness both personal and epochal—structures Whitman's poetic enterprise as it develops across multiple post-Civil War editions of *Leaves*. Whitman would grow increasingly concerned with his own lateness, with the coming of old age and its ranging political, cultural, physiological, and aesthetic resonance."[21]

Vander Zee implies, correctly, that Whitman didn't lose his indomitable hopefulness even as it became increasingly difficult to date his poems according to their time of composition. The continuous shifting of poems within thematic groups obscured their chronology of composition. To be able to align poems from 1891 into groups of poems written in 1871 argues against any sense that, old and frail as he was, the poet did not relinquish his optimistic attention—whether he summoned that attention to comment on the times, on his friends, or on his country.

Critic Karen Karbiener provides a telling anecdote to help express the vigor of Whitman's very late years. Thomas Edison was one of Whitman's heroes; although Jeff was the engineer in the family, Walt had always been fascinated by technology. Edison had patented the phonograph in 1878, and Whitman had visited the New York Exposition Building to see it. Edison asked Whitman to make a recording, and he chose to read his short, late poem, "America." Speaking into a microphone attached to the recorder with a flexible tube while Edison turned the crank, Whitman can be heard clearly—until the device fails after only four of the six lines.

It is probable that few other nineteenth-century poets were so recorded.[22] The reader, and now listener, can envision this audible version of "America"

---

[20] Whitman, "So Long!," Library, 609–12.

[21] Anton Vander Zee. "Late Whitman: Critical Pasts, Critical Futures," *Resources for American Literary Study* 40 (2018): 90–144, this 91.

[22] Karen Karbiener, "Introduction," *Leaves of Grass,* xiv–xv.

constituting yet a new dimension of travel for the energetic and curious poet. What is recorded are the poem's first four lines:

> Centre of equal daughters, equal sons,
> All, all alike endear'd, grown, ungrown, young or old,
> Strong, ample, fair, enduring, capable, rich,
> Perennial with the Earth, with Freedom, Law and Love,
> A grand, sane, towering, seated Mother,
> Chair'd in the adamant of Time.[23]

The unrecorded last two lines take the poem into the more encompassing thematic group of the spiritual so to omit the "grand, sane … Mother" robs the short work of its considerable reach. Still effective, however, it provides us with an example of late Whitman. He wrote this poem in 1888; he recorded it in 1889, just three years before his death.

---

23 Whitman, "America," Library, 616.

17

The Last Years

Still writing about "America" in 1888, Whitman lived under his own adage: "really great poetry is always the result of a national spirit."[1] He was an American; he wanted to both love his country and create for it a voice. That aim ran through much of what he wrote. In one of the earliest passages of "Specimen Days," he explained further:

> I have said somewhere that the three Presidentieds preceding 1861 show'd how the weakness and wickedness of rulers are just as eligible here in America under republican, as in Europe under dynastic influences. But what can I say of that prompt and splendid wrestling with secession slavery, the arch-enemy personified, the instant he unmistakably show'd his face? The volcanic upheaval of the nation, after that firing on the flag at Charleston, proved for certain something which had been previously in great doubt, and at once substantially settled the question of *disunion*. In my judgment it will remain as the grandest and most encouraging spectacle yet vouchsafed in any age, old or new, to political progress and democracy. It was not for what came to the surface merely—though that was important—but what it indicated below, which was of eternal importance. Down in the abysms of New World humanity there had form'd and harden'd a primal hard-pan of national Union will, determin'd and in the majority, refusing to be tamper'd with or argued against, confronting all emergencies, and capable at any time of bursting all surface bonds, and breaking out

---

[1] Whitman, "A Backward Glance O'er Travel'd Roads," Library, 672.

© The Author(s), under exclusive license to Springer Nature
Switzerland AG 2021
L. Wagner-Martin, *Walt Whitman*, Literary Lives,
https://doi.org/10.1007/978-3-030-77665-7_17

like an earthquake. It is, indeed, the best lesson of the century, or of America, and it is a mighty privilege to have been part of it. ... .[2]

As Whitman's poems from the 1887–1888 period show, his identification of himself as the voice of America was changing. Now there were many poems about his aging, and about the loss of the vitality that had previously marked his life.

It is as if in many of these late poems, the country, to a certain extent, has disappeared. References to his being housebound (and during one year, bedroom-bound) transformed the very fact of geography. In "You Lingering Sparse Leaves of me," he plays on the readers' recognition that, as he has often said, he *is* his book, that book being the countless versions of *Leaves of Grass*:

> You lingering sparse leaves of me on winter-nearing boughs,
> And I some well-shorn tree of field or orchard-row;
> You tokens diminute and lorn—(not now the flush of May,
>   or July clover-bloom—no grain of August now;)
> You pallid banner staves—you pennants valueless—you
>   overstay'd of time,
> Yet my soul-dearest leaves confirming all the rest,
> The faithfulest—hardiest—last.[3]

"Old Age's Lambent Peaks" recounts the metamorphosis in the views that Whitman had both seen and presented in his own embodiment:

> The touch of flame—the illuminating fire—the loftiest look
>   at last,
> O'er city, passion, sea—o'er prairie, mountain, wood—the
>   earth itself;
> The airy, different, changing hues of all, in falling twilight,
> Objects and groups, bearings, faces, reminiscences;
> The clamer sight—the golden setting, clear and broad:
> So much i' the atmosphere, the points of view, the situations
>   whence we scan,
> Bro't out by them alone—so much (perhaps the best)
>   unreck'd before;
> The lights indeed from them—old age's lambent peaks.[4]

---

[2] Whitman, "Specimen Days," Library, 706–07.

[3] Whitman, "You Lingering Sparse Leaves of Me," Library, 633.

[4] Whitman, "Old Age's Lambent Peaks," Library, 635.

Whitman wrote two very uncharacteristic poems that he placed in this group. "Orange Buds by Mail from Florida" takes the reader back to the ways even a house-bound Whitman can keep savoring the natural world; as does the surprisingly personal, and colloquial, "After the Supper and Talk."

> After the supper and talk—after the day is done,
> As a friend from friends his final withdrawal prolonging,
> Good-bye and Good-bye with emotional lips repeating,
> (So hard for his hand to release those hands—no more will
>   they meet,
> No more for communion of sorrow and joy, of old and
>   young,
> A far-stretching journey awaits him, to return no more,)
> Shunning, postponing severance—seeking to ward off the
>   last word ever so little,
> E'en at the exit-door turning—charges superfluous calling
>   back—e'en as he descends the steps,
> Something to eke out a minute additional—shadows of
>   nightfall deepening,
> Farewells, messages lessening—dimmer the forthgoer's
>   visage and form,
> Soon to be lost for aye in the darkness—loth, O so loth to
>   depart!
> Garrulous to the very last.[5]

Poignant as this description of a final leave-taking is, the ending line quiets the sorrow. It is rare we see much humor in Whitman's poems—it is more often within his prose. Even with this closing, however, the sadness of this event is not much ameliorated.

"The Dismantled Ship" is a much more somber poem:

> In some unused lagoon, some nameless bay,
> On sluggish, lonesome waters, anchor'd near the shore,
> An old, dismasted, gray and batter'd ship, disabled, done,
> After free voyages to all the seas of earth, haul'd up at last
>   and hawser'd tight,
> Lies rusting, mouldering.[6]

As Whitman had done throughout his long writing career, he often shaped his prose writing so that it was congruent with his current poetry, or occasionally,

---

[5] Whitman, "After the Supper and Talk," Library, 636.
[6] Whitman, "The Dismantled Ship," Library, 634.

as if it would answer some of those poems. His various modes were frequently in a subtle conversation. The opening of his very late essay, "The Old Poets," came into play as a means of supporting the work that the old poets he discussed—Whittier, Longfellow, Bryant, Emerson—had accomplished, but also as a way of supporting his own writing. He begins by comparing these aged writers to "some very large, very old, entirely sound and vital tree or vine, like certain hardy, ever-fruitful specimens in California and Canada ... beyond the chronological records—illustrations of growth, continuity, power, amplitude and *exploitation*, almost beyond statement, but proving fact and possibility, outside of argument."

> Perhaps, indeed, the rarest and most blessed quality of transcendent noble poetry is ... from sane, completed, vital, capable old age. The final proof of song or personality is sort of matured, accreted, superb, evoluted, almost divine, impalpable diffuseness and atmosphere or invincible magnetism, dissolving and embracing all—and not any special achievement or passion, pride, metrical form, epigram, thought, or what is call'd beauty.

In Whitman's calm and calming voice, he rails here against the single work of perfection and his word choice reminds the reader how typical this effulgent prose is for the man who values the process of "accretion," his building from one style to a further style—i.e., his catalogs—as well as his process of "evolution," a way of creating that each successive edition of *Leaves of Grass* proves valuable beyond definition. When he coins "impalpable diffuseness and atmosphere," he is taking harsh critical comments and deifying them. Eventually, Walt Whitman found ways to answer the critics that he knew were—for the most part—narrow-minded, confined by traditional prescriptive rules, and—much of the time—mean-minded.

As he concludes this central paragraph:

> The bud of the rose or the half-blown flower is beautiful, of course, but only the perfected bloom or apple or finish'd wheat-head is beyond the rest. Completed fruitage like this comes (in my opinion) to a grand age, in man or woman, through an essentially sound continuated physiology and psychology (both important) and is the culminating glorious aureole of all and several preceding. Like the tree or vine just mention'd, it stands at last in a beauty, power and productiveness of its own, above all others, and of a sort and style uniting all criticisms, proofs and adherences.[7]

---

[7] Whitman, "Old Poets," Library, 1252–53.

For all his defenses of aging, Whitman's last years were not easy. In 1886, his niece, Hattie, Jeff's older daughter, died of enteritis; she was only 26. Whitman began to search for places to give his Lincoln lecture, but his presentations usually brought in little money. Then a New York City event was organized at the Madison Square Theater. Whitman was offered hotel accommodations. From that one event he garnered nearly $600. More important, several hundred callers came to visit him at the hotel, and Mark Twain, Edward Eggleston, and John Hay were among the audience members for the talk. Later, an even better publicized Lincoln lecture earned Whitman over $2500.

At one of the earlier talks, Whitman had met a young printer, Horace Traubel, who would become not only a friend and a helper, but his scribe, writing down much of the poet's conversations. Perhaps a gift worth more than money, the Traubel books were valued by the hundreds of Whitman scholars to come.

From the start of 1888, it was clear that Whitman's health was in rapid decline. His eyes were failing as were his kidneys; walking was more difficult than it had been. He enjoyed the May 31 birthday party given by friends but on June 2, the first of a handful of strokes began—covering several days, they left the poet hallucinating and delirious. At the advice of friends, he named some reliable literary executors, already having made his will. The strokes nearly ended his life. He was unable to leave his second-story bedroom for close to a year, cared for by a series of male nurses—their wages often paid by Whitman's reliable friends.[8]

During that year, frequently bedridden, Whitman put together a new collection, a mix of recent poetry and prose, titled *November Boughs*. Then he began work on a 900-page book, titling it *Complete Poems and Prose of Walt Whitman*. Because David McKay and Company could never invest in those production costs, he regretfully had the massive book printed himself, at Ferguson Brothers in Philadelphia. The finished copies came to Mickle Street in early 1890.[9]

Friends were, at least subconsciously, already mourning Whitman's death but they continued their support—physically, emotionally, and financially. One friend purchased a wheelchair for him, which his then nurse, Ed Wilkins, pushed for afternoon walks, sometimes lasting hours, in Camden and in the parks Whitman loved. Being outdoors brought Whitman a reprieve from thinking about his physical wasting. But finally, as his sensory balance diminished, he found those outdoor walks frightening, so they ended.

---

[8] Loving, *Walt Whitman*, 458–62.
[9] Loving, *Walt Whitman*, 461–66.

Truly housebound, Whitman sometimes pored over all the versions of *Leaves of Grass*. He tried to systematize the many other printed books crowding his upstairs. Trying to create order, finally, seemed futile: there was a great deal of work to be done, but he had no physical stamina to undertake it.

For the last thirty years of his life—and perhaps longer, Whitman was a man willing to accept help. He stored extra copies of all those printed books in various friends' homes. He accepted invitations to meals, to get-togethers, to trips. When his biographer, Richard Bucke, invited him to visit Canada, Whitman stayed for four months, allowing Bucke to become a tour guide through much of that country. He accepted cash, single contributions, or fund-raising events that would bring him the horse and buggy he enjoyed in New Jersey. He accepted years and years of physical help—friends walking with him out in the natural world he so enjoyed, cleaning various rooms and, finally, his Mickle Street house, helping to read printed pages he could no longer see in the process of publishing yet another book; writing favorable essays and comments about his poetry; providing care during the lengthy months while he was housebound after his paralytic strokes; giving parties on every May 31; and buying the wheelchair that made his last few years a different kind of convalescence. There was a strange generosity of spirit in his *acceptance*: not everyone could accept so graciously, and show such evident pleasure.

There is no way to record such truly generous occasions, but his friends' support might perhaps be seen as a kind of compensation for the common belief that Whitman was *not* praised in his own country—at least not so much as among his British readers. Perhaps any artist's reputation becomes exaggerated through time. Perhaps Whitman throughout his career felt *more* appreciated than sales records for his books indicated. Within all his poems there is a sense of community, that when "I" speaks it is less individual than it is communal—a kind of expansive "I" sharing the vicissitudes of life rather than representing an isolated speaker.

Many of Whitman's later poems focus on the coming of death, but they do so in a variety of ways. "As They Draw to a Close," for example, is reminiscent of his early catalog poems although it brings in the soul as a part of this tapestry:

> As they draw to a close,
> Of what underlies the precedent songs—of my aims in
>   them,
> Of the seed I have sought to plant in them,
> Of joy, sweet joy, through many a year, in them,
> (For them, for them have I lived, in them my work is done,)

Of many an aspiration fond, of many a dream and plan;
Through Space and Time fused in a chant, and the flowing
    eternal identity,
To Nature encompassing these, encompassing God—to the
    joyous, electric all,
To the sense of Death, and accepting exulting in Death in
    its turn the same as life,
The entrance of man to sing;
To compact you, ye parted, diverse lives,
To put rapport the mountains and rocks and streams,
And the winds of the north, and the forests of oak and pine,
With you O soul.[10]

The first poem in Whitman's late category "Songs of Parting" is the very direct "As the Time Draws Nigh":

As the time draws nigh glooming a cloud,
A dread beyond of I know not what darkens me.

I shall go forth,
I shall traverse the States awhile, but I cannot tell whither or
    how long,
Perhaps soon some day or night while I am singing my
    voice will suddenly cease.

O book, O chants! Must all then amount to but this!
Must we barely arrive at this beginning of us?—and yet it is
    enough, O soul;
O soul, we have positively appear'd—that is enough.[11]

Relatively little commentary concerns Whitman's very late poems, but among the poems chosen for discussion is his "Song at Sunset," one of the longest of his closing poems. It also has the sense of a community voice:

Splendor of ended day floating and filling me,
Hour prophetic, hour resuming the past,
Inflating my throat, you divine average,
You earth and life till the last ray gleams I sing.

---

[10] Whitman, "As They Draw to a Close," Library, 607–08.
[11] Whitman, "As the Time Draws Nigh," Library, 597.

Open mouth of my soul uttering gladness,
Eyes of my soul seeing perfection,
Natural life of me faithfully praising things,
Corroborating forever the triumph of things.

Illustrious every one!
Illustrious what we name space, sphere of unnumber'd
    spirits ...
Illustrious the attribute of speech, the senses, the body, ...

Good in all,
In the satisfaction and aplomb of animals,
In the annual return of the seasons,
In the hilarity of youth,
In the strength and flush of manhood,
In the grandeur and exquisiteness of old age,
In the superb vistas of death ... .

O amazement of things—even the least particle!
O spirituality of things!
O strain musical flowing through ages and continents, now
    reaching me and America!
I take your strong chords, intersperse them, and cheerfully
    pass them forward.

I too carol the sun, usher'd or at noon, or as now, setting,
I too throb to the brain and beauty of the earth and of all
    the growths of the earth,
I too have felt the resistless call of myself. ... .

The long poem continues, growing more inclusive with each segment; the penultimate section concludes, "Wherever I have been I have charged myself with contentment and triumph." Then come the final eight lines:

I sing to the last the equalities modern or old,
I sing the endless finales of things,
I say Nature continues, glory continues,
I praise with electric voice,
For I do not see one imperfection in the universe,
And I do not see one cause or results lamentable at last in the
    universe.

O setting sun! though the time has come,
I still warble under you, if none else does, unmitigated
    adoration.[12]

Perhaps the most evocative of these late poems, replete as it is with Whitman's perfect sense of balance and timing, is "A Clear Midnight":

This is thy hour O Soul, thy free flight into the wordless,
Away from books, away from art, the day erased, the lesson
    done,
Thee fully forth emerging, silent, gazing, pondering the
    themes thou lovest best,
Night, sleep, death and the stars.[13]

The simplicity of both language and thought parallels what the poem says, as the writer strips away all his learning, his art, leaving only the natural world in which he has grown, and to which he will return. To include the adjective "clear" in the title continues that metaphoric force.

Whether or not Whitman's poems showed conclusively that life was about to end, his body could barely continue to exist. In November of 1890 his brother Jeff died of typhoid pneumonia. There would be one more birthday celebration on May 31 of 1891. Whitman was now living with an electric light in the Mickle Street parlor: he could finally make out some words as he sat in his reading chair. He had been offered a free cemetery lot of his choice in the new cemetery that was being constructed. He chose a place on a hillside within a wooded area and planned a granite house-shaped tomb where he hoped to move the caskets of his parents and siblings. The structure would cost $4000, twice as much as had his house. But he had accumulated over $8000 and friends assured him that there would be money enough to keep Eddy where he received good care. He had published one last edition of *Leaves of Grass* which included "Sands at Seventy" and "A Backward Glance." He felt that he could do no more.[14]

On the evening of March 16, 1892, a few months before his 73rd birthday, Whitman died of bronchial pneumonia. The autopsy showed a completely collapsed left lung and a right lung that had only one-eighth area available for breath. His longevity had been a feat almost beyond his body's capability.

Four days later Whitman was buried in the new structure at the Harleigh Cemetery. According to Jerome Loving, the public viewing was open to

---

[12] Whitman, "Song at Sunset," Library, 602–04.
[13] Whitman, "A Clear Midnight," Library, 596.
[14] Loving, *Walt Whitman*, 462–79.

mourners at the Mickle Street house for several hours, and over a thousand neighbors and friends paid their respects. Then "thousands lined Haddon-field Pike as the bier was taken by carriage to the cemetery. They filled the hillsides around the tomb, which was fronted by an open-flapped tent for the speakers and special guests."[15]

Whitman would have enjoyed the celebration. He would have enjoyed being taken to rest by the community of real people who loved him, those members of what he called the "divine average," a group to which he himself belonged—and for whom he had written long and well, until he had no more strength to hold the pen.

---

[15] Loving, *Walt Whitman*, 480.

Walt Whitman, Selected Bibliography

Primary

Walt Whitman. *Complete Poetry and Collected Prose*. Ed. Justin Kaplan. New York: Library of America, 1982.

———. *Complete Prose Works (Specimen Days and Collect, November Boughs and Good Bye My Fancy)*. Boston: Small, Maynard, 1901.

———. *Faint Clews and Indirections, Manuscripts of Walt Whitman and His Family*. Ed. Clarence Gohdes and Rollo G. Silver. Durham, North Carolina: Duke University Press, 1949.

———. *Franklin Evans or The Inebriate: A Tale of the Times*. Ed. Christopher Castiglia and Glenn Hendler. Durham, North Carolina: Duke University Press, 2007.

———. *The Half-Breed and Other Stories by Walt Whitman*. Ed. Thomas Ollive Mabbott. New York: Columbia University Press, 1927.

———. *Leaves of Grass, First and "Death-Bed" Editions*. Ed. Karen Karbiener. New York: Barnes and Noble, 2004.

———. *Leaves of Grass and Selected Prose*. Ed. John Kouwenhoven. New York: Modern Library, 1950.

———. *Life and Adventures of Jack Engle: An Auto-Biography*. Ed. Zachary Turpin. Iowa City: University of Iowa Press, 2017.

———. *Manly Health and Training: To Teach the Science of a Sound Mind and a Beautiful Body*. Ed. Zachary Turpin. New York: Regan Arts, 2017.

———. *The Uncollected Poetry and Prose of Walt Whitman*. Collected and Edited by Emory Holloway. Garden City, New York: Doubleday, Page, 1921.

———. *Walt Whitman's Memoranda During the War [and] Death of Abraham Lincoln*. Ed. Roy P. Basler. Bloomington: Indiana University Press, 1962.

© The Editor(s) (if applicable) and The Author(s), under exclusive license to Springer Nature Switzerland AG 2021
L. Wagner-Martin, *Walt Whitman*, Literary Lives,
https://doi.org/10.1007/978-3-030-77665-7

———. *Walt Whitman's Selected Journalism*. Ed. Douglas A. Noverr and Jason Stacy. Iowa City: University of Iowa Press, 2014.

Secondary

Aaron, Daniel. *The Unwritten War: American Writers and the Civil War*. Madison: University of Wisconsin Press, 1987. New York: Knopf, 1973.

Allen, Gay Wilson. *The New Walt Whitman Handbook*. Albany: New York University Press, 1975.

———. "A New Look at Emerson and Science," *Literature and Ideas in America: Essays in Honor of Harry Hayden Clark*. Ed. Robert Falk. Athens: Ohio University Press, 1975.

Anderson, Quentin. *Imagined Communities: Reflections on the Origin and Spread of Nationalism*. London: New Left, 1983.

———. "Whitman's New Man," Walt Whitman: *Walt Whitman's Autograph Revision of the Analysis of "Leaves of Grass" (for Dr. R. M. Buche's Walt Whitman)*. New York: New York University Press, 1974:45–46.

Aspiz, Harold. *So Long! Walt Whitman's Poetry of Death*. Tuscaloosa: University of Alabama Press, 2004.

Asselineau, Roger. *The Evolution of Walt Whitman*. Cambridge, Massachusetts: Harvard University Press, 1960.

Barrett, Faith. *"To Fight Aloud Is Very Brave": American Poetry and the Civil War*. Amherst: University of Massachusetts Press, 2012.

Basler, Roy R. "Introduction," *Walt Whitman's Memoranda During the War and the Death of Abraham Lincoln*. Ed. Roy R. Basler. Bloomington: Indiana University Press, 1962:1–46.

Bauerlein, Mark. *Whitman and the American Idiom*. Baton Rouge: Louisiana State University Press, 1991.

Baym, Nina. "The Rise of the Woman Author," *Columbia Literary History of the United States*. Ed. Emory Elliott. New York: Columbia University Press, 1988 :289–305.

Beidler, Philip. "Veterans, Trauma, Afterwar," *War and American Literature*. Ed. Jennifer Haytock. New York: Cambridge University Press, 2021:71–86.

Belasco, Susan, Ed Folsom, Kenneth M. Price, ed. *Leaves of Grass: The Sesquicentennial Essays*. Lincoln: University of Nebraska Press, 2007.

Benfey, Christopher. "'Best Grief Is Tongueless': Jerome Liebling's Spirit Photographs," *The Dickinsons of Amherst*. Lebanon, New Hampshire: University Press of New England, 2001:169–209.

Berlant, Lauren and Michael Warner. "Sex in Public," *Critical Inquiry* 24 (1998):547–66.

Blasing, Mutlu. "Whitman's 'Lilacs' and the Grammars of Time," *PMLA* 97 (1982):31–39.

Blight, David W. *Race and Reunion: The Civil War in American Memory.* Cambridge, Massachusetts: Belknap, 2002.

Boudreau, Kristin. *Sympathy in American Literature, American Sentiments from Jefferson to the Jameses.* Gainesville: University Press of Florida. 2002.

Bradford, Adam. *Communities of Death: Whitman, Poe and the American Culture of Mourning.* Columbia: University of Missouri Press, 2014.

Breslin, James E. "Whitman and the Early Development of William Carlos Williams," *PMLA* 82 (December 1967):613–21.

Buell, Lawrence. "The Transcendentalists," *Columbia Literary History of the United States.* Ed. Emory Elliott. New York: Columbia University Press, 1988:364–78.

Buinicki, Martin T. *Walt Whitman's Reconstruction.* Iowa City: University of Iowa Press, 2011.

Burbick, Joan. "Bio-democracy in *Leaves of Grass,*" *Healing the Republic: The Language of Health and the Culture of Nationalism in Nineteenth Century America.* New York: Cambridge University Press, 1994:113–36.

Cabe, Delia. *Storied Bars of New York: Where Literary Luminaries Go to Drink.* New York: Countryman, 2017.

Cady, Joseph. "Not Happy in the Capitol: Homosexuality and the *Calamus* Poems," *American Studies* 19 (1978):5–22.

Callow, Philip. *Walt Whitman: From Noon to Starry Sky.* London: Allison and Busby, 1993.

Carlisle, E. Fred. *The Uncertain Self: Whitman's Drama of Identity.* East Lansing: Michigan State University Press, 1973.

Chase, Richard. *Walt Whitman.* Minneapolis: University of Minnesota Press, 1961.

Chauncey, George. *Gay New York: Gender, Urban Culture, and the Making of the Gay Male World.* New York: Basic, 1994.

Colacurcio, Michael J. "Idealism and Independence," *Columbia Literary History of the United States.* Ed. Emory Elliott. New York: Columbia University Press, 1988:207–26.

Columbia Book of Civil War Poetry. Ed. Richard Marius. New York: Columbia University Press, 1994.

Cook, Robert J. *Civil War Memories: Contacting the Past in the United States Since 1865.* Baltimore, Maryland: Johns Hopkins University Press, 2017.

Coviello, Peter. "Intimate Nationality: Anonymity and Attachment in Whitman," *American Literature* 73.1 (March 2001):85–119.

Crain, Caleb. *American Sympathy: Men, Friendship, and Literature in the New Nation.* New Haven, Connecticut: Yale University Press, 2001.

Creeley, Robert. *On Earth: Last Poems and an Essay.* Berkeley: University of California Press, 2006.

Cull, Nicholas J. "Propaganda for War from the Revolution to the Vietnam War," *War and American Literature.* Ed. Jennifer Haytock. New York: Cambridge University Press, 2021:27–41.

Cunningham, Michael. *Specimen Days.* New York: Farrar, Straus, Giroux, 2005.

Cushman, Stephen. *Belligerent Muse: Five Northern Writers and How They Shaped Our Understanding of the Civil War*. Chapel Hill: University of North Carolina Press, 2014.

———. *Fictions of Form in American Poetry*. Princeton, New Jersey: Princeton University Press, 1993.

Davis, David A. "African American Literature, Citizenship, and War, 1863–1932," *War and American Literature*. Ed. Jennifer Haytock. New York: Cambridge University Press, 2021:166–79.

Davis, Robert Leigh. *Whitman and the Romance of Medicine*. Berkeley: University of California Press, 1997.

Davis, Theo. *Ornamental Aesthetics: The Poetry of Attending to Thoreau, Dickinson, and Whitman*. New York: Oxford University Press, 2016.

Deleuze, Gilles. *Essays, Critical and Clinical*. Trans. Daniel W. Smith and Michael A. Greco. Minneapolis: University of Minnesota Press, 1997.

Denning, Michael. *The Cultural Front*. New York: Verso, 2010.

———. *Mechanic Accents: Dime Novels and Working Class Culture*. New York: Verso, 1998.

Diffley, Kathleen. *Where My Heart Is Turning Ever: Civil War Stories and Constitutional Reform, 1861–1876*. Athens: University of Georgia Press, 1992.

Dimock, Wai Chee and Michael T. Gilmore. *Rethinking Class: Literary Studies and Social Formations*. New York: Columbia University Press, 1994.

Donaldson, Scott. *The Impossible Craft: Literary Biography*. University Park: Pennsylvania State University Press, 2015.

Donoghue, Denis. *The American Classics, A Personal Essay*. New Haven, Connecticut: Yale University Press, 2005.

Dow, William. *Narrating Class in American Fiction*. New York: Palgrave Macmillan, 2009.

Doyle, Laura. *Bordering on the Body: The Racial Matrix of Modern Fiction and Culture*. New York: Oxford University Press, 1994.

Erkkila, Betsy. "Emily Dickinson and Class," *Mixed Bloods and Other Crosses: Rethinking American Literature from the Revolution to the Culture Wars*. Philadelphia: University of Pennsylvania Press, 2005:37–61.

———. *Walt Whitman's Songs of Male Intimacy and Love: "Live Oak, with Moss" and "Calamus."* Iowa City: University of Iowa Press, 2011.

———. "Whitman and Political Theory," *Whitman East and West: New Contexts for Reading Walt Whitman*. Ed. Ed Folsom. Iowa City: University of Iowa Press, 2002:115–44.

———. *Whitman the Political Poet*. New York: Oxford University Press, 1989.

Fahs, Alice. *The Imagined Civil War: Popular Literature of the North and the South*. Chapel Hill: University of North Carolina Press, 2001.

Faint Clews and Indirection: Manuscripts of Walt Whitman and His Family. Ed. Clarence Gohdes and Rollo G. Silver. Durham, North Carolina: Duke University Press, 1949.

Faust, Drew Gilpin. *The Republic of Suffering: Death and the American Civil War.* New York: Knopf, 2008.

Fishkin, Shelley Fisher. *From Fact to Fiction: Journalism and Imaginative Writing in America.* Baltimore: Johns Hopkins University Press, 1985.

Fletcher, Angus. "The Book of a Lifetime," *A New Literary History of America.* Ed. Greil Marcus and Werner Sollors. Cambridge, Massachusetts: Harvard University Press, 2009:306–12.

———. *A New Theory of American Poetry: Democracy, the Environment, and the Future of Imagination.* Cambridge, Massachusetts: Harvard University Press, 2004.

Folsom, Ed. "Lucifer and Ethiopia: Whitman, Race, and Poetics Before the Civil War and After," *A Historical Guide to Walt Whitman.* Ed. David S. Reynolds. New York: Oxford University Press, 2000:45–95.

———. "So Long, So Long! Walt Whitman, Langston Hughes, and the Art of Longing," *Walt Whitman: Where the Future Becomes Present.* Ed. David Haven Blake and Michael Robertson. Iowa City: University of Iowa Press, 2008:127–45.

———. "Walt Whitman's Invention of a Democratic Poetry," *The Cambridge History of American Poetry.* Ed. Alfred Bendixen and Stephen Burt. New York: Cambridge University Press, 2015:329–59.

Folsom, Ed and Kenneth M. Price. *Re-Scripting Walt Whitman: An Introduction to His Life and Work.* Malden, Massachusetts: Blackwell, 2000.

Foner,, Eric. *Reconstruction: America's Unfinished Revolution, 1863–1877.* New York: Harper Perennial, 1989.

Fuller, Randall. *From Battlefields Rising: How the Civil War Transformed American Literature.* New York: Oxford University Press, 2011.

Fussell, Edwin. *Lucifer in Harness: American Meter, Metaphor, and Diction.* Princeton, New Jersey: Princeton University Press, 1973.

Fussell, Paul. *The Great War and Modern Memory.* New York: Oxford University Press, 1975.

Gardner, Sarah E. "Civil War Literature and Memory," *War and American Literature.* Ed. Jennifer Haytock. New York: Cambridge University Press, 2021:151–65.

Gass, William H. "Emerson and the Essay," *Habitations of the Word: Essays.* New York: Simon & Schuster, 1985:9–49.

Gates, Henry Louis. *Figures in Black: Words, Signs, and the 'Racial' Self.* New York: Oxford University Press, 1987.

Gelpi, Albert. *The Tenth Muse: The Psyche of the American Poet.* Cambridge, Massachusetts: Harvard University Press, 1975.

Genoways, Ted. "A Common Language," *New York Times Book Review* (September 3, 2017):21.

———. *Walt Whitman and the Civil War: America's Poet During the Lost Years of 1860–1862.* Berkeley: University of California Press, 2009.

Gilbert, Sandra M. and Susan Gubar. *The Madwoman in the Attic. The Woman Writer in the Nineteenth-Century Literary Imagination.* New Haven, Connecticut: Yale University Press, 2000.

Giles, Paul. *American World Literature, An Introduction.* Malden, Massachussetts: Wiley, 2019.

Gilmore, Paul. *Aesthetic Materialism, Electricity and American Romanticism.* Stanford, California: Stanford University Press, 2009.

Goodman, Susan. "Edith Wharton's Sketch of an Essay on Walt Whitman," *Walt Whitman Quarterly Review,* 10:1 (Summer 1992):3–9.

———. *Republic of Words, The Atlantic Monthly and Its Writers, 1857–1925.* Hanover, New Hampshire: University Press of New England, 2011.

Grant, Douglas. *Walt Whitman and His English Admirers.* Leeds: Leeds University Press, 1962.

Gray, Richard. *A Brief History of American Literature.* Chichester: Wiley Blackwell, 2011.

Greenspan, Ezra. "The Poetics of Participle-Loving Whitman," *The Cambridge Companion to Walt Whitman.* Ed. Ezra Greenspan. Cambridge: Cambridge University Press, 1955.

———. *Walt Whitman and the American Reader.* Cambridge: Cambridge University Press, 1990.

Grossman, Allen. "The Poetics of Union in Whitman and Lincoln: An Inquiry toward the Relationship of Art and Poetry," *The American Renaissance Reconsidered: Selected Papers from the English Institute, 1982–83.* Ed. Walter Benn Michaels and Donald E. Pease. Baltimore, Maryland: Johns Hopkins University Press, 1985:183–208.

Gruesser, John Cullen. *Edgar Allan Poe and His Nineteenth-Century American Counterparts.* New York: Bloomsbury, 2019.

Gura, Philip F. *American Transcendentalism, a History.* New York: Hill & Wang, 2007.

Habegger, Alfred. *"My Wars Are Laid Away in Books": The Life of Emily Dickinson.* New York: Modern Library, 2002.

Halperin, David and Valerie Traub. *Gay Shame.* Chicago: University of Chicago Press, 2010.

Hawkins, Ty. "War and Morality," *War and American Literature.* Ed. Jennifer Haytock. New York: Cambridge University Press, 2021:13–26.

Haytock, Jennifer. *The Routledge Introduction to American War Literature.* New York: Routledge, 2018.

———. "Representing Soldiers," *War and American Literature.* Ed. Jennifer Haytock. New York: Cambridge University Press, 2021:42–56.

Hendler, Glenn. *Public Sentiments: Structures of Feeling in Nineteenth-century American Literature.* Chapel Hill: University of North Carolina Press, 2001.

Herreshoff, David Sprague. *Labor into Art: The Theme of Work in Nineteenth-Century American Literature.* Detroit, Michigan: Wayne State University Press, 1991.

Hoffman, Daniel. "'Hankering, Gross, Mystical, Nude': Whitman's 'Self' and the American Traditions," *Walt Whitman of Mickle Street: A Centennial Collection.* Ed. Geoffrey Sill. Knoxville: University of Tennessee Press, 1994.

Hollis, C. Carroll. *Language and Style in Leaves of Grass*. Baton Rouge: Louisiana State University Press, 1983.

Holloway, Emory. *Aspects of Immortality in Whitman*. Westwood, New Jersey: Kindle Press, 1969.

Howe, Irving. *The American Newness: Culture and Politics in the Age of Emerson*. Cambridge, Massachusetts: Harvard University Press, 1986.

Howe, Susan. *The Birth-Mark: Unsettling the Wilderness in American Literary History*. Hanover, New Hampshire: University Press of New England, 1993.

Hutchinson, Coleman. "Civil War Today, Civil War Tomorrow, Civil War Forever," *American Literary History* 30.2 (Summer 2018):331–42.

Hutchinson, George B. *The Ecstatic Whitman: Literary Shamanism and the Crisis of the Union*. Columbus: Ohio State University Press, 1986.

Isenberg, Nancy. *White Trash, The 400-Year Untold History of Class in America*. New York: Viking, 2016.

James, Henry. *Autobiographies*. Ed. Philip Horne. New York: Library of America, 2016.

Jarrell, Randall. *Poetry and the Age*. New York: Knopf, 1953.

Jensen, Beth. *Leaving the M/other*. Madison, New Jersey: Fairleigh Dickinson University Press, 2002.

Jones, Gareth Stedman. *Languages of Class, Studies in English Working Class History, 1832–1882*. Cambridge: Cambridge University Press, 1984.

Kammen, Michael. *Mystic Chords of Memory: The Transformation of Tradition in American Culture*. New York: Vintage, 1993.

Kaplan, Justin. *Walt Whitman, A Life*. New York: Simon & Schuster, 1980.

Karbiener, Karen. "Whitman at Pfaff's: Personal Space, A Public Place, and the Boundary-Breaking Poems of *Leaves of Grass* (1860)," *Literature of New York*. Ed. Sabrina Fuchs-Abrams. Newcastle upon Tyne: Cambridge Scholars, 2009:1–38.

———, ed. "Introduction," *Leaves of Grass, First and 'Death-Bed' Editions*. New York: Barnes & Noble, 2004.

Katcher, Philip. *The American Civil War, Day by Day*. Gloucestershire: Spellmount, 2007.

Katz, Jonathan Ned. *Love Stories: Sex Between Men Before Homosexuality*. Chicago: University of Chicago Press, 2001.

Keenaghan, Eric. "War and Queerness," *War and American Literature*. Ed. Jennifer Haytock. New York: Cambridge University Press, 2021:271–85.

Kennedy, William Sloane. *Reminiscences of Walt Whitman*. London: Alexander Gardner, 1896.

Killingsworth, M. Jimmie, ed. *The Cambridge Introduction to Walt Whitman*. New York: Cambridge University Press, 2007.

———. *Walt Whitman and the Earth: A Study in Ecopoetics*. Iowa City: University of Iowa Press, 2004.

———. *Whitman's Poetry of the Body: Sexuality, Politics, and the Text*. Chapel Hill: University of North Carolina Press, 1989.

Kinder, John M. "War and Disability Studies," *War and American Literature*. Ed. Jennifer Haytock. New York: Cambridge University Press, 2021:286–300.

Klammer, Martin. *Whitman, Slavery, and the Emergence of Leaves of Grass*. University Park: Pennsylvania State University Press, 1995.

Kinnell, Galway. "'Strong Is Your Hold:' My Encounters with Whitman," *Leaves of Grass, The Sesquicentennial Essays*. Ed. Susan Belasco, Ed Folsom, and Kenneth M. Price. Lincoln: University of Nebraska Press, 2007:417–25.

Krieg, Joann. *A Whitman Chronology*. Iowa City: University of Iowa Press, 1998.

Kreyling, Michael. *A Late Encounter with the Civil War*. Athens: University of Georgia Press, 2014.

Lalor, Eugene T. "Whitman and the New York Literary Bohemians, 1859–1862," *Walt Whitman Review* 25 (1979):131–45.

Lawson, Andrew. *Walt Whitman and the Class Struggle*. Iowa City: University of Iowa Press, 2006.

Leaves of Grass Imprints. Ed. Joel Myerson. Columbia: University of South Carolina Press, 2012.

Levin, Joanna and Edward Whitley, ed. *Walt Whitman in Context*. New York: Cambridge University Press, 2017.

Lewis, R. W. B. "Adam Creates a World," *Critics on Whitman, Readings in Literary Criticism*. Ed. Richard H. Rupp. Coral Gables, Florida: University of Miami Press, 1972:36–44.

Logan, William. *Dickinson's Nerves, Frost's Woods: Poetry in the Shadow of the Past*. New York: Columbia University Press, 2018.

Loving, Jerome. *Emerson, Whitman, and the American Muse*. Chapel Hill: University of North Carolina Press, 1982.

———. *Walt Whitman: The Song of Himself*. Berkeley: University of California Press, 1999.

Lowell, Robert. "*Paterson II*," *Critical Essays on William Carlos Williams*. Ed. Stephen Gould Axelrod and Helen Deese. New York: Hall, 1995:80–82.

Luckhurst, Roger. "War and Whiteness," *War and American Literature*. Ed. Jennifer Haytock. New York: Cambridge University Press, 2021:315–29.

Maffly-Kipp, Laurie. "Religion 1700 to the Present," *Oxford Companion to Women's Writing in the United States*. Ed. Cathy N. Davidson and Linda Wagner-Martin. New York: Oxford University Press, 1995:755–57.

Mancuso, Luke. *The Strange Sad War Revolving: Walt Whitman, Reconstruction, and the Emergence of Black Citizenship, 1865–1876*. Columbia, South Carolina: Camden House, 1997.

Martin, Justin. *Rebel Souls, Walt Whitman and America's First Bohemians*. New York: Da Capo Press, 2014.

Martin, Robert K. "The Disseminal Whitman: A Deconstructive Approach to *Enfans of Adam* and *Calamus*," *Approaches to Teaching Whitman's Leaves of Grass*. Ed. Donald D. Kummings. New York: Modern Language Association of America, 1990:74–80.

————, ed. *The Continuing Presence of Walt Whitman*. Iowa City: University of Iowa Press, 1992.

Maslan, Mark. *Whitman Possessed: Poetry, Sexuality, and Popular Authority*. Baltimore, Maryland: Johns Hopkins University Press, 2001.

Matthiessen, F. O. *American Renaissance: Art and Expression in the Age of Emerson and Whitman*. New York: Oxford University Press, 1941.

Meyerson, Joel, ed. *Whitman in His Own Time*. Detroit, Michigan: Omnigraphies, 1991.

Miles, Josephine. *Eras and Modes in English Poetry*. Berkeley: University of California Press, 1957.

Miller, Edward Haviland, ed. *The Artistic Legacy of Walt Whitman, A Tribute to Gay Wilson Allen*. New York: New York University Press, 1970

Miller, James E., Jr. *A Critical Guide to Leaves of Grass*. Chicago: University of Chicago Press, 1957.

————. *"Leaves of Grass": America's Lyric-Epic of Self and Democracy*. New York: Twayne, 1992.

Miller, Stephen. *Walking New York: Reflections of American Writers from Walt Whitman to Teju Cole*. New York: Fordham University Press, 2016.

Millner, Michael. "The Fear Passing the Love of Women: Sodomy and Male Sentimentalism Citizenship in the Antebellum City," *Arizona Quarterly* 58.2 (Summer 2002):19–52.

Moon, Michael. *Disseminating Whitman:: Revision and Corporeality in Leaves of Grass*. Cambridge, Massachusetts: Harvard University Press, 1991.

———— and Eve Kosofsky Sedgwick. "Confusion of Tongues," *Breaking Bounds: Whitman and American Cultural Studies*. Ed. Betsy Erkkila and Jay Grossman. New York: Oxford University Press, 1996:23–29.

Morris, Roy, Jr. *The Better Angel: Walt Whitman in the Civil War*. New York: Oxford University Press, 2000.

Murray, Aife. *Maid as Muse: How Servants Changed Emily Dickinson's Life and Language*. Durham: University of New Hampshire Press, 2009.

Nathanson, Tenney. *Whitman's Presence: Body, Voice, and Writing in "Leaves of Grass."* New York: New York University Press, 1992.

Obama, Barack. *A Promised Land*. New York: Crown, 2020.

Oliver, Charles M., ed. *Critical Companion to Walt Whitman*. New York: Facts on File, 2006.

Olney, James. *The Languages of Poetry: Walt Whitman, Emily Dickinson, Gerard Manley Hopkins*. Athens: University of Georgia Press, 1993.

O'Neill, Bonnie Carr. *Literary Celebrity and Public Life in the Nineteenth-Century United States*. Athens: University of Georgia Press, 2017.

Pearce, Roy Harvey. *The Continuity of American Poetry*. Princeton, New Jersey: Princeton University Press, 1961.

Perlman, Jim, Ed Folsom, Dan Campion, ed. *Walt Whitman, The Measure of His Song*. Duluth, Minnesota: Holy Cow Press, 1998.

Poets of the Civil War, ed. J. D. McClatchy. New York: Library of America, 2005.

Polito, Robert. "A Judgment of Art," *A New Literary History of America*. Ed. Greil Marcus and Werner Sollors. Cambridge, Massachusetts: Harvard University Press, 2009:564–69.

Pollack, Vivian. "'Bringing Help for the Sick': Whitman and Prophetic Biography," *Leaves of Grass, The Sesquicentennial Essays*. Ed. Susan Belasco, Ed Folson, and Kenneth M. Price. Lincoln: University of Nebraska Press, 2007:244–65.

———. *The Erotic Whitman*. Athens: University of Georgia Press, 2000.

Porte, Joel. *Representative Man: Ralph Waldo Emerson in His Time*. New York: Columbia University Press, 1988.

Powers, Lyall H., ed. *Henry James and Edith Wharton: Letters: 1900–1915*. New York: Scribner's, 1990.

Price, Kenneth M. *To Walt Whitman, America*. Chapel Hill: University of North Carolina Press, 2004.

———. *Whitman and Tradition: The Poet in His Century*. New Haven, Connecticut: Yale University Press, 1990.

Rattray, Laura. *Edith Wharton and Genre: Beyond Fiction*. London: Palgrave Macmillan, 2020.

Reynolds, David S. *Walt Whitman's America: A Cultural Biography*. New York: Knopf, 1995.

———, ed. *A Historical Guide to Walt Whitman*. New York: Oxford University Press, 2000.

Rich, Adrienne. "Six Meditations in Place of a Lecture," *What Is Found There: Notebooks on Poetry and Politics*, second edition. New York: Norton, 2003.

Richards, Eliza. *Battle Lines: Poetry and Mass Media in the U.S. Civil War*. Philadelphia: University of Pennsylvania Press, 2018.

Robertson, Michael. "The 'Long Foreground' of *Leaves of Grass*," *Resources for American Literary Study* 39 (2017):293–99.

———. *Worshipping Walt: The Whitman Disciples*. Princeton, New Jersey: Princeton University Press, 2008.

Ropp, Theodor. *War in the Modern World*. Durham, North Carolina: Duke University Press, 1959.

Rorabaugh, W. J. *The Craft Apprentice: From Franklin to the Machine Age in America*. New York: Oxford University Press, 1986.

Rosenthal, M. L. and Sally M. Gall. *The Modern Poetic Sequence*. New York: Oxford University Press, 1983.

Rowe, John Carlos. *At Emerson's Tomb*. New York: Columbia University Press, 1997.

Salska, Agniezka. *Walt Whitman and Emily Dickinson: Poetry of the Central Consciousness*. Philadelphia: University of Pennsylvania, 1985.

Salzman, Jack. "Literature for the Populace," *Columbia Literary History of the United States*. Ed. Emory Elliott. New York: Columbia University Press, 1988:549–67.

Sanchez-Eppler, Karen. *Touching Liberty: Abolition, Feminism, and the Politics of the Body*. Berkeley: University of California Press, 1992.

Saunders, Judith. "Literary Influence," *Edith Wharton in Context*. Ed. Laura Rattray. New York: Cambridge University Press, 2012:325–34.

Schaffer, Talia. *Romance's Rival: Familiar Marriage in Victorian Fiction*. Oxford, UK: Oxford University Press, 2016.

Schmidgall, Gary. *Containing Multitudes: Walt Whitman and the British Literary Tradition*. New York: Oxford University Press, 2014.

———. *Walt Whitman: A Gay Life*. New York: Dutton, 1997.

Schmitz, Neil. "Forms of Regional Humor," *Columbia Literary History of the United States*. Ed. Emory Elliott. New York: Columbia University Press, 1988:306–23.

Sedgwick, Eve Kosofsky. "Whitman's Transatlantic Context: Class, Gender, and Male Homosexual Style," *Delta* 16 (May 1983):111–22.

Seery, Richard, ed. *A Political Companion to Walt Whitman*. Lexington: University of Kentucky Press, 2011.

Sharpe, William Chapman. *Unreal Cities*. Baltimore: John Hopkins University Press, 1990.

Sherman, Nancy. *Afterwar*. New York: Oxford University Press, 2015.

Shklar, Judith N. *American Citizenship: The Quest for Inclusion*. Cambridge, Massachusetts: Harvard University Press, 1991.

Showalter, Elaine. "American Bards and American Poetesses," *A Jury of Her Peers*. New York: Knopf, 2009:72–74.

Silber, Nina. *The Romance of Reunion: Northerners and the South, 1865–1900*. Chapel Hill: University of North Carolina Press, 1997.

Sill, Geoffrey M. "You Tides with Ceaseless Swell: A Reading of the Manuscript," *Walt Whitman Quarterly Review* 6.4 (1989):189–97.

Stacy, Jason. "Containing Multitudes: Whitman, the Working Class, and the Music of Reform," *Popular Culture Review* 13. 2 (2002):137–54.

Stansell, Christine. *City of Women: Sex and Class in New York, 1789–1860*. New York: Knopf, 1986.

Stokesbury, James L. *A Short History of the Civil War*. New York: Morrow, 1995.

Stovall, Floyd. *The Foreground of Leaves of Grass*. Charlottesville: University Press of Virginia, 1974.

Taylor, Andrew. "Nineteenth-Century America, 1843–1870," *Henry James in Context*. Ed. David McWhirter. New York: Cambridge University Press, 2010:3–13.

Thomas, M. Wynn. *The Lunar Light of Whitman's Poetry*. Cambridge, Massachusetts: Harvard University Press, 1987.

———. *Transatlantic Connections, Whitma,n, U.S., Whitman, U. K*. Iowa City: University of Iowa Press, 2005.

———. "Whitman, Tennyson, and the Poetry of Old Age," *Something Understood: Essays and Poetry for Helen Vendler*. Ed. Stephen Burt and Nick Halpern. Charlottesville: University of Virginia Press, 2009:161–82.

Traubel, Horace, ed. *With Walt Whitman in Camden* (9 volumes). Boston, Philadelphia, New York: Appleton, 1908. 1906–1996.

Trout, Steven, "Mourning, Elegy, Memorialization from the Civil War to Vietnam," *War and American Literature*. Ed. Jennifer Haytock. New York: Cambridge University Press, 2021:87–102.

Tuggle, Lindsay. *The Afterlives of Specimens: Science, Mourning, and Whitman's Civil War.* Iowa City: University of Iowa Press, 2017.

Tytell, John. *Reading New York..* New York: Knopf, 2003.

Vander Zee, Anton. "Inventing Late Whitman," *ESQ: A Journal of Nineteenth Century American Literature and Culture* 63.4 (2017):641–80.

———. "Late Whitman: Critical Pasts, Critical Futures," *Resources for American Literary Study* 40 (2018):90–144.

———. "Whitman's Late Lives," *Walt Whitman Quarterly Review* 35.3 (2017):174–200.

Vendler, Helen. *Poets Thinking: Pope, Whitman, Dickinson, Yeats.* Cambridge, Massachusetts: Harvard University Press, 2004.

Waggoner, Hyatt H. *American Poets: From the Puritans to the Present.* Boston: Houghton, 1968.

———. *American Visionary Poetry.* Baton Rouge: Louisiana State University Press, 1982.

Wagner, Linda W. "Modern American Literature: The Poetics of the Individual Voice," in (Wagner) *American Modern, Essays in Fiction and Poetry.* Port Washington, New York: Kennikat, 1980:95–114.

Wagner-Martin, Linda. *Emily Dickinson, A Literary Life.* New York: Palgrave Macmillan, 2013.

———. "*Foreword*" to Richard Ruland and Malcolm Bradbury, *From Puritanism to Postmodernism.* New York: Routledge, 2016.

———. "Overview of American Literature," *Encyclopedia of American Studies.* Ed. Miles Orvell. New York, 2001:11–18.

Walker, Jeffrey. *Bardic Ethos and the American Epic Poem: Whitman, Pound, Crane, Williams, Olson.* Baton Rouge: Louisiana State University Press, 1989.

Warner, Michael. "Whitman Drunk," *Breaking Bounds: Whitman and American Cultural Studies.* Ed. Betsy Erkkila and Jay Grossman. New York: Oxford University Press, 1996:30–43.

Warren, Craig A. *Scars To Prove It: The Civil War Soldier and American Fiction.* Kent, OH: Kent State University Press, 2009.

Weinstein, Cindy. *Family, Kinship, and Sympathy in Nineteenth-Century American Literature.* New York: Cambridge University Press, 2005.

Whitman among the Bohemians. Ed. Joanna Levin and Edward Whitley. Iowa City: University of Iowa Press, 2014.

Wichelns, Kathryn. *Henry James's Feminist Afterlives: Annie Fields, Emily Dickinson, Marguerite Duras.* New York: Palgrave Macmillan, 2018.

Wilentz, Sean. *Chants Democratic: New York City and the Rise of the American Working Class, 1788–1850.* New York: Oxford University Press, 1984.

Wilkerson, Isabel. *Caste, The Origins of Our Discontents.* New York: Random, 2020.

Williams, C. K. *On Whitman.* Princeton, New Jersey: Princeton University Press, 2016.

Williams, William Carlos. "Against the Weather," *Selected Essays of William Carlos Williams.* New York: Random House, 1954:196–218.

————. "America, Whitman and the Art of Poetry," *Poetry Journal* 8 (1917):30–31.

————. "An Essay on *Leaves of Grass*," *Leaves of Grass: One Hundred Years After*. Ed. Milton Hindus. Stanford, CA: Stanford University Press, 1955:22–31.

————. "Lincoln," *In the American Grain*. New York: New Directions, 1925:234–35.

————. "On Measure—Statement for Cid Corman," *Selected Essays of William Carlos Williams*. New York: Random House, 1954:337–40.

————. "Preface" to *Selected Essays of William Carlos Williams*. New York: Random House, 1954: n.p.

Wilson, Edmund. *Patriotic Gore: Studies in the Literature of the American Civil War*. New York: Oxford University Press, 1962.

Winters, Yvor. *In Defense of Reason*. Chicago, Illinois: Swallow, 1947.

Woodward, Kathleen. *Aging and its Discontents: Freud and Other Fictions*. Bloomington: Indiana University Press, 1991.

Wortham, Thomas. "William Cullen Bryant and the Fireside Poets," *Columbia Literary History*. Ed. Emory Elliott. New York: Columbia University Press, 1988:278–88.

Zeitlin, Michael. "Bodies, Injury, Medicine," *War and American Literature*. Ed. Jennifer Haytock. New York: Cambridge University Press, 2021:57–70.

Zweig, Paul. *Walt Whitman: The Making of the Poet*. New York: Basic, 1984.

Index

© The Editor(s) (if applicable) and The Author(s), under exclusive license to Springer Nature Switzerland AG 2021
L. Wagner-Martin, *Walt Whitman*, Literary Lives,
https://doi.org/10.1007/978-3-030-77665-7